KILLER

KILLER

Charlie Seiga

Published by John Blake Publishing Ltd,
3 Bramber Court, 2 Bramber Road, London W14 9PB, England

First published in paperback in Great Britain in 2002

ISBN 1 903402 86 7

British Library Cataloguing-in-Production Data:
A catalogue record for this book is available
from the British Library.

Typeset by Jon Davies

Printed and bound in Great Britain by
Bookmarque Ltd, Croydon, Surrey

1 3 5 7 9 10 8 6 4 2

I would like to dedicate this book
to my late brother Jimmy, whose loyalties
— not only as a brother, but also as a friend —
were beyond compare.

And also to all my family and friends,
for all of their continuing loyalty and support.
There are too many names to mention,
but you know who you are.

Chapter One

I had heard some horrendous stories about this ruthless character. He had no mercy when it came to extracting money from other criminals. He was known as the 'Tax Man'. He was known to have shot, stabbed and tortured many young people. Even as far as having a pregnant woman tied up in a body bag, which ultimately caused her to miscarry her child. Most of the criminals in Liverpool were terrified of him, especially the drug-dealers.

I had arranged a meeting with this villain. He said he would definitely call to my home between 5.00pm and 6.00pm that evening. It was Tuesday, 18 November 1997. It was getting very dark outside. Winter was setting in fast and the weather wasn't too good either; it was very cold and drizzling rain. The time was ticking away by now. It was 5.00pm, then it was coming up to 5.30pm and still no sign of him. 'Where the hell is he, is he going to show up or what?' Ten more minutes, and my doorbell rang. I opened my front door, and he stood there with a slight smile on his face. I always noticed every time he smiled that his eyes never showed any emotion. He wasn't a tall man but the rest of him was powerful looking: thick neck, big arms and a barrel chest. I thought, He looks more stocky than he usually does, and then I realised he was most probably wearing his body armour again. He was standing there with his mountain bike.

'All right, Charlie,' he said. 'Can I bring my bike in? It's worth a couple of grand. It might go missing if I leave it outside.'

'Yeah, bring it in. Leave it in the hallway.'

Little did he realise that, a few minutes later, three bullets would be pumped into his head and his brains blown away.

It all happened so fast. He is now on the floor in my home as I look down on him. He is still moving and making gurgling sounds. It's a miracle he is still alive. I turn, pick up my phone and dial 999.

* * *

My name is Charlie Seiga; I was born on 7 April 1940 at 59 Barkbeth Road, Huyton, Liverpool 14. I am presently awaiting trial at Liverpool Crown Court on a murder charge. I have been accused of committing a contract killing, that is 'shooting to death a notorious Liverpool villain'. If found guilty of this offence, I will never be set free and probably die in prison.

A few months ago, if someone had told me I'd be facing a murder charge and would spend the rest of my life in prison, I would have told them it was impossible. But then again, anything is possible with the sort of lifestyle I've led. I am now 57 years of age and time might have finally run out for me.

This is my story from the beginning …

Chapter Two

I hold no one responsible for the life I've led — except myself. No one forced me to become a criminal; no one persuaded me to become a thief; in fact, no one forced me to do anything I didn't want to do. It was down to me. No one else took any decisions on my behalf. It's easy to blame others for mistakes you've made in life, especially when you've been involved in crime your entire life.

So often, I've heard the same old story from many a villain who has led a life of crime: 'I was led astray' ... 'somebody showed me how to steal' ... 'I had a rotten childhood'. Well, I can honestly say that no one corrupted me and I had a pretty good childhood. From the very beginning of my life of crime, I knew perfectly well what I was doing and, more importantly, I knew exactly what I wanted.

I wasn't born into a life of crime — far from it. Both my parents were as straight as they come. They were both honest, hard-working people.

I think from an early age I wanted the good things in life, like fine clothes, cars and holidays. I had no intention whatsoever of earning my living honestly. When I left school, I had no qualifications but I was offered the opportunity to learn a trade such as plumbing, bricklaying or joinery. In those days, you would serve your time from the age of 16 until you were 21. When you're 16, 21 seems like a million years away. No, that life wasn't for me.

I became a villain from the age of 12, but I still maintained certain qualities and rules. When I hear of old ladies getting mugged for their pensions and the like, and drugs being peddled to schoolchildren, it makes me sick. Yet those sorts of scum pretend to be gangsters. Well, I know there is no comparison, especially when it comes to child-killers, rapists and all the other filthy beasts that go with them. No, I don't compare myself to scum like that. There's a certain line to be drawn; I was brought up with a bit of decency and qualities from my parents, whom I will always treasure.

Both my parents were Liverpool born and bred. My mother's name was Jane Brown and my father's name was Frederico Seiga. The name Seiga is of Italian origin and my dad's father — my grandfather — was a sailor. He arrived in England on one of his sea trips and met my grandmother who had been born and bred in Liverpool. I never knew my grandparents on my father's side; they had passed away long before I was born. I do know they raised a family in Liverpool and lived in a house in Beaufort Street, which is to the south end of the city.

My dad and his brothers were all born in Beaufort Street, and I believe in those days, in the early 1900s, it was a terrible, poverty-stricken area. The housing conditions were appalling; no running water in the houses, communal lavatories at the back of the terraces and the only available water was drawn from standpipes in the streets. It must have been unbearable to have lived in a place like that. It makes you wonder how people put up with those sorts of conditions.

Those were some of the reasons my father ran away from home and joined the Merchant Navy at the age of 13. He must have taken after his father wanting to run away to sea, seeking adventure and seeing the world. I understood that all the Seigas were merchant seamen. Even my three older brothers ended up going to sea.

In those days, Liverpool was a big, cosmopolitan, thriving sea port and many young men from Liverpool joined the Merchant Navy. Seafaring was a good steady job with reasonable pay and a touch of excitement and adventure which attracted many of Liverpool's young teenage lads. And yet my dad never told us much about his life at sea or his life in foreign countries. I was always curious about that side of things but he kept it all to himself. In fact, he kept most things to himself and, as a result, I never really got to know my old fella. Understandably, he was rarely at home particularly during the first part of his married life and, as I later discovered, he wasn't really a family man, more a loner who happened to come home occasionally.

I do know that he had been at sea some three years before he met my mother. They were both teenagers and they met one Saturday night at the Rialto dance hall in Liverpool. My dad was handsome and smartly dressed. My ma was a beautiful, dark-haired, olive-skinned, slim young woman who came from a completely different background to his. Her parents were shrewd business people and were considered wealthy, well-to-do and highly respectable. They owned a wholesale food warehouse, a thriving business, and lived in a large, elegant house in Parliament Street which, in the 1920s, was one of the élite areas of Liverpool. Like every good Catholic, my ma and her family went to church every Sunday and every Saints day without fail. It was driven home to them that to miss attending church on Sundays was a sin.

From the moment my dad was introduced to my ma's parents, they took an instant dislike to him. They could see he was handsome but they never liked my dad and strongly disapproved of their daughter courting a sailor who was likely to spend most of his life away from home. They could envisage their beloved daughter bearing children every year and then having to bring them up all on her own while he gallivanted back to sea for a few more months.

They feared that their beloved Jane would marry a young, no-good adventurer who would spend his life far from home and the family, leaving them to survive as best they could. My ma's parents wanted something better for their daughter. One of my ma's brothers would later work for the British Government in South Africa and one of her sisters would become Headmistress at the College of Notre Dame in Liverpool. They tried their best to put an end to the relationship but Ma was a determined young woman with a mind of her own. She told me later how much she was in love with her handsome young sailor and was determined to marry him.

So they married in secret at a Liverpool Register Office, although they were both only teenagers. I respected her for that because it must have taken some guts to go against her parents' wishes and secretly marry a young man of whom they totally disapproved. Years later, my mother told me that her early married life was bizarre because for the first 12 months they didn't live together. After spending an evening out with my dad, she would go home to her parents' house pretending she was still single. And he would do the same. No one knew they were married. Can you imagine that happening in this day and age? It must have been hilarious.

I did learn they were both terrified of their secret being revealed. Both sets of grandparents were staunch Catholics and to get married in a Register Office instead of the church was considered one of the worst sins a Catholic could commit in those days.

Their secret did finally get out and all hell broke loose! After everything had simmered down, they got married once again, this time in a Catholic church. Some time later, my father was eventually accepted by the family and even employed in the family business.

After some time, my parents settled down and the children arrived — three boys and two girls. Their names were Edward, Delia, Frederick, Gerald and June. But June died when she was only four years old so I never knew her. My ma never talked to me about her so I never knew what really happened but I think it was an illness, not an accident.

I suppose that with both my parents working and having their own house, my ma and dad were content in their own way. When my mother's father passed away, things improved further. He left his money to be shared out amongst his children. With her share, my mother had the foresight to buy a shop in the south of Liverpool and turn it into a fish and chip shop, the first in that part of the city. It was situated in Hill Street. As I understand it, she was also the first chippie to put a big bottle of lollipops on the counter for the kids and everyone who bought any fish and chips could have a free lollipop. The idea worked brilliantly and the shop took off with queues outside most nights. My mother worked hard but the money came in thick and fast. Things looked up and they soon began to live comfortably.

Then the war broke out. Liverpool was targeted almost daily because of its big docks and its shipping importance.

In a bid to escape the bombing, my parents moved the family to Huyton and, at that time, Huyton was a semi-rural area on the outskirts of Liverpool.

Not long after the move, I was born, followed by three younger brothers — William, James and Joseph. The family was now large with seven brothers and one sister but it was divided into two quite separate parts with ten years dividing us. William, James, Joseph and I were always called 'the four youngsters'. I don't know why there was a ten-year gap between my parents' children. They might just have been having a rest.

Growing up as a child in Huyton in the late '40s and early '50s was great for me and my brothers. The war was over and we had all survived. My parents were both working and my three older brothers were all in the Merchant Navy, again following the family way of life. We were all comfortable and happy at home and we young ones wanted for nothing.

My mother made sure we were always well dressed, unlike a lot of the other poor kids. Poverty was still widespread in Liverpool, especially just after the war. Lots of families of my school mates seemed to survive on bread and dripping or butties. Incidentally, there was a large variety of butties in Liverpool at that time — sugar butties, syrup butties, jam butties and 'connie honey' (condensed milk) butties. We were lucky. We always seemed to have plenty in our house. There was never a shortage of food, even though everything was still rationed.

I found out later why we had been so fortunate. There were a lot of goods being sold on the black market by the end of the war when I was aged six. I didn't quite understand it at first. I thought it meant the stuff had been stolen but it hadn't really. It seems when my older brothers came home from sea they would bring all kinds of goodies with them which they called 'contraband'. They would buy goods cheap abroad and sell them at vast profits in Liverpool to anyone who could afford little luxuries. They would then give some of those profits to my ma so that she was able to buy anything she needed for the family.

I remember how exciting it was when my brothers came home from sea. There would be presents for everyone. We had toys that other poor kids could not get; no wonder we felt so privileged.

In those days after the war, Huyton was a lovely place to live. My brothers and I had many happy childhood memories. The place was full of parks and woodland and people were friendly. We used to go fishing or bird nesting for eggs. I recall the village being a beautiful place to live. Many of the houses and cottages were Tudor style and the shops seemed full of character. The shopkeepers were cheery and everyone said 'Good morning' to one another. Most people seemed kind and sociable. People would do anything for a friend or a relative or even a neighbour.

I remember Huyton Police Station — I should do, as I got handcuffed to a drainpipe outside it a few years later. I will elaborate on this later. I cannot understand how a beautiful village like Huyton was pulled down, bulldozed out of existence. For some godforsaken reason, in the early '60s the local council decided to demolish the entire place and sent in the bulldozers. It seemed that my childhood was being destroyed before my very eyes. I had loved the old place and I knew so many people. 'Progress' they called it. In place of the village, they built a couple of so-called supermarkets and some drab council buildings. I called it 'vandalism', not progress.

My younger brothers and I went to a school called Longview. It wasn't very far from our house so we could easily walk there and back. The school was Church of England or Protestant. It was a fairly good school, a little bit strict on discipline but still a good school. It was my father's idea to send us to a Protestant school. Even though he was a Catholic, he reckoned that Protestant schools provided a better education. My younger brothers and I were happy there and I used to enjoy myself. We had lots of mates to play with and all the teachers were very good to us.

Discipline was also quite strict at home. Both my parents believed in making us do as we were told. Every day we arrived back home from school we would all inspect each other before going into the house, checking that our clothes were tidy and that our hands, faces, knees and particularly our shoes were clean. If they weren't, we would be in trouble.

Saturday night was bath night and my ma used to bath the lot of us — using carbolic soap. She would give each of us a good scrubbing to ensure we were spotlessly clean.

She was also worried about 'nits' — hair lice. Every evening she made us kneel down on the floor in front of her and place our head on her knees. Armed with a fine-toothed comb, she would diligently examine our heads making sure there were no lice. I recall everyone being happy in those early years. At school I heard dreadful stories of kids being hit by their parents and having little food to eat, but I was fortunate. Thanks to our ma, we always had plenty to eat and good clothes to wear and our home was nearly always a place of happiness.

My dad had some odd ideas though, ideas which I believed he inherited from his Italian background. One was his passion for growing herbs in our little back garden; there were all kinds of herbs but garlic was his favourite, his cure-all. He was absolutely convinced that garlic was the great protector of good health, and particularly wonderful for children. He was certain that garlic prevented colds, coughs, 'flu and nearly every other illness under the sun.

Each day he would make us drink a revolting, foul concoction of a whole clove of garlic, which he crushed in a saucer with a steel fork. Into the saucer he would pour some tea and we would be made to drink it as he stood and watched us. Sometimes it made us feel sick but we still had to drink it.

As a result, the other children at school used to tease us something terrible because we stank of garlic. I remember the teacher could never look at us when we spoke to her because of the stench of garlic on our breath. I was so embarrassed. I would plead with my father not to make us drink his garlic tea but he insisted. In those years, tuberculosis and diphtheria were rife around Liverpool and I believe he made us drink the garlic tea because he fervently believed it was the best way of keeping us healthy. He may have been right, because we were never ill and never away from school. None of us ever suffered from coughs, colds, sore throats or the 'flu, unlike most of the other kids.

Then trouble came crashing into our young lives and, from that moment on, my life changed for ever.

* * *

I came home from school with my three younger brothers to find my ma crying her eyes out. She was sitting in the living room, tears flowing down her cheeks and she was surrounded by all kinds of strange men I had never seen before. I had no idea what was happening, what was going on, but I knew my mother had been scared out of her mind and that my older brothers were in some sort of trouble.

I found out later that my elder brothers, Edward and Frederick, had been charged with armed robbery along with another man. The strange men in our house had been plain-clothed detectives from the CID. Apparently, my brothers and their mate had held up a tailor's shop in the city centre. My brother Freddy had taken a gun with him and he'd been caught with the gun in his possession. In the 1950s, criminals rarely used guns, so their offence was considered to be unusually serious. All three were charged with a string of offences relating to the crime.

The tailor's shop they'd robbed used to sell clothes to the young men coming home from sea. I believe it was a popular or 'trendy' shop in those days. Anyway, some time later both my brothers were sent for trial and were found guilty. We had no idea that my brothers were involved in anything criminal, particularly my ma and dad. They had brought up all their children to believe that stealing was a sin, which kids from good Catholic families would never consider for one moment.

Until that moment, my brothers had never been in trouble but the fact that a gun had been used in the robbery meant that they received long prison sentences. Edward got five years and Frederick ten. Frederick was only 19. For some reason, the other man with them got only three years. He gave evidence against Edward and Frederick. My other brother, Gerald, had also been charged with robbery and he was sent to prison for three years.

My parents were devastated at what had happened. One minute we were one big happy family, and the next, disaster had torn apart the family and ruined my parents' lives. Our family had always been considered a good, stable, respectable family in which the children were well cared for and provided for and who were always clean and well turned out, a credit to their hard-working parents. My ma had always been able to hold her head high in Huyton and she was proud of that.

The armed raid by my brothers brought a terrible disgrace and humiliation to us all, having to endure the added shame of having the family name plastered all over the local paper. It was headline news that the Seiga brothers had been sent to prison for armed robbery. People shunned us in the streets and the shops. Those who had been family friends did not call, not even to commiserate with my mother in her hour of need. My poor mother took the humiliation and the disgrace very badly. She seemed to believe that she had been in the wrong, that she had made mistakes in the way she had brought up her sons. I hated to see my ma so terribly down-hearted.

For the first time ever, I saw her spirit had been broken and she felt a deep sense of shame. She took it all so personally and yet she should not have done so. My ma was a clean-living, decent lady, as she had been throughout her life, but she felt hurt and humbled when neighbours — her friends for many years — began to look the other way and ignore her whenever she walked down the street.

I remember going to school at that time with my younger brothers and being treated like lepers in the playground. All our mates had been told by their parents not to play with us. My mate said to me, 'Charlie, my mam told me to keep away from you in case I get into trouble with the police.'

'Why's that?' I asked him.

'Because she says that all the Seigas are robbers,' he replied.

Imagine young children like us, who had done

nothing wrong, being told that we were criminals although we had done absolutely nothing wrong in our lives. Even the teachers treated us differently after the trial, looking down on the Seiga family as though we were some sort of 'scallies' — riff-raff. Before the trial, we had all been treated like children from a respectable family. Afterwards, some of the teachers seemed to dismiss us, take no notice of us in the classroom or the playground, as though we were no longer at the school. I hated the fucking lot of them.

The lovely home where we had been so happy for so long had to be sold. At that time, legal aid was not available, regardless of income, and lawyers' fees had to be paid. Our brothers had to be legally represented and my parents had to find the money from somewhere. The only money they had was in the house so that had to go. We were on our own with no one to help us.

Things went from bad to worse. We had to go on free meals at school. It was so humiliating for us. Those who paid for their meals obviously got top priority. They were served first while we had to wait at the end of the queue. I felt so small, so insignificant. It was degrading and I hated that feeling. So many people at school treated us like dirt. They looked down on us and I hated that, too. I vowed then that, one day, I would be back on top. But, at that time, our world had come crashing down and we could do nothing about it.

But it was my ma who somehow found the strength to carry on. She somehow made us feel that our world had not ended. In those days and weeks, I saw the strength in my mother's character as she fought to overcome the disgrace and I admired her.

It was during that family crisis that I first saw my old fella for what he really was — a weak, pathetic bastard. In my eyes, he had always been the man of the house. I would see how my mother always made us respect him, as she did. He would always have his own chair, the comfortable one near the fire, and no one else was permitted to sit in it.

Sometimes I would sit in his chair as a dare or just for devilment, and my ma would walk in from the kitchen and tell me to get off the chair. If I didn't move quickly enough, she might sometimes give me a clout round the ear to make me obey. I never argued with my ma because she was always right.

But now I watched my old fella sitting, slumped in his favourite chair and it seemed the fight had gone out of him. He had changed so much. I suppose it must have been that he, too, felt ashamed but he never said anything. I don't even recall him saying anything to us kids, like telling us that what happened to our older brothers would happen to us if ever we thought of breaking the law by thieving or stealing. But he said nothing, not a word of warning.

Within a matter of a few weeks, he had become useless. He started drinking. I hadn't noticed it at first but then I realised that he was drinking lots, he was never out of the ale house. And he was becoming sullen and morose. He suddenly found life a struggle but he had no guts to fight it, unlike my ma. Money was short and, having been used to having little luxuries and good food on the table, it was hard to accept.

But my ma was so very different. From the moment what had happened to our family eventually passed, my mother was always preaching to both me and my younger brothers — 'never ever steal'. We had it drummed in to us every day before going to school in the morning and when we came home at night. I remember going to some lad's house for tea one day after school and, as we left to go home, the boy's ma gave me some toys — a red fire engine and a little train set — to take home. As soon as my ma saw me with those toys I saw anger in her eyes and, in that instant, she was convinced I had stolen them. She questioned and cross-questioned me, her eyes burning into me as she fired questions at me. She was convinced that I had stolen the toys and she was determined that I should learn, once and for all, that I must never steal. When I still refused to admit that I had stolen the toys, my ma grabbed hold of me by the scuff of the neck and marched me out of the house.

She dragged me round to the lad's home as I protested my innocence and fought to release her grip on my arm. But to no avail. I had tried 100 times to explain to her that the boy's mother had given them to me but she refused to believe me, convinced of my guilt. I was so terribly hurt and embarrassed. I was hurt that she wouldn't believe me and embarrassed that I was being marched along the street with everyone looking at me.

My ma banged on the neighbour's door and asked the woman who opened the door, 'I'm sorry to trouble you but did you give Charlie these toys?'

'Yes,' she replied.

'He didn't take them, then?'

'No,' she replied, 'he was playing with them and so I asked him if he would like to take them home with him. He looked so happy that I let him take them.'

'That's all right then,' said my ma, releasing her grip on my arm. 'I thought for one moment he might have just taken them.'

'No,' replied the woman. 'I understand. But I did give them to him.'

'Thanks, sorry to have troubled you.'

'That's all right, I understand,' and she smiled at me and then at my ma.

When the woman told my ma that she had given me the toys, I felt as though a great weight had been lifted from me.

But the thought that we three younger boys might follow in our brothers' footsteps and get into trouble with the law obviously played on my ma's mind. She became increasingly worried. Whenever we returned home from school or were a little late returning home, she would question and cross-question us. Finally, it seems the worry became too much for her, so she began keeping us at home, forbidding us to play in the streets or the parks, or with other kids, fearful that we might get into some sort of trouble and bring more disgrace on the family. I don't think she would have been able to take any more.

But the restrictions became too much for me. Because I was older than my three brothers, I was made to feel responsible for them. I had to take them to school every day and bring them home. My ma told me that I had to look after them, make sure they didn't get into trouble or into any fights at school. She also told me that I had to make sure they didn't steal anything from other children or shops.

When I was about 12 or 13, I sort of rebelled against everything that was going on. I felt I was being picked on at home and picked on by the teachers at school. Of course, at school, things did get stolen from time to time and when that happened we would be picked on and questioned as though we were the culprits. If anything went missing, we would be the first to be asked if we had taken the stuff or knew where things might be, intimating that we had robbed them.

Even where we lived, the neighbours would always blame the Seigas for anything that went wrong or, more importantly, went missing. It became intolerable for my poor ma because she was being treated in the street and in the local shops like I was being treated at school.

My mother decided that she had had enough of this treatment and moved the family to a different part of Huyton. We moved to St David's Road, Page Moss, which was not too bad at first. By then — the early 1950s — Huyton was becoming a built-up area with houses, flats and shops going up everywhere. People were moving to Huyton from Bootle and the city as the rows of slum houses were being demolished.

My first bit of dishonesty, if you can call it that, took place in 1952. It was during the summer holidays and my three younger brothers and I had just broken up from school. We had six weeks off but because money was still very tight in our house with little food, we would go to the school every day for a free meal. My mother's pride was hurt but she had no choice because she realised it was more important to get good food in us. So each day at around 12.00pm I would take my brothers to the school for their free meal.

On one of those days, as we were about to leave the house, my dad told us we would have to take our dog to the dogs' home which was on the way to the school. Our dog, Snowy, was a bitch and she was on heat. My father wanted her out of the house because all kinds of stray dogs had been hanging around our house trying to get near Snowy. But my brothers and I were gutted at being made to abandon Snowy. We loved her. She was our dog and we couldn't bear to think of her being destroyed for no good reason. My dad told us that Snowy would be well looked after in the dogs' home but we knew they might put her down. We had had Snowy since she was a pup but, like everything else, we had to do as we were told.

No matter how much I protested and pleaded, my old fella was having none of it; Snowy had to go.

So off we went with our dog. I found an old tie which belonged to one of my older brothers and tied it around Snowy's neck as a lead. While we were on our way to the dogs' home, which was about two miles away, our Billy, one of my younger brothers, found a Post Office savings book. It was full up with loads of 2s 6d stamps, each worth about £5 at today's value. But our Billy and my other two brothers didn't realise the value of its contents. Being the eldest, I realised this savings book was worth a small fortune — perhaps today's equivalent of about £500. At first, I had every intention of handing it in to the nearest Post Office, then I thought, Here we are, four young kids, hungry and fed up with everything and miserable at the thought of having to give away our dog.

My brothers kept saying, 'What shall we do with it? What shall we do with Snowy?'

'I don't know,' I kept saying. 'I don't know ... just calm down ... let me think.'

After considering the consequences of disobeying my father and of what might happen to Snowy, I said, 'Well, I don't think we should take Snowy to the dog's home; they'll only put her down if they can't find some family to have her.'

My brothers agreed. Then I had to think what we could do with her. I had no idea and my brothers just looked to me for inspiration. We decided to take Snowy to the park so she could have a run around while we thought how we could save her from the dog's home.

When we arrived at Dovecote Park, I noticed an old lady sitting on her own on a wooden bench. She kept looking at me and Snowy. While my three brothers were playing around, I got talking to the old lady. She seemed very nice and kept asking me about our dog. I told her the dog's name and what had happened at home regarding my father and what he had told us to do — to get rid of Snowy. To my surprise, the old lady said she would keep the dog for us and give her a good home. She even said we could always visit her house and see Snowy whenever we wanted. In fact, I lost the lady's address and we never saw Snowy again. Sometimes, I would go to the various parks to play hoping to see Snowy or the old woman but I never did. I just hoped Snowy had a nice life. I'm sure she did because she was a good little dog.

After much thought, I finally decided to keep hold of the savings book. After all, we had found it; it wasn't as though we had deliberately gone out of our way to steal it. But I wasn't sure how we should spend the money. It seemed at that moment that I was walking around Huyton with a small fortune in my pocket. I had never in my life experienced such a feeling of happiness. Now I knew what it was like to feel rich and that I could buy anything I wanted. It felt great.

Dovecote Park was just past Huyton, and was one of my favourite places which I had always found exciting. It was always packed with people enjoying themselves. There was a Punch and Judy Show for the kids and a big fishing pond with ducks. Sometimes in the summer, there would be fairs and the whole place would hum with excitement and noise and the shouts of the gypsies urging people to spend their money. There were strangers around and lots of people laughing and joking and enjoying themselves in a friendly, innocent way. It was a place of wonderful memories for me when I was just a kid and now, some 40 years later, it is nothing but a desolate field, overgrown with long grass and weeds.

I decided that we should try to draw some money out of the savings book and, if that worked, then we would go mad and spend the money on ice creams and sweets and chocolate, all the tasty things we hadn't enjoyed for some time. I knew my ma had been having a hard time making ends meet and she had no money to spend on luxuries.

The first Post Office we came to was in Page Moss, Huyton. Our Billy and I went in. I told Jimmy and Joe to hang on outside. I asked the lady behind the counter if I could withdraw ten shillings. I remembered to say 'please'. I wondered if she was going to ask any questions, or call the police or ask how I had so much money in my savings book. My heart was thumping, I could almost hear it. But she said nothing. She just took the book from me, took four stamps out and passed it back with a big ten bob note. I couldn't believe it had been so easy. I walked out holding the savings book and the ten bob note, holding my breath in case she called me back to check whether the book was really mine.

I didn't breathe or say a word to our Billy until we were out of the shop and some distance away. I was worried that she might have been watching us to see our reaction. I turned only once to check she wasn't following us. It was only then that I began to relax. Once I fully realised how simple it had been to get the money I felt on top of the world, a fantastic feeling of happiness.

I waved the ten bob note in the air and shouted to my brothers, 'No crap school dinners for us today. Come on, let's go and buy a load of good scoff.'

We were going to celebrate big style.

The school meals were always the same, especially the pudding. It was always semolina with a blob of red jam in the middle. We used to stir it up and the four of us would have four plates of pink pudding. My brothers wouldn't eat it unless they stirred it up first to make it look like something else.

I was the oldest and I knew they needed the food, so I would tell them every day as we sat and stirred our sick-making semolina, 'Pretend it's pink ice cream and it'll make it taste nice.'

Well, this time we were going to get real ice cream and cakes and sweets. I had the 'readies' and we were going on the first spending spree of our lives. The first shop we came across was a cake shop. I bought four bags of cakes. There were cream slices, buns, little trifles and some others as well. We were all so excited. But I was worried that someone might come along and wonder what four kids were doing with four bags of cakes and I realised that could bring it on top for us — trouble. So I told them that I would hold the bags until we found somewhere quiet, where no one would see us having our secret party.

We walked to Woolfall Field not far from where we lived in Huyton. The field had a river running across it called the River Alt. It was one of our favourite play areas where we used to knock about as kids. We went to a sheltered spot to ensure no one would see us and I laid all the goodies down on the grass. The four of us got stuck into our wonderful big feast. The cakes tasted brilliant and we could hardly eat them quick enough.

But as we were getting stuck into the scoff, a crowd of dirty, scruffy kids spotted us and ran over to see what we were eating. They gathered round and began to look enviously at our party, making remarks. The kids worried me, so I picked up a couple of stones just in case they wanted a fight. I knew these kids were from over the Alt, lads who had been our enemies for years. They had been evacuees from Liverpool and Bootle who came to live there to escape the bombing during the war. Two or three times a week, the kids who were born in Huyton used to fight the Alt kids. There would frequently be pitched battles with both sets of kids hurling stones, bricks and grass sods. Some even used catapults which were really dangerous. One shot from a catapult could put a kid's eye out. These were quite ferocious battles in which kids sometimes got seriously hurt.

But this day was different.

'Give us a cake,' one of the Alt kids asked.

I looked at him and said nothing.

'Don't be tight, give us one,' he said.

I could see they were as hungry as we had been, so I gave them some cakes. Within a few minutes, every scrap of food had gone. I thought, We'll have some more of this, and off we went to Twig Lane Post Office. I felt like the Pied Piper with all the kids following me.

Twig Lane was very near where we had been holding our party. This time I went alone into the Post Office and drew out another ten shillings' worth of stamps. I was learning fast and buzzing with confidence. We ran off to another shop. This time I bought loads of sweets and ice cream for everyone. It was great. We went back to the park to enjoy our feast and some more kids came along. It became a party, a big party, with maybe 20 or so kids all enjoying our money.

We would go to different shops to buy the goodies but most of the stuff I bought was the same — cakes, sweets, ice creams, chocolate. But after an hour or so, I began to feel full up and a little sick. In fact, four or five of the kids *were* sick, and they all started to vomit. That didn't look very nice and they made us all feel sick. We had had enough. It was time to sack it all and go home.

None of us had ever had it so good; well, not for a long time anyway. After our little party was over we all made our way home. Just before we got to our house, I had a good talk to my brothers.

'Listen to me,' I said. 'Don't say a word about any of this to my ma or it'll be the end. We will all get battered and won't be allowed to play out.' I added, 'If we all keep quiet and keep this secret to ourselves, we will be able to go out and do the same tomorrow.'

They were all with me and I knew I could trust them to say fuck all. I decided to hide the savings book under a stone in our garden and then we all went into the house. No one said anything. As usual, my old lady had prepared our tea and put it on the table and, as usual, there wasn't very much to eat, just a few jam butties. Without fail we would always dive into our tea and wolf it down in minutes, especially as there usually wasn't very much. But this day we just looked at the butties and could only nibble a little.

Right away, my ma was suspicious. She was no fool. At first she thought we were all sick and appeared worried. She asked whether we had been swimming in the River Alt but we shook our heads.

'No, Ma, honestly,' I said, which was the truth. Occasionally, in the summer we did swim in the river despite the fact that we all believed dead cats and sometimes dead dogs were to be found in it. My ma had always told us never to swim in the Alt because everyone believed it to be contaminated.

So I said, 'We've all had bad stomachs. That's why we're not very hungry. We haven't been feeling well all afternoon.'

But I could tell she was still suspicious. The next minute the ice cream man was ringing his bell outside. My mother went out to him and came back with a special treat for us — an ice cream each! In those hard-up days it was a real treat to be bought an ice cream but the last thing any of us wanted that day was another ice cream. Just the look of the ice cream made me want to throw up.

Now Ma became even more suspicious. She took hold of our Jimmy and went into the back kitchen to talk to him. We waited in terror, looking at each other, trying to hear what was going on. We could hear them talking but we couldn't hear what they were saying. I feared the worst. I knew my ma. I knew there was every probability that she would get the truth from our Jimmy. Within minutes she was back.

My mother walked straight over to me and held out her hand. 'Give me that savings book,' she said.

Our Jimmy had 'blown me up'. Mind you, he was only about eight at the time. I have forgiven him since. I knew there was no point in arguing so I went outside, got the book and handed it over to my mother. Even worse, my old fella had just arrived home and my mother explained what had happened.

The four of us were immediately sent up to bed and told not to speak to one another. I never heard anything more about that savings book but I did wonder what became of it. I do know we all had good food on the table for the next couple of weeks and we also had new shoes bought for all four of us. I often wondered where the money had come from. I would just like to say whoever lost that savings book in Princess Drive, Huyton in 1952 made four hungry little kids happy for a short while!

Chapter Three

I was just a few months short of my fourteenth birthday when my life changed for ever.

Due to the fact we were born in Huyton, most of the local kids started to resent the city kids and, because of this, gangs began to develop and — guess what — I was in one of them. I had just about enough of everything; always being accused of stealing and everything! This was the 1950s and I wanted a piece of the action. I started 'sagging' (playing truant) from school, although I still made sure my three younger brothers never did. I still maintained my responsibilities towards them. I used to make them swear never to tell my mother what I got up to. We were all loyal to one another in that sort of way. Our William went on to win his scholarship to a grammar school. My other two brothers, James and Joe, did all right for themselves, too. They all kept out of trouble which was one good thing.

Not me, though — by now I was running wild. We had one of the best little firms in Huyton. We were up to all kinds of things — fighting, robberies, you name it. Nobody could stop us, or so I thought. I was scared of nothing and of nobody. At 14, I was making plenty of money. We would break into shops and steal anything we came across.

The alarm systems on properties in those days were a joke; all you had to do was go around the back of the shop and 'brace-and-bit' the wooden door and you were in. It was so easy. We took pride in the fact that we were a well-organised gang. We took care; we kept a look-out during our graft, and we even cased places and checked when the people arrived and left their shops or work or whatever we were breaking into. We were professionals, or so we thought.

I am always asked what started me off stealing and in crime in general. It began some time after I met Joey Hannigan and Yank Myers. We were about the same age with the same determination. In those days, there were no supermarkets and, of course, most kids would be sent down to the shops for their parents, or act as messengers, usually when they had just returned home from school. It was just the done thing. You would always see a kid with a shopping bag or running a message.

My mother would give me a shopping list with the items I had to buy. There were always things like tea, butter, bread, slices of bacon, and so on. So Joey, Yank and I put our heads together and decided that we should start robbing the goods we wanted from the various shops and keep the money our parents gave us. Every day, I would volunteer to do the shopping and meet my mates. We would then tour around the various shops stealing everything we wanted when the shopkeepers and their staff were not looking and make a tidy little sum every day.

But I started feeling guilty about keeping my mother's money. As I was getting all the shopping for nothing, I knew in my heart that meant I was stealing from my ma and I felt guilty for doing that. I didn't care about the shopkeepers because I knew they could afford it. But my ma couldn't. I knew she used to go without to make sure we were properly fed and clothed. So I used to sneak some of the stolen money back to her without her knowing. She always left her purse on the mantelpiece and when she wasn't in the room, I would slip some money into it. That not only made me feel better but it also meant my ma had some money to spend on herself.

The shoplifting was OK to start with but it wasn't long before we became more ambitious. By now, two more lads had joined up with us and so our gang became six. We came up with the idea of breaking and entering shops with the idea of stealing as much stuff as we could carry. We calculated that the proceeds would be much bigger.

But things didn't go according to plan because the alarms would go off whenever we tried to break into a shop. Of course, the bizzies would come running along the road or arrive on their old push bikes. We had some mad chases with the police and some narrow escapes. We knew that if we continued like that it wouldn't be long before one of us was caught.

So, eventually we started planning the raids properly. We decided to become more professional and use a brace-and-bit. The brace-and-bit was a valuable tool to a robber in those days. It would drill through any wooden door. The door was then never opened, and so the alarm was never triggered. Once you'd bored a panel out of the door, you were in. That worked really well for a few months and then the shopkeepers got wise and began putting steel plates on the shop doors so we couldn't brace-and-bit them open. We had to plan something different.

All the time this was going on, I used to come home and fill our house with 'little goodies'. The larder was never short of food and I used to try and force money on my mother. She would go mad at me. She would threaten me with going to the police, warn me that I would end up in jail like my elder brothers, plead with me to stop robbing and stop sagging school. But I took no notice. I was enjoying myself, having a great time. Life was good to me now and I thought I was so clever that the police would never catch me.

In the end, I think my ma just gave up on me. She couldn't control me any more. She would warn me to behave myself before I left the house each morning but I would take no notice of her pleas. I was beyond her control. I knew she was worried for me; I knew she cared for me; I knew she wanted me to do well at school, and get a good job. I knew all these things but they made no difference to me. I knew what I wanted. She tried everything to stop me becoming a villain but I just would not listen to her.

My father was still drinking heavily and stupidly trying to make money by gambling on the horses. He was a mess. He seemed to have lost interest in us kids. He seemed more interested in his next drink. He even started getting violent towards my ma. I began to hate him. He would come home drunk and we would all be terrified of him, including my ma. She seemed to be a slave to him and I hated that. Despite the fact that he was half-drunk all the time, my ma still treated him with respect; she still insisted that he was the head of the family and should be treated with respect by all of us.

I envied my mates — their dads always seemed all right. I saw them going to a football match or the pictures with their fathers. But not us. Me and my younger brothers got nothing like that. We didn't even get a toy from him or anything, even at Christmas or on our birthdays. Our ma did everything for us.

I was nearly 15 and the thought of leaving school for good made me want to start my own life and really begin earning good money. I was, in fact, spending less and less time at school, I was sagging two or three times a week! At school and at home I was getting pressured to start planning my future — deciding what apprenticeship I should go for, serving my time as a bricklayer, plumber, joiner or electrician. My dad wanted me to become a toolmaker. I didn't want to know. I was dreading the idea of spending the next few years working for someone else and for virtually no pay.

When I finally left school in the summer of 1955, the world seemed so exciting. Rock 'n' roll was born. By now, Huyton had become a fairly tough place. There were gangs of youths roaming around and fights were breaking out virtually every night.

In our gang there must have been 15 to 20 and people always referred to us as Teddy Boys. You had to be in a gang if you wanted to stay out of big trouble. The gang stopped you getting worked over by other gangs. Most of the time we stayed around our own area of

Huyton but if we ever strayed into other territories, there would be fights. Hardly a day went by without some form of pitched battle with other gangs.

Most of the time we carried studded belts and 'dusters'. For the belts we would buy steel studs and hammer them into the leather belts so they would do real damage when you smashed someone across the head or face. They hurt enough if someone hit you across the arm or the body, but those belts could really make a mess of someone's face. The knuckle dusters came in handy when having it off (fighting) with somebody. After you twatted them and they went down you just made sure they never got back up. Sometimes knives were used but not as often as the belts and the dusters.

But all of the gangs only fought amongst ourselves. We would never have dreamt of mugging an old woman or hitting or robbing an old person for their pension or for fun. There was never anything like that. It was unheard of. A young girl could walk from one end of the city to the other without fear of being molested or attacked.

Many people condemned Teddy Boys as violent young thugs and many older people believed we should have all been cleared off the streets and locked up. But those people didn't realise that in those days there was a code of behaviour which we all followed. Teddy Boys had no wish to harm anyone except other gangs. People were safe in those days, violence only existed between ourselves.

Yet here we were, young 'tearaways' running wild everywhere. I loved it all, especially the clothes, the fights and, of course, the girls — they were something else, dressed in skin-tight jeans and sweaters. To make all this possible, however, you had to have money and I only knew one way to acquire it.

I did have a try at working 'straight' for a living. I remember taking a job on some building site once and I was working six full days a week for a measly £8 per week. By the time I gave my mother her housekeeping money and paid for my bus fares, there was nothing left. I couldn't afford to buy even a shirt, let alone a suit!

I tried one other job as a jobber's mate. But that only lasted a few days. I had to push the jobber's hand cart along the streets in the south end of Liverpool. I felt a right knob-head walking along pushing this fucking old cart and I would always look down at the cart, praying that someone I knew would not see me and take the piss. The jobber, called Old Jack, walked by my side. We would walk miles like this in one day, taking things from one place to another. Most days I suppose I must have pushed that old cart five miles at least. By the end of the day I was shattered.

The end came when Old Jack made me deliver a new lavatory to someone's house some miles away. On the cart was a ladder and the lavatory, and I felt everyone was looking at me pushing this fucking lavatory through the streets of Liverpool. I felt a right dope. It didn't help that it was pissing down with rain that day, making me feel even worse. I imagined doing this every day for the rest of my life and the thought sent a shiver through me. I knew I couldn't last long doing that job. I hated every moment of it but only stuck it for my ma's sake.

On the way back, pushing the stained, dirty old lavatory to the yard, the wheels of the cart became trapped in the tram lines and, as I tried to extricate the cart, the whole thing tipped over, and the dirty lavatory and the ladder were flung across the road. The tram came to a halt and the driver and conductors came to help me put the stinking lavatory back on the cart. The girls from the jeans factory, which was in a place called Edge Lane, wondered what the commotion was about — they were just knocking off from work. They were giggling and laughing at what had happened and I was totally embarrassed. When I saw all those girls laughing at me I just panicked and ran away. In fact, I ran all the way home and told my ma what had happened. I also told her that I could never stick that job. So like a real good old lady she went to see Old Jack and came back with my cards. I thought she was brilliant doing that, saving me the embarrassment of explaining everything to Old Jack who was a decent sort of fella.

I suppose that if I had been prepared to save up every week, I might have one day been able to buy a set of clothes, but no, that wasn't for me. I told myself that I had been trying to go straight, I had given it a go, I had done what my ma wanted me to do. But I simply just wasn't cut out for work. After a few weeks of going straight, I had jacked in the job and went back to doing what I knew best, earning a living using only my wits. I had finished my last straight job. I was just 16.

* * *

One day, while breaking into a shop, my two pals got caught by the police and my other pal and I got away. The shop had one of those new-fangled alarm systems which, when triggered, would set off the alarm in the local police station. We hadn't known about this new system, so we were caught by surprise. We hadn't heard any ringing and were happily robbing everything we could when we heard a police car racing towards us. When we realised they were coming straight for us, we got off as quickly as we could. My pal and I went to a girlfriend's house nearby and just lay low for an hour or so. When we thought it was safe, we came out of hiding and both returned home. When I eventually arrived at my mother's house, the police were waiting for me. Apparently, the police had had a good idea that I had also taken part in the robbery. But, I discovered later that one of my so-called pals had 'grassed' on me. My worst fear was not worrying about the police and what they might do to me, but what my ma would say.

I stood in the kitchen not daring to look at my ma. After all the promises I'd made to her about keeping out of trouble, I just found it hard to face her. I hardly heard what the police were saying. I just wanted them out of the house so that I could try and square it with my ma. But I knew I could never do that. I had broken my promise to her and I hated myself for doing that. She had been let down by my older brothers and now I had let her down, too. This was the first time I'd been caught, but only because of a friend who had betrayed me. I couldn't believe one of my so-called loyal pals could do this, not just to me but the rest of our gang.

I was remanded overnight in Huyton Police Station. This was my first experience at the hands of the police and they weren't about to let me off lightly. They started playing their silly head games with me. I was interrogated all through that night, questioned and cross-questioned until I didn't know whether I was coming or going. They wanted a detailed list of every other job I had done in the past because they weren't stupid. They had an idea that I had been involved in loads of other similar robberies and they wanted to pin them on me. But I refused to co-operate with them which infuriated them still further. It was raining heavily that night and, in a desperate effort to make me confess to all the other jobs, they took me outside and handcuffed me to a drainpipe. They left me out there for a couple of hours.

'As soon as you're ready to tell us what you've done,' the coppers said, 'give us a shout, and you'll be allowed inside.'

I said nothing, preferring to stand in the rain all night if necessary rather than tell them what I had done. I recalled the heavy prison sentences my brothers had done and I had no wish to spend the next few years inside. Not if I could help it. I knew that I had to say nothing, tell them nothing, own up to nothing and eventually I would be safe.

I was soaked to the skin. The rain had soaked my shirt and trousers and had run down my neck, making me feel cold, shivery and very, very wet. I must have been out there for two hours or more. They wanted a confession out of me.

In the end, they had me by the balls. They read out the confessions of the other lads and one had named me as being the organiser of the robberies and break-ins. As the police told me, 'You may as well co-operate because your mates have told us you're guilty.'

I didn't want to give in but I now felt there was little point in pleading not guilty. The police also warned me that, if I refused to co-operate, the punishment I received would be far worse than if I agreed to help them solve all the other identical robberies. That made sense to me and so, reluctantly, I gave in. However, my obstinacy cost me. When I was hauled before the magistrates the following day, I was refused bail and the magistrates remanded me in custody to a place called Woolton Vale Remand Home — Woolton is a suburb of Liverpool.

When I arrived at the home, I was made to stand on a wooden box in a reception room. All the staff were brought in to gawp at me. This was because I was dressed like a Teddy Boy. They were all walking around me, inspecting and examining me and my clothes and making all kinds of comments.

'This is the uniform of the juvenile of today,' one said. Another commented, 'This is the teenager's way of showing off, drawing attention to themselves.' Another said, 'When they dress like Teddy Boys, they think they can get away with murder.'

I may have been only 16 but, fortunately, I was fairly well-built for my age which proved a great asset to me during the couple of weeks I was there. Anyway, after being marched up and down and paraded for all to see, and make their silly remarks, I was taken to the bath house and given a scrubbing brush. I thought they wanted me to scrub the floor or something. The next thing I knew two grown men, so-called warders, wanted to scrub underneath my feet with that brush. No way I thought to myself. I thought they were trying it on to show how hard they were.

'What the fuck do you think you're doing?' I asked in a loud voice.

'You've got to be properly scrubbed,' one said.

'I can bath myself,' I replied. There was no way I would let two hairy men touch my body — they would have to kill me first.

The two warders looked at each other and then fucked off. One said, 'Well, you had better scrub yourself well, otherwise we'll be back.'

Before arriving at Woolton Vale, I had heard all kinds of stories from kids on the outside about what went on there.

Some of the staff were beasts. At night in the dormitory it would sometimes happen. One of the staff would come in pretending he was just saying goodnight and then select one of the little kids and the filth would start. Some of those kids were only about nine or ten years old. The beatings I witnessed were terrible, too. How these people got these jobs was beyond me. Those days, 45 years ago, everything was 'hushed up' and it would be 20 years before the outside world faced up to the problem and accepted that for decades it had been the kids telling the truth and the warders and staff who had been lying. I knew then that nobody would believe the kids if they complained. I was fortunate nobody tried anything on me — maybe it was because I was bigger and older and could handle myself.

I was finally released and placed on two years' probation. I thought it wasn't a bad deal, really, considering the circumstances. But as I left the court, I could hear the Magistrate's words ringing in my ears, telling me that, if I re-offended at any time during the next two years, I could be sent away to a home for young offenders for a long time.

A man by the name of Mr Cubbins was appointed as my Probation Officer. A quiet, slightly balding 45-year-old man, Mr Cubbons always wore a tweed jacket and flannels. He was quite kind actually, a decent sort of fella, and he did seem genuinely concerned about my welfare. The first thing he wanted was to get me into work and secondly to keep me out of trouble. He did try his best with me but I had now had a taste of the good life and of the hard life, and I had decided by then that I was only interested in the good life.

Free once more, I felt confident enough to take on the world. I may have been only 16 but I felt far older than my years. Looking back, I realise that I hadn't got that much experience; in fact, very little. But when I was a teenager, I felt I could take on the whole world and win. Within a couple of days, I was back to my old ways again. My two best pals, Joey Doyle and John Connor, had joined up with me and we were ready for action.

John was 17 and had started driving, which was just what we wanted for our firm. A new craze had exploded among the young teenage tearaways — joyriding. We realised that the car was the ultimate tool for carrying out criminal activities. It was so easy to steal a car in those days. The police were very limited and most of the coppers still relied on bicycles. Indeed, most of the police force was still pounding the streets on foot. In those days, you could steal a car and keep it for weeks before it was discovered.

John Connor was a brilliant car 'bandit'. He could look at any car and within no time he would have it away. John Connor was our main 'wheel man' and I was now the organiser of our little gang, planning our raids and robberies. When we got chased by the police we could guarantee that he would lose them. Now that we could get around by car we began to plan bigger, more daring robberies and the car was the all-important element of surprise and escape.

Everything seemed to be happening fast in the '50s. The music was crazy, and becoming more wild and irreverent. The clothes we wore were so totally different to everyone else's and all the girls were wild. After all, we were only teenagers. My two mates and I were only 17.

I know they were crazy years but I loved it all — everything was exciting. We never took drugs those days to get a 'buzz' or 'high', we didn't need them. In fact, drugs weren't around like they are today. People are complaining about these 'smack heads' or 'druggies' of today. Our nuisances were 'drunks' or 'winos'. I will admit there were a lot more drunks around then than there are today. Every pub you walked past you would always find one or two men outside asking for money to buy a pint or trying to bum a ciggie. But that was the low life of the 1950s.

Talking about drunks — my old fella was fast becoming one. He was never out of the ale house and he was also becoming increasingly violent, which worried me. I wasn't scared for myself, only my ma. Even she had become scared of him and so was the rest of the family. Me and my younger brothers worshipped my mother and when my father started knocking her about, we began to hate and despise him.

I remember when I'd come home after being on one of my money-making rackets. He guessed I had been out thieving or selling contraband goods and would use that as an opportunity to turn me over. He would make me stand against the wall and then search me, feeling in all my pockets, even down my socks, for money I may have concealed from him. He was a typical hypocrite. He would 'confiscate' the money and then he would give me a short lecture about stealing. Of course, in reality, he just stole it from me to buy ale for himself.

This had been going on for some time and I had just about had enough of it and of him. I came home on Christmas Eve in 1956 with presents for my ma and the rest of the family, and this time I had paid for them honestly — well, with the money I had stolen, obviously!

I hadn't been in the house more than a few minutes when my old fella came over to me and told me to hand over the presents to him. They weren't for him and I told him, 'No. I've bought them for the family, not for you.'

'You've just been and robbed them, haven't you?' he said, accusing me.

'No, I haven't,' I said. 'I've just bought them with my own money.'

'Where did you get enough money from to buy Christmas presents?'

'Mind your own fuckin' business,' I told him.

'Don't you talk to me like that,' he shouted.

I knew what was coming next — there was going to be a kick-off.

I had had enough of my father. I had grown up and now I would prove that I was no longer a kid to be fucked about by him. He turned, picked up the poker and swung round in a bid to smash me across the head. One hit would have cracked my head open and probably knocked the fuck out of me. If he'd wanted to kill me, then he was going about it the right way.

In that instant, I ducked the poker which went over my head and I lunged at him, butting him as hard as possible in the face. He went down on the deck. It was the first time in my life that I had ever retaliated against my father. He struggled to his feet with blood pouring from a gash on his forehead and tried to have another go at me. I was determined to teach him a lesson, to make him pay for the way he had treated my ma, hitting and punching her all those years.

I then started to knock fuck out of him.

'This one's for my ma,' I said as I twatted him in the face.

I smashed him time after time until he couldn't get up. My younger brothers were glad I had done him. But my poor mother was upset and shaking with fear.

She said to me afterwards in a whisper, 'You must watch your back because one day he will want revenge.'

Before leaving the house, I told him, 'If you ever lay a finger on my ma again, I'll kill you.'

He didn't reply.

I knew that my dad would never again have a go at me because he now knew that I could and I would knock fuck out of him. I was, however, still worried for my ma.

Three days later, I returned and I was in the house talking to my ma when my dad walked in the back door. He saw me and looked the other way. He didn't stop but walked through the kitchen and up the stairs to their bedroom. My ma was afraid and shaking, fearful that another fight would start.

I put my arm around my ma to comfort her and reassure her.

'Don't worry, Ma,' I told her. 'He knows that if he so much as touches a hair of your head I'll be up those stairs and will kill him. He knows that, I promise you.'

My dad never touched my ma again and he never looked me in the eye from that day on.

As a result of that set-to, I became the bread-winner in our house. I used to make sure we would have food in the house and that Ma had enough money to buy the food she needed. As well as that, I was always sneaking money into Ma's purse, making sure she had enough money for a few little treats for herself. But I never told her what I was doing. I would just put money in her purse whenever I had done a good little earner. I also gave my younger brothers pocket money, because I knew they would never get any from my father. He was mean that way. He would never give any of his children as much as a penny, and yet the same father would buy his mate a pint in the pub. I just can't understand how some men can be the popular life and soul of the pub, buying people drinks all the time, and yet not put a loaf of bread on the table for their family.

Can you imagine what the poor wives and kids had to go through? There were hundreds — if not thousands — of men around like my dad, happy to get pissed every night and forget they had a wife and kids at home to feed, clothe and support. It seemed as though they just didn't want to know and didn't give a fuck as long as they had enough in their pockets for a couple of pints. Most of my pals — hard villains — who committed all kinds of robberies, would give their kids and wives the best. Many believed that one of the joys of the job was to have enough money to take their family on a shopping trip and 'splash out'. Later, I adopted the same attitude. And I loved spoiling my kids. It gave me a buzz and they loved it, too.

Don't get me wrong — I admire any man who earns a living, whether it be through hard, honest work or stealing. I respect a man who earns his living brushing the streets for he is getting out there and doing something to earn a crust. But these other 'dogs' who spend most of their time in pubs and betting shops, spending their family's benefits — I've no respect whatsoever for them.

They reckon drink was a big problem among the poor families in the days when I was a kid. You would always see kids hanging around outside these Liverpool pubs waiting for their drunken parents to come out and take them home. No wonder the kids became drunks later in life. Some of the pubs in Huyton were very rough. One in particular was called the Eagle and Child in Page Moss. This pub was known all over Liverpool. It was mainly notorious for the villains who frequented the place. It was also notorious for the many fights that broke out there on a daily basis.

The Eagle — as it was more usually known — earned its infamous name in the late 1940s. It was also famous for one of the biggest gun fights ever fought in a British pub. Apparently, the gun fight erupted after two fellas fell out over a woman. Apparently, this attractive young woman had a date with an American soldier in another pub called The Bluebell which is also in Huyton. It seems that the American GI got fed up waiting for his date and believed she might have stood him up or blown him out. So he went to the Eagle which wasn't far away. When he arrived, the first person he saw was his date, the young woman who had promised to meet him in The Bluebell. And she was in the company of another American GI who happened to be black. That's what caused the battle that followed.

After a big slanging match, both men pulled their guns on each other. The bar was full of both black and white GIs who, of course, were all half-pissed and there was a major shoot-out with bullets flying everywhere. The bar staff and regulars dived for cover and others ran outside to safety, leaving the American GIs to shoot it out with bullets flying around the pub. Apparently, most of the American soldiers in the pub joined in. The police were called and so were the US military police — who arrived in their Jeeps and army trucks. They arrested every US soldier in the bar and marched them outside. Then, they literally threw the men in the back of the vehicles before driving away. I don't know what happened to the soldiers and I don't know if anyone was actually killed or wounded in that gun battle. But there were bullet marks still embedded in the walls of that pub until it closed in 1995.

* * *

My two pals, Joey and John, and I were starting to earn bigger 'pay-offs' now that we were pulling off all kinds of smash-and-grab jobs. To execute these jobs, you had to be very quick. I had learned that speed was essential. So the car became our most important asset ensuring quick getaways. Usually, John selected the Ford Consul, because he believed those cars were the best for that type of work; fast but not too flashy. He would, of course, steal a different car a few hours before every job and we would ditch the stolen vehicle within minutes of pulling the job. We used to drive round a particular area of a town selecting the right shop to have off and then we would cruise about checking there were no police in the vicinity. Once the coast was clear, we would first drive the car on to the pavement outside the shop parking it close to the shop window. Then I would jump out and smash the window. A big iron bar was the best method. Joey and I always wore industrial gloves to protect ourselves from the broken glass. We would first grab everything in sight. Radios were the main target in the 1950s but we quickly discovered that practically all electrical goods were in great demand on all the housing estates. We had no shortage of customers. People were only too happy to buy the goods from us with no questions asked.

These smash-and-grab jobs were all the rage amongst the young criminals of the day. In fact, the shops became such easy targets that we started to run out of shops to raid. Sometimes we would be driving around the city looking for a good store to rob and then you might see another gang in another car looking for exactly the same opportunity. We started running out of electrical stores. Then, on police advice, shop owners began putting steel grids on the windows and, in no time, every other electrical store had followed suit. So we had to move on, and find other ways of earning a living, if you can call it that.

Our new money-spinner was furniture stores. We would take a small piece of newspaper with us and wander around the store as though inspecting the furniture. Considering we were still only teenagers it seemed surprising that the salesmen didn't get on to us in their shops. But that was our luck. We would wait until the salesmen were busy with other customers and then light the paper, place it in a wardrobe or chest of drawers and walk away. Within a few minutes someone would draw attention to the fact that smoke was coming from the piece of furniture and the salesmen would immediately rush to see what was happening. We would then calmly walk over to the till, grab all the pound notes, and slowly walk out of the store. One of the beauties of these operations was the fact that as soon as the shoppers saw the smoke, they, too, would usually make for the exit and we would walk out with them so that no one noticed us leaving the store. It worked like a treat for several months.

By now, we were becoming more ambitious. We were hungry for real money, big money. We felt we had ended our apprenticeship on the smaller shops where we just stole small amounts of money or goods which would never make us rich. We had read in the newspapers of gangs raiding jewellery stores, particularly in London, and decided that if those were the shops raided by the big-time gangs then we should follow suit and have a crack at the big time ourselves. We agreed that having been so successful in targeting electrical shops, we should have the same success raiding local jewellers.

But we first had to find a way of getting rid of the stuff we robbed. We knew that the people on the estates who bought the electrical goods just hadn't the money for real jewellery, so we had to find a fence. It took some time before we were finally introduced to someone who said he was a fence and would gladly pay us 'good money' for tidy stuff. But he warned us that he didn't want any cheap rubbish, only the best. We had to put our faith in that fence because we didn't know if he was reliable or honest. He could even have been a copper's nark for all we knew.

The first jeweller's we robbed was very nearly a total disaster! The shop we selected was in the centre of Liverpool. We arrived in our stolen car at about 2.00am. The area was quiet and almost deserted. Most streets were quiet those days; there wasn't a lot of nightlife or clubs then.

We carried out our usual recce, driving up and down the street making sure there were no police cars around and no plod pounding the beat. We discovered two bizzies on foot at one end of the half-mile-long street and there were another two on foot patrol at the other end.

The shop we had targeted was about half-way between the four bizzies on patrol. After a quick discussion, the three of us decided to go ahead as planned and have the shop away. I thought we could have smashed the window and grabbed everything we wanted before the police could get anywhere near us. I guessed that we would be well out of the way before they even reached the shop.

We used the same routine. John drove the car — which we had stolen earlier that evening — on to the pavement right next to the shop. I caved in the window with a sledgehammer and we started grabbing the jewels, watches, rings, bracelets and so on. Then the alarm bell went off, bringing it on top for us all. It sounded very loud. Of course, this alerted the police and all of a sudden we had bizzies running like mad towards us. John, who was sitting in the car, was screaming for us to hurry but Joey was a little bit greedy, stupidly determined to grab as much as he could. We had brought a large shallow box with us, the idea being to scoop as much as we could, as quickly as we could, into the box and then put everything into the car. We believed we stood a far greater chance of grabbing more stuff that way. Joey kept scraping everything into it, even loads of glass from the broken window, as we yelled at him to get into the car.

Finally, Joey realised how close the bizzies were and jumped into the car. John put his foot down and accelerated as fast as possible away from the shop. Suddenly, a stupid bizzie came hurtling into the road and leapt on the bonnet of the car, throwing his baton at the windscreen. Fortunately, it simply bounced off. Somehow, the copper clung on as John veered left and right in an effort to throw him off as he sped down the road. For 20 yards or more the copper clung on until he was thrown from the bonnet and we drove off.

Within a minute or so, we heard the sound of police cars, their bells ringing. It seemed there were police cars everywhere and we were chased for miles. Somehow, after ten minutes or so, John managed to lose them and saved us once again. When he arrived at our safe house in Huyton, the fence was already there waiting for us. He went through the stolen goods, checking every item before offering us the magnificent sum of £3,000 for the lot. In today's value that must have been worth about £30,000. We were well pleased because we had not the slightest idea we would earn that sort of money from just one hit. It took him a few days to get the money together but he paid us the full amount when next we met.

We had carried out a brilliant smash-and-grab raid

and had made ourselves a fortune. Never in my life had I ever believed I would have so much money and there I was — not yet 17 years of age — pulling £1,000 all for myself. We all believed we were now in the big time; nothing could hold us back.

The job we pulled off was all over the local paper that week and everyone was talking about it. I felt on top of the world. I'd never had so much money before.

I walked around Huyton that week with some of the money in my pocket feeling terrific. I also believed at that time that the fences — the receivers — had been really generous to us. It was years later that I came to realise that no fence was ever generous. Many villains believe that receivers are worse than robbers for they take very few risks but usually end up ripping off the criminals. I can certainly recollect the many times in my younger days when I was ripped off by so-called reliable receivers. At first they'll promise you a good price for the spoils and when you get the goods to them they make excuses — prices have dropped, some of the stones are not real — any excuse to bargain you down. There was also another problem with fences, one which I knew nothing about until I was a good many years older — many fences are also police informers!

I remember on one occasion that we had some beautiful antique silverware to sell. But the fence who had agreed to buy the silver told us that the goods were so hot that he could only give us scrap price for the lot. He told us he would just about take it off our hands for a few quid and he would then get rid of the lot — as scrap metal.

I didn't believe a word he was saying. So I said to him, 'Fair enough,' and I walked outside, pulled a hammer out of the car and walked back inside.

'I'll break it up for you,' I said and raised the hammer above my head as if I was about to smash the silver.

'Don't do that,' he said.

'I may as well smash it for you; to save you the trouble,' I said and raised the hammer again. I was only bluffing, of course.

'No,' he said, 'I'll see what I can do with it. I'll try to sell it for you but I can't promise much.'

He started offering us a bit more. I had learned to my cost how devious some fences can be. I also knew that if I didn't come to a deal with this dog, there was a good chance that he would 'grass' to the bizzies. So after he had offered a reasonable price I agreed to the deal despite the fact I knew that he was ripping us off.

It was some years later that I learned that some detectives occasionally allow receivers to buy a certain amount of stolen goods from criminals providing they grassed on a few fellas. That way both the fences and the police ended up happy.

After our first brilliant success, we decided we should let everything cool down. We heard that the police were sniffing around the area, asking questions and talking to fences so we thought it would be sensible to get out of Huyton for a while. Joey and I decided we should go on a holiday. In those days, no one I knew went away on holidays except for day trips to places like New Brighton. People would still take a coach for a day trip to Blackpool but they would always return that evening, never thinking of staying the night away from home. I didn't know anyone who went on holidays abroad like to Spain or even France. To us, holidays meant a break from school.

Most kids I knew had never been out of Liverpool. When Joey and I decided to go away on holiday, we had no idea where to go or what we should do to organise a holiday. Neither of us had ever been very far from Liverpool. I think Wales was the furthest place I'd ever been to and that was on a school trip.

However, Joey Doyle and I heard that the Isle of Man was a good place to go on holiday and we knew we could get there by ship. John Connor, our other pal, decided to stay put. He didn't like the idea of taking a holiday. When Joey and I finally got to the Isle of Man, I couldn't believe the colour of the sea. It was a wonderful green-blue colour, the like of which I had never seen before. The only sea I'd ever seen was at the mouth of the Mersey which was always dark and murky.

We had a fantastic time there. We stayed for a week and really enjoyed ourselves. The guest house where we stayed had good food and I loved their big, slap-up breakfast with tea and toast. The Isle of Man was buzzing like mad in those days with dance halls and arcades and hundreds of holidaymakers from Britain enjoying the good food and the lively pubs. I shall never forget that holiday because it was there that I met and fell in love with my first ever girlfriend. I loved her from the moment I first set eyes on her. She was so beautiful.

Her name was Joyce Valante whose parents had come to the Isle of Man from Italy. She was my age, just 17. I invited her out and started dating her and the more time we spent together the more her parents took a liking to me. Of course, neither Joyce nor her parents knew how I earned my living. They thought I was just a hard-working lad from Liverpool.

When I got back home, I used to keep in touch with Joyce and I had all kinds of plans for the two of us. I knew that we loved each other and, for me, Joyce was my dream girl. As I sailed back to Liverpool at the end of that holiday, I knew that one day we would get married. I would sit at home and plan our life together. I wrote postcards to her, telling her how much I missed her and how much I loved her. And she wrote cards to me telling me the same. It was magic. I still have those postcards; I've always treasured them.

One day, two months later, I received a letter from one of Joyce's friends who knew that she and I were in love. The girl wrote that Joyce had been killed in a freak accident when she fell from a train while on holiday with her parents in Africa. I never knew exactly what happened but I was devastated. The girl also sent me the Mass card of her funeral service. I tried to pretend that she wasn't dead but the Mass card proved it. I knew that was the end and I was shattered. I had loved her so much. I felt a part of me had died as she had been killed. It took me a long time to get over her. For weeks and months I went around in a kind of daydream, absolutely broken-hearted at what had happened.

In those lonely weeks, I would also walk around Huyton as though in a trance and didn't want to know about carrying out any more jobs. The guts had been ripped out of me and I had no fight, no ambition. I didn't even want any money; I just wanted Joyce back again but that, I knew, was an impossibility.

I had been out with other girls before going to the Isle of Man in 1957 but they had been more for a laugh than anything serious. The girls I had gone out with before were nothing compared to the beautiful feelings I had for Joyce. She was my first true love.

I have been with lots of women throughout my life but I don't think anyone can ever recapture that first young, innocent love. I will never forget those glorious summer days we spent together. We would just walk along the beach together or through the town and I would just think nothing can feel this good, not even Heaven. We would laugh together, smile together, and just want to be with one another. She seemed so honest and straightforward, warm and generous. She was fun to be with and when she kissed me I felt a beautiful, tender love for her. I would have done anything for Joyce because during those days together we were as one, thinking and planning our young dreams together.

I remember years later going back to the Isle of Man for a holiday with my wife and daughter but it just wasn't the same. The place had lost its holiday charisma, maybe because people were going abroad to Spain or Greece and because the Isle of Man had lost most of its trade to the sun-drenched beaches of southern Europe. I think I went back there to capture the nostalgia of my teenage years and to reminisce about my first true love. Wonderful memories never die.

However, in a matter of a few months I had overcome my grief and returned once more to the life I knew.

We all agreed that jewellers should now become our number-one target. I knew the smash-and-grab raids in our area would soon come to an end because the jewellery shops were having unbreakable glass put in their windows. We were also warned that their alarms were getting more sophisticated and more difficult to silence. There was only one thing left to do, and that was to start working outside Liverpool.

We decided to branch out to some of the little towns and districts on the outskirts of Liverpool. So we drove around places like St Helens, Warrington and Prescot which we believed were still some way behind the times. We were proved right. We must have plundered a dozen or more of them over the next few months and we would read of our raids in the local newspapers. It was easy money but we still went through our strict planning procedure to ensure we targeted the right shops where there were no police hanging around.

Other gangs from Liverpool were doing the same as us. Eventually, you had all kinds of raiding parties driving out to these premises and just stealing everything. No wonder Liverpool earned itself such a terrible name for crime, which seems to have lasted to this day.

Towards the end of the 1950s, my older brothers were being released from prison. Our Freddy was the last to be set free. He was then 27 and had served seven years of his ten. My ma seemed so happy now that they were all out of prison but things didn't seem the same at home. Something seemed to be missing but maybe it was simply the fact that I had grown up. Anyway, our Freddy and I started hitting it off straight away. There was an understanding between us, a close relationship and I respected him. He was determined to make up for lost time and wanted to 'go at it' right away.

Of course, I told him everything that I had been doing over the past few years and he was quite surprised at the number of jobs we had pulled. But we agreed that smash-and-grabs were getting played out because of the steel grilles and the sophisticated alarms and Freddy wanted to branch out into more sophisticated and daring jobs where there was a real chance of picking up big money.

While our Freddy was doing his time, he'd learnt a lot from his prison mates about crime. He surprised me with his knowledge. He seemed to know about everything. A few of his friends came to visit him; he still lived at my mother's. Eventually, my ma's became our meeting place. My mates would come to our house and with my brother's mates calling it was getting pretty hectic. We would usually sit around drinking tea and my old lady just came to accept it. She never said anything to either Freddy or me but I had suspected for some time that she knew I had been up to no good. She wasn't stupid and yet she had simply turned a blind eye to the fact that I had become the family breadwinner, that I kept putting a few quid in her purse each week. I think she had given up on me long before Freddy came out of jail.

But we all had the greatest respect for my ma. We always made sure she was shown the utmost respect from everyone who called at the house. Nobody was allowed to swear or anything while my ma was around. All my friends accepted the situation and behaved well in front of her. That was good manners. It also showed my ma that we respected her.

When our mates dropped round my ma would usually go to the kitchen and begin sorting a meal for us all. I think she genuinely wanted to be generous to our friends but I knew she also didn't want to know what was going on and, by busying herself in the kitchen, she avoided any embarrassment she may have felt about the graft we were discussing. She also liked the fact that her scoff was so good and the lads would wolf down everything she dished out, especially the scouse and pea soup.

One day, not long after our Freddy's release, a friend of his called at the house to see him. His name was Charles Connolly. He had just got out of jail after serving ten years for murder. He had been involved with a man called George Kelly in a famous case in Liverpool which became front-page news and was known as the 'Cameo Murder'. The Cameo was a popular picture house in Liverpool which, like many cinemas at that time — before the television age — was packed most nights. During a robbery at the Cameo, the manager was shot dead and Charlie Connolly and George Kelly were charged with his murder.

Kelly was hanged at Walton Prison and Connolly was sentenced to a long jail term. Before the trial, Charlie had turned King's evidence and for doing so he was snubbed and ostracised by the Liverpool criminal fraternity who believed he had grassed on his mate George Kelly. But those that rushed to judge him and brand him a 'grass' didn't know the truth of the matter. Charlie had no choice but to turn King's evidence. In fact, George Kelly had signed his own death warrant when he had confessed to a prosecution witness — a police informer — that he had shot the cinema manager. The policeman in charge of the murder case planted the informer in Walton Jail in an effort to get Kelly to talk. It worked brilliantly. During walks around the prison yard, Kelly confessed to shooting the manager. The police informer also tried to get a confession out of Connolly in the same way but Charlie knew he wasn't guilty and wasn't having any of it. Connolly continued to deny that he had played any part in the shooting.

All these details came to light at the trial at Liverpool Assizes. It also came to light that Kelly himself had been an informer when he was mixing with Liverpool villains. But, of course, because Charlie had been on the same job with Kelly he, too, was guilty of armed robbery and technically guilty of the manager's murder. In the end, Charlie Connolly pleaded guilty and that's why he got a long sentence. But there was no way Charlie had anything to do with the actual shooting. He didn't even know that Kelly was carrying a gun, let alone that he might use it. Charlie had just been in the wrong place at the wrong time.

I liked Charlie Connolly. He was a kind and generous man and he was greatly respected by my family, including my ma. He became a frequent visitor to our house.

I wasn't far off my eighteenth birthday and talking to Freddy, Charlie and all their mates, who were all many years older than me, I started to feel the time was ready to join the big time.

Chapter Four

I started working with our Freddy and his mates, who were right villains. They were all professionals and I was made up that they accepted me in their firm. Although to them I was still just a kid, I was making lots of money with them. At that time the average wage was probably around £12 to £15 a week and I was pulling in about £150 a week. I thought I was a millionaire. We were planning jobs, raiding offices and firms and blowing safes.

In those days, the criminal world considered safe-blowing to be the very top of the crime list, reserved only for experts and real professionals. I was over the moon to be included in their firm and I would lie awake at night excited by the thought that somehow I had made it right to the top of the ladder. I couldn't believe my luck and I was certain that this magic would never end. My old mates were still doing smash-and-grabs and other robberies.

I parted company from John and Joey and they went

their own way after recruiting two other mates. We remained the best of pals and I would gladly have helped them if ever they needed advice or help or found themselves in trouble. Though I had moved on, we still remained good mates and I knew I could always rely on them if ever I needed their help. That's the way it was with most villains; a member of one firm would sometimes just join up with some other firm or sometimes you could get two firms joining together. It all depended on whether you needed a few extra hands.

At the time, I believed that our trade — safe-blowing — was the pinnacle of excellence, requiring excellent technique, daring, planning and a high level of knowledge of how explosives worked, how they should be placed and how much was needed at any one time. All that could only be learned from experience and that was why many criminals were frightened to get involved with safe-blowing. Perhaps they thought they might blow themselves up and get killed.

But looking back on all the safes we blew, the operations were basically quite easy as long as a few basic rules were followed. The builder's office soon became our main target because we knew that every Wednesday night the wages money was guaranteed to be in the safe waiting to pay the workers the following day. We nearly always got our vital inside information from the building workers. There were always one or two building workers prepared to give us the nod and if the job was successful then he would be properly looked after. All the worker had to do was give a few details of the office layout and the best method of gaining entry. These fellas were called 'card-markers' and there were numbers of villains who made a career out of card-marking, gathering information from building workers and passing it on to safe-blowing firms like ours. A good, reliable card-marker could earn himself good money providing accurate information.

Sometimes, however, we came across a bad card-marker. These were the ones who were just guessing there would be money in a firm's safe, hoping they would be right with their lies and expecting a good pay-day after the job was completed. They never gave a fuck for the risks we were taking in blowing open a safe only to find nothing in it. If we had been caught, it would have been long jail sentences, particularly for the men who had already done time.

The first safe I actually witnessed being blown open fascinated and intrigued me. I also felt a sense of bewilderment and excitement. I watched the safe-blowers in operation and was impressed at the professional way they went about the task. These fellas were experts. We had just broken into a builder's offices in Liverpool and our Freddy and his mate manhandled the safe on to its back so the safe door was facing upwards. They then stuffed some gelignite into the keyhole and gently pushed a detonator right into the centre of the keyhole. Then I helped pack all kinds of clothes and sacking we had found in the offices around the safe in an effort to muffle the noise of the explosion.

Once the detonator had been lit, everyone had to keep well away from the safe, hiding behind a wall or a partition. It was a very dangerous game. Too much explosive and the entire office building could have been blown to smithereens with all of us with it. And if too little explosive was used, or placed in the wrong place, then a decision had to be taken very quickly whether the whole process should be repeated immediately. Some men believed that in those circumstances it was better to sack the job off and get out of there fast, just in case the explosion had been heard by some patrolling bizzies.

If all went well, we would immediately rush to the safe to see how well the door had been blown. The minute it was blown we would just grab the money and the contents and get out of the place as quickly as possible. Sometimes the noise of the explosion did alert the police and, of course, safe-blowers were sometimes caught bang to rights. They always received very long sentences. We wanted none of that. At my first job, we collected £2,500 from the safe, equivalent to something like £25,000 in today's money. It was a good night's work.

Sometimes, there were funny moments and there were other occasions when there was nearly death and disaster. One night we had just taken a safe from some premises. We had to move the safe because the place was not far from a police station and we couldn't risk the possibility of them hearing the explosion. So we had no option but to remove the safe and blow it some miles away.

We were just driving away from the place with the safe in the van when a copper spotted us. We knew he was suspicious and we were convinced that he would immediately make a call to the local police station and they would not be too far behind us. We had two choices, either abandon the safe and the van we had stolen or take the risk of carrying on. We put it to the vote and we agreed it was worth the risk of going on.

It must have been about 3.00am and we expected we would be able to hide somewhere unnoticed, blow the safe, grab the money and do one sharpish. Our Freddy spotted a park and told the driver to park up. We drove in, parked the van in a secluded spot and decided to blow the safe there and then. One of the men accompanying us was a big strong fellow named 'Tosh' Smith. We often employed him because of his strength more than anything else. He was very handy when it came to lifting safes that weighed a couple of hundredweight.

Tosh and one of the other lads pulled the safe from the van and our Freddy set about blowing it. Once he had put the explosives in place, we scattered out of the way and we checked to see whether there was any police activity around the park. There was none. We decided to blow the safe as quickly as possible, grab the money and then make our way home on foot, abandoning the van which we felt sure they would be searching for.

We had been led to believe that the safe contained two weeks' wages so we knew it was worth taking a risk to blow it. It wasn't often one managed to find a safe containing double wages.

Freddy lit the fuse and we all ran from the immediate area and spread out, lying on the grass. Nothing happened. Not even a splutter. We waited for another minute and still nothing happened. We were, of course, more anxious than usual because we knew the police were searching for us and we were worried in case they decided to search the park.

Still nothing happened.

'Give it one more minute,' Freddy said. 'We can't

take any risks. It might have just been a slow burn.'

We waited and I could almost hear my heart thumping. I was becoming nervous. Nothing happened. It just didn't explode. Freddy and one of his mates, decided to go and check what had happened. I watched with my heart in my mouth as they walked very slowly and cautiously towards the safe to check what had happened to the detonator. The detonator had failed to go off. They decided to have one more go. Despite the fact that the fuse was now a lot shorter, they quickly re-lit the fuse and ran back to where they had been lying low in the grass.

Meanwhile, Tosh Smith had started walking towards the safe, totally unaware of what had been going on. He had gone to park the van further out of sight of any passing vehicles, behind some tall trees. We were shouting to him to keep away from the safe which we knew was about to blow. It was too late. He was walking right past it when the detonator and the explosive blew, catapulting the safe door through the air and missing Tosh by inches. He must have been the luckiest man alive. By the time we reached him, he was just standing there, a look of shock and disbelief on his face. He just kept repeating, 'Fuckin' hell, fuckin' hell, fuckin' hell.'

But our luck had held that night and we took away a very big lump of money. We split up and all took different ways back to our homes. As we walked home, we kept our eyes peeled for police road-blocks. We encountered two but we managed to skirt around them so we were never roped in, not even a pull. For Tosh, it was a night that he would never forget. His head was nearly ripped off his shoulders.

At this time we must have carried out about five jobs

a month and we were making really good money. But our success had a headache. The jobs we were pulling off were attracting all kinds of attention, especially from the media, as well as the police. Our firm enjoyed so much success that some of our number became too high-profile.

It wasn't just the graft that was making the headlines and bringing us to the notice of the bizzies, but it was also our lifestyles. Our Freddy had different mates who were now wanting to join the firm. One of these was a fellow called Johnny Oats. Now Johnny was a very well-known villain around Liverpool at that time. He came from the famous Bull Ring in the city centre.

Johnny was a good bloke, except for one problem. First and foremost, Johnny was a party man, a big party man. He could never resist a party and looked for any excuse to have one. I believe he liked the parties and the champagne lifestyle because they attracted the beautiful women and Johnny also loved beautiful women. He was never happier than when in a nightclub enjoying the music and the goings-on and being surrounded by pretty girls. It was his idea of heaven. Every single time we had a 'good touch' Johnny would blow all his money on women and parties within a couple of weeks. Then, of course, he would be keen to make another hit so that he could get his hands on more money to splash around. Now, we were well aware that the local detectives — the 'filth' in our language — knew that villains hung about in Liverpool's nightclubs. And they would often put one or two of their own in those places to keep their eyes open for anybody throwing their money around who might have got their pile of cash by criminal means. As a result, of course, villains like Johnny Oats stood out like a sore thumb. They just knew he had been at it, but they couldn't touch him for anything specific. But the very fact that the filth knew he had been at it meant he could bring it all on top for the rest of us.

Johnny Oats had two brothers, Kieran and Francis, who were both good blokes. They were known for being smart dressers and were popular with the rest of the villains in Liverpool during the the late 1950s and early 1960s. Kieran Oats became our Freddy's best friend. Our Freddy and I, together with Kieran, decided to branch out on our own. The three of us felt that the rest of the firm were bringing too much attention to themselves, so we broke away from them. There were no hard feelings or anything like that.

It wasn't as though we were taking anyone else's livelihood. The rest of the firm knew all the ins and outs of blowing safes so nobody was being done out of earning a living. We also felt it was becoming more risky now that so many other local firms were trying their hand at safe-blowing. And there was another big problem. The media were making the safe jobs headline news. Local business was up in arms, demanding action. As a result, the bizzies were constantly on the alert.

Sometimes, the noise of a safe exploding would be deafening and the police would know right away what had caused that noise. The minute they heard a suspicious bang, they would immediately cordon off areas and erect road-blocks, stopping and searching anyone they thought might be a suspect. Builders' merchants were taking advice from crime prevention officers, changing their regular collection days, and not leaving pots of money in their firms' safes overnight. With all this tightening of regimes, we knew our little earners would become far more difficult to pull off. We had to think of new ways to earn a crust.

Once again, our Freddy came up with a brainwave. We remembered that Charlie Connolly had been caught as he and his mate were robbing a cinema. Now, we all knew that cinemas were taking big money every night of the week at that time and we knew that the takings were left overnight in safes kept in the manager's office — especially Sunday nights. We found out that they never banked the weekend's takings 'til Monday. There was another vital point to knocking over cinema safes; they were sound-proof. We were certain that even a loud explosion wouldn't be heard outside in the streets whatever the time of night.

So we went to work, selecting the biggest cinemas from which we hoped to bag the biggest hauls. We would go to the pictures, see the film and then hide somewhere in the lavatories or wherever. No one bothered to check if the place was empty before locking the doors and going home for the night, leaving the night's takings securely locked up in the manager's safe. So, here we were, once or twice a week, happily blowing safes in picture houses knowing that nobody could hear us outside.

I have actually been keeping watch inside while our kid and his mate have been working on the safe and a copper has walked past testing the doors of the premises. We would just blow the safe, stay in place for a few hours and move out into the street to mingle with the people going to go to work. That way we never brought attention to ourselves. It went like a treat.

This went on for quite some time. We might take a

few hundred quid on every hit and no one was any the wiser. We were making plenty of money. I was living well, enjoying myself, looking after my ma and the family and still having enough to buy myself good clothes and jewellery and spend what money I wanted. But sometimes there were snags.

We had turned over so many cinemas in and around Liverpool that we were fast running out of places to hit. We decided we would have to move away from Liverpool, into totally new areas where we had never before operated. It was good common sense.

And there was another major problem. Other firms who read of our escapades in the local papers began to adopt the same technique — hitting cinemas and, as a result, the police became more active which also made our lives more difficult. Kieran Oats had split up with me and our kid and had gone off to join a London firm. After a few months, however, he was caught bang to rights and was given seven years.

Me and Freddy and another mate of ours went into Wales on a job we were put on to. A card-marker had told us there was a very large sum of money in a safe in a big laundry in Wrexham, North Wales.

We drove down, located the place and in no time we were in. My part was to keep look-out. Our kid and his mate went to work on the safe, packing clothes, blankets and sheets around it in a bid to muffle the explosion. They blew the safe but it never opened. Now there was a golden rule which we had always followed when blowing a safe in any building; if the safe didn't open right away we never tried again because somebody could have been alerted by the noise of the explosion. It was simply too risky and therefore madness to try a second time. I knew we were doing the wrong thing and I said so. I just had a bad feeling about the whole place, but our kid and his mate wanted to give the safe one more go and so, somewhat reluctantly, I went along with them.

Just as they had the device all set up once again, we heard the sound of whistles. We knew instantly that these were police whistles and we knew we were in a mess. I looked outside and it seemed as though we were surrounded by the entire Welsh police force. I rushed from place to place but wherever I looked, I could see police. They had us completely cut off; there was no escape.

Disturbed by the noise of whistles and clanging bells it seemed all the neighbours wanted to join in the excitement. Everyone seemed to come out of their houses to stare at us and people came crowding around us, looking us up and down and inspecting us. I don't think they had ever seen safe-blowers before. The on-lookers weren't hostile at all, simply curious. While we were being escorted to waiting vehicles, we could see the police officers were congratulating one another on their result. I was fucking gutted.

Catching safe-blowers in the act of blasting open a safe in Wrexham was obviously a very big deal for the local police as well. When we were put in the police cells, the bizzies kept coming in to stare at us. Mostly, they said nothing but simply stared. We heard them chatting amongst themselves as soon as they left the cells but they didn't speak in front of us. Overnight, we had become famous. I thought to myself, If this is what fame's all about, you can fucking keep it. I don't think anything big had ever happened in Wrexham before.

While we were in custody, other police officers came to visit us from all over the north of England, the Midlands and mid-Wales. They wanted us to admit to other jobs that had been done in their areas. It was madness. Most of the jobs they tried to pin on me were in places on the map that I had never visited in my life and many places I had never even heard of, let alone visited.

I had been warned by those more experienced than me that the one rule I had to follow if ever I was picked up by the police for questioning was to say fuck all. Keep my mouth shut and admit to nothing, even when caught red-handed. It was the golden rule. And that's exactly what I did, though it obviously really annoyed the filth who wasted so much of their time questioning me.

Eventually, we were all sent to Chester Assizes and my brother, Freddy, having pleaded guilty, was given three years. His mate also copped three years and I was sent for Borstal training.

* * *

I had never even seen the inside of a prison before and what a shock I got when I first walked in there. It wasn't the conditions that shocked me so much as some of the prisoners. Before being sent to a Borstal, young villains like me were sent to an adult prison for six weeks. Officially, a YP (young prisoner) is sent there so that he can be 'assessed'. I think young villains are sent there to show them how bad life is in an adult prison in an effort to persuade them to go straight in future. Most young people sent to Borstal know that if they re-offend they will end up in jail the next time. I was sent to Walton Prison which then had a notorious name for the number of hard-cases, tough villains and gangsters housed there.

I was amazed because instead of the young, tough gangsters I'd expected, I discovered the majority of prisoners were the dregs. I couldn't believe how so-called hardened convicts could creep and crawl around some of the screws, even going as far as grassing on one another. I found that despicable. Every city has its local prison and they mostly cater for people who have been sentenced to short terms — three months, six months, but usually never more than three years. They're called 'calendar cons' because they're always in and out of jail, getting short sentences for petty crimes.

After two months, I was transferred to Latchmere House, an allocation house in Surrey. Two weeks later, two other lads and I were taken to our final destination a 'Borstal Camp' in Yorkshire called Gringley. In fact, it was an old RAF camp, totally remote in the middle of windswept Yorkshire. The place consisted of five wooden huts where we all slept and a single brick building which consisted of offices and the dining area. When I and the other two lads arrived, we were marched into the Chief's Office and ordered to sit on the floor and wait.

After a few minutes, the office door opened and I had the shock of my life. A giant of a man walked in. He must have been more than 6ft 6in tall, with massive shoulders and large strong arms and legs. He must have weighed around 20 stone but he looked fit. There wasn't an ounce of fat on him. I gulped, overcome by seeing such a giant of a man.

I thought, I'm not going to get on the wrong side of him, he would kill you in a fight.

'I'm the Chief,' he said in a loud, forceful voice as he looked at each of us as though examining our innermost thoughts and secrets. 'I'm in charge here.'

There was a stunning, eerie silence. No one said a word. I looked around and I could see in the faces of the other lads that they also were overcome by the size of the man who would be in charge of us for the next few months.

'Understand?' he asked.

We nodded, not sure whether we should speak or not.

In silence, he then inspected each of us in turn as we sat in silence on the floor.

Then he said, 'Now listen to me and listen well.'

He paused for effect. Then he said very slowly, 'I am the "hard-case" here; there's no bullying here. Understand?'

We nodded.

He went on. 'I'm the only bully. Understand?'

Again we all nodded.

He then told us in no uncertain terms that we were all young men who were going to work hard and behave ourselves throughout our stay.

He added, 'By the way, there's no queers in here. None of that stuff is allowed. Understand? You will all do as you are told and work hard, harder than you have ever worked in your lives.'

After that brief, no-nonsense talk he relaxed a little and I felt that he began to talk to us in a fatherly sort of way. We all relaxed. The lad sitting next to me became a bit cheeky, trying it on with the Chief. Within two seconds the Chief had stepped forward, grabbed the kid by his shoulder, hauled him to his feet and whacked him. The kid hit the deck with the Chief still standing in front of him. As I watched the kid's face screwed up in pain, I made a vow to myself that I was never going to answer him back or make any sort of cheeky remark. The Chief put the lad back on the floor and carried on as if nothing whatsoever had happened.

The Chief's name was Mr Marshall. Despite that hair-raising introduction to the giant, I learned later that he was both a fair and an honest man. I came to respect him and so did most of the lads. But he was strict and he would put up with no nonsense from any of us. He kept telling us, 'I want you all to think of your parents and how you're ruining their lives.'

The rest of the staff were also big, well-built, fit men and they were not to be argued with either. In a fight you would stand no chance with them — they looked and were hard bastards.

Everything in Gringley was run like clockwork. We were up early and out to work. We were employed mostly in farm work. Mr Marshall had been right. He did work us hard, usually from morning until night. But it was the winter months that were the toughest. It was murder being out in the foggy, freezing weather, our hands blue with cold, our bodies shivering so much that you couldn't feel your hands or your feet. I remember picking carrots in such freezing weather and because the ground was frozen it was almost impossible to collect any of the carrots. But no one dared to complain. Somehow we stuck at it but I vowed never to return to the place again even if that meant getting a job and going straight.

One lad became so distraught with the cold that

penetrated every part of our bodies that he decided he was going to make a run for it. He had only recently arrived and he believed that if he made a run for it he might escape or he might be sent somewhere else. He said that he would do anything to get out of the place. We all encouraged him to have a go and attempt an escape which was bang out of order of us. The reason we egged him on was because whenever anyone tried to run away, those left in the fields were immediately ushered back inside. The screws feared that if one made a run for freedom, everyone would try and escape which would have meant the masters would have had an almost impossible task rounding up 40 or so lads who had all fucked off in different directions. We wanted him to run off because it meant we would be called into the warmth of the huts, escaping from the bitter cold that numbed our very bones.

Others had discussed the possibility of running away but the main stumbling block was the fact that Gringley was situated on a vast plateau and the land was flat as far as the eye could see. There was no place to hide and lie low for a while. You could be spotted for miles. But this particular day was foggy and so this stupid lad made a run for it. As soon as the masters realised one boy was missing, they called us all inside and took off in their Land Rover to find him and bring him back.

When we heard the Land Rover returning, we were all ordered outside to witness the return of the runaway. The Chief obviously wanted us to see what happened to lads who tried to run away. The lad was half-running and half-walking, handcuffed to the back of the Land Rover by a long chain. The poor kid was white with frost covering him. They just untied him and ordered him to do press-ups to thaw out. We all had to stand in the freezing cold and watch as the poor, exhausted kid tried to carry out their orders.

After I had been there a few months, I found that I was quite enjoying myself, which amazed me.

I thought to myself, This is fucking madness. I must have lost my fucking head.

But it was true. I had actually come to enjoy the discipline, the rigorous training schedule. The young lads who had all become my mates. Some of them were no-hopers, but the majority were staunch kids who I would have trusted to take on a bit of graft on the outside.

When I had first arrived at the desolate Second World War aerodrome, I thought I was going to die in the place; it was so forbidding, the environment was hostile and uninviting. I expected to hate every waking moment at Borstal. The staff kept us all working hard but we did have hours of PT and games which I came to enjoy.

And every week we were given several hours of what they called 'rehabilitation'. The Chief spent a lot of time talking to us and trying to teach us the difference between right and wrong. By the time I was released from the place, he had nearly convinced me that I should lead an honest life.

Throughout my months at Gringley, members of my family came to visit me on a couple of occasions but though my ma wanted to come and see me and even pleaded with me to let her come and see me, I didn't want her to visit because I was certain that she would become upset; and I had done enough to upset her already.

I was still at Borstal when I received the terrible news that my mate John Connor had been killed in a car accident in London Road, Liverpool. He had died at the wheel of a stolen Jaguar during a police car chase. It was typical of John. He was only 19 when he died, exactly the same age as me, and his death made me think long and hard about what I should do with my life. John had been a good mate of mine and I always worked with him because he was good at his job. He used to steal cars not only for fun, but also to teach himself how to handle different vehicles. He would then go practising how to drive hard and fast under difficult circumstances. And there was nothing John liked more than a fast, 100mph car chase with the bizzies on his tail.

We had done some crazy things together; we must have been involved in so many chases with the bizzies and I admire John for the way he would leave them behind, despite the half-a-dozen or so cars chasing us. But John had trained himself. He knew Liverpool and the surrounding area better than most taxi drivers. He studied routes he would take and he led the bizzies all over Huyton and would still lose them. He was brilliant. I just felt so very, very sad.

But his death at the wheel of a really fast car was probably the way he would have wanted to die. He loved to compete against good police drivers. Sometimes, I felt he had to have that buzz. I would have been far happier with no car chase at all.

John's death made me wonder whether I would die young, too. During those years at the end of the 1950s, everyone seemed to be dying young. The terrible tragedy of the 'Busby Babes', the Manchester United footballers, who were killed in the Munich air crash; Buddy Holly, one of my favourite singers at the time, killed in another plane crash; and the famous young Hollywood film star, the rebel James Dean, who was only 24 when he, too, died in a car crash. James Dean was the star of such legendary films as *East of Eden* and *Rebel Without a Cause*, and I remember feeling down when I heard of his death. Throughout the '50s, it seemed that many of the Top Ten singles were about people dying. 'Teen Angel' and 'Tell Laura I Love Her' were two I loved and the Everley Brothers cut a disc about a young girl being killed in a plane crash. John Connor's favourite song was 'It's Only Make-Believe' by Conway Twitty.

It seemed in the 1950s as though it had become fashionable to die young and many of the kids just didn't want to grow old. When someone like James Dean was killed, we talked of our lives and whether we, too, wanted to go on living boring, ordinary lives like our parents or whether we would prefer to enjoy life to the full while still young and face an early death. But I wasn't one of those kids who wanted that sort of short life. I wanted to go on living a fast, hard life so that I had money to burn on the good things that life could offer me. I had dreams, young dreams, and too much to live for.

Thirteen months after arriving at the old RAF base in Yorkshire, I was driving away from the place and, believe it or not, part of me was sorry to be leaving. The place had grown on me. When I arrived home after so long away, I realised that I was still young but now I was super fit. I had never been so fit and athletic in my life and never would be again. But it made me feel good. All that hard work, physical training and discipline had done me a power of good. I felt as though I was walking on air.

When I arrived back home, I had every intention of going straight. Mr Marshall had convinced me that I should get a proper job and lead an honest life. And he had been honest enough to tell me that the reason I would take that decision was because of the amount of rehabilitation I had received. However, there was another, more important reason — my ma. She had been a good mother to me and my three younger brothers. I could see the worry in her face every time I came home, knowing that I had been into some villainy or other. And yet she didn't want to know exactly what I had been up to because that would only make her worry more. And I hated to see her upset and worried. It wasn't fair to her and yet it was me who was making my mother miserable, so I decided to go straight, give it a go.

One of my mates who I had done a lot of graft with had been caught and sentenced to some years in jail and I couldn't get out of my brain the fact that my best mate John Connor had been killed in a car chase with the police. His death had really cut me up far, far more than I had realised at the time. It was as though I had lost part of my own life because we had been so close.

And Mr Marshall had made me realise that although I wasn't married and although I didn't have any kids, I still had responsibilities. I had three younger brothers who looked up to me and I didn't want them turning to crime and ending up dead or banged up inside some nick. I wanted to make sure my three younger brothers kept out of trouble and so, I thought to myself, if I went straight, they would also.

Our Billy who was two years younger than me had

gone to live with my older sister, Delia. She was a decent, hard-working person and so was her husband Joe.

Billy had just left grammar school, which was in a small town outside of Liverpool called Prescot. He was on his way to having a good career ahead of him. He was just 18 and I was going on 20. My brother Billy and I were inseparable. We had always been that way from the first time we both could walk, right up to our mid-twenties. We just went everywhere together — clubs, parties, dances and every other social activity we were involved in. But when it came to my criminal way of life, I wouldn't let him take any part in it.

When you come to think about it all, there we were, two brothers trying to make the grade, both determined to try and crawl out of the quagmire, so to speak. One by honest means and the other by criminal ones.

Take, for instance, the time when our Billy had passed the 11-plus exam and won a place at grammar school. My mother and sister and my grandmother — who was still alive in 1953 — clubbed together and bought him a bike. In those days, it was a big occasion for a boy of 11 to have his own bike. That wouldn't impress the kids of today, as they have practically everything handed to them on a plate; even my own children have wanted for nothing. Only recently, I bought my youngest daughter a new car, which at today's standards is 'just the norm', but even when she was a child, a new bike didn't mean a great deal, as everyone had one. But when we were kids, it was a very big thing.

However, with our Billy having the bike bought for him, I felt a little bit jealous. After all, I was only a kid myself. I knew that my poor mother couldn't afford to buy me one and, if she could have afforded it, she would have had no hesitation. But with me being the way I was, I went out and stole one. In fact, it was two bikes we stole, one each for me and my mate.

My mate at the time was a lad called Joey Hannigan who lived in Winbourne Road, just around the corner from our house. Joey and I stripped the two bikes we had stolen in his backyard. We hung the frames on the washing line after taking the wheels off and painted the frames different colours.

Mine was blue and I was thrilled to bits when it was finished. I put the wheels back on and made a few more adjustments and I had myself one of the best bikes around. It was a truly wicked bike — all the kids used to go mad for a ride on it. I used to make all kinds of excuses to my mother, saying it belonged to my mate. Our Billy knew where the bike had come from, but he said nothing because secretly he was pleased for me, but that's the way Billy was with me. I knew deep down he idolised me being his big brother and everything.

We were, and still are, very loyal to one another. Even after all these years, I'm proud of him and I know he worked very hard to achieve his goal in life. He is now a successful businessman in New Zealand. We still correspond regularly, and in fact it was Billy who gave me the inspiration to write this book.

But back to the story. My other two brothers, Jimmy and Joe, had become a little unruly whilst I had been away. I had to keep my eyes on them, and by that I mean try and keep them out of trouble and not upset my mother. She had gone through enough with me and my older brothers. My old fella was not interested in his family; he was too fond of the drink by now.

Well, here I am trying to take care of things at home and doing it the hard way — working honestly for a living. My former probation officer, Mr Cubbons, was more than pleased that I had turned over a new leaf and had managed to get employment.

I started work for Colin Bleasdale, who owned Sefton Building Company which was situated in Aintree, just outside Liverpool. It was a good firm to work for and Mr Bleasdale was prepared to give me a chance, knowing where I had been and what I was regarding my past. I was put to work helping some other fella who had the works van, which is how I learned to drive, incidentally. We used to do all the deliveries to various building sites, which wasn't too bad as far as a job goes.

I was coming home each week with my wages and paying my ma her share to help with the household bills and everything. My other brother, James, had also started work; he was 16 by now and had so far kept out of trouble. It was still a bit of a struggle as far as money went, but my mother seemed to manage somehow.

Now that I was living the honest way of life and trying to be a decent citizen, it was the usual routine of getting paid Friday and ending up skint by Monday. Can you imagine me keeping this up? I still had my mates calling to see me and pestering me to jump in with them on all kinds of robberies. To be honest, I was tempted on more than one occasion, but the answer was always 'No.' The reason — I had met my wife to be.

Her name was Veronica Morgan. She was from St John's estate in Huyton. It was the usual 'boy meets girl' situation. My pals and I used to hang around the same places as Veronica's friends. Most teenagers frequented what we called 'milk bars'. They were just like McDonald's are to the kids of today, but there was also a big difference then — you could walk into one of these milk bars or cafés and there would be a jukebox with all the best rock 'n' roll music playing, such as Elvis, Little Richard, Eddie Cochran and many others. I know it might seem nothing to today's kids, but let's have it right, we thought everything was brilliant then. All over the city, kids would hang around in these milk bars; in fact, there was one on nearly every corner. It was the same at the dance halls and the picture houses, they'd all be full up with teenagers and when you were courting your girlfriend, these were the places to be seen in. You could even go for nice walks in the parks, which, I might say, were something else! They had beautiful boating lakes and fun fairs and shows. I know it sounds a bit primitive compared to the activities enjoyed by teenagers today, but that was the way life was in the 1950s.

I had just turned 20 when I met Veronica, and she was just 17. She was so beautiful and I fell in love with her immediately. She had dark hair in a pony tail and her eyes were a lovely green and fascinating; she was truly outstanding. We were both madly in love and wanted to be together for ever. At that time, it was a big thing for a girl to have a ring and to be able to say she was engaged to her boyfriend. I don't know why, but it was a sort of craze to be engaged and to boast about it to everyone. Veronica's sister was always going on at her, saying, 'Why aren't you two engaged?' Her sister was always bragging about the ring her boyfriend had given her which had cost him £40.

It was 1960 and £40 was nearly five weeks' wages to me at that time. For me to save that much would have taken months. Now Veronica's family never knew anything about my past. They were straight people and had good, well-paid jobs. I myself was earning a pittance compared to their salaries. I had told Veronica about my past deeds and everything I had done and how I was trying to go straight, but the temptation was too strong for me. I wanted more than anything in the world to be able to buy her a ring and become engaged. I knew I couldn't afford to wait for ever, and on my meagre wages that is how long it would take!

There was only one way I could get my hands on some real money — steal it!

Just before I was sent to Borstal, I remembered some insurance agent marking my card about a nice little safe job.

I got in touch with him and, having had a good talk, he told me that everything was still the same, nothing had changed as far as it goes. My brother Freddy had just got out of prison and, of course, we both put our heads together. The safe-blowing we both used to do a couple of years earlier was getting played out.

But there were other ways of stealing — one method was called 'the creep' (cat burglary). The job we were put on to was a big, posh Conservative Club in an old-style house in its own grounds; inside, in the safe we would find the week's takings. The club steward, so we were told, always carried the safe keys on him. Every Saturday night when all the staff and customers had gone home, the steward would sneak out of the club and go around to some woman's house who he was having an affair with.

The house the woman owned was not too far away from the club and the steward would always stay the night with her, then return to the club the next day.

This is what you call a good 'card mark'. There was only one small problem — we had to get the safe keys from the steward, which, as I said, he carried at all times. The plan was to capture him as he was coming out of the club on the Saturday night and then force him back in and make him open the safe.

After keeping a close watch for a couple of Saturday nights we decided to do it, but on the Saturday we were waiting for him, he came out with the woman he was knocking off.

I said to Freddy, 'There's no way I'm doing it with her on the scene.' I just didn't fancy hurting a woman. It just wasn't me when it came to women and kids getting hurt.

So we decided to follow them back to her house and try and work out another plan. We watched them go into the house, having followed them for a short while, and we 'sat off' and waited in a park opposite. I thought we would have a better chance of creeping the house if they both fell asleep. After all, it was Saturday night and most people have a good drink, never mind other things that they would be getting up to!

I knew in a couple of hours they would be well away (fast asleep). It must have been about 4.00am when we made our move. The problem was that there weren't any downstairs windows open. It is true to say that people actually left windows open in those days — well, most people did. The only window open, though, was at the gable end or side of the house upstairs. Directly underneath the window was a parked car. At first, I thought of standing on the roof of the car and reaching up to the window, but it was far too high. When you're doing a job like this, you have to be very, very quiet; there is no forcing doors open or breaking windows or anything like that. If you make too much noise and wake people up, then you have blown it!

We had a look around and decided that the best way in was through that window. As luck would have it, along the fence in the next door garden was a ladder, one of those old, wooden extending ones. After getting the ladder from next door, we put it up to the top-floor window, which was very awkward because of the car parked below it. We extended the ladder as much as we could, to the very last rung, in fact, and placed it over the car. Having done this, it was decided that I would be the one to go up the ladder and climb through the window.

Freddy was positioned at the very base of the ladder to steady it because of its awkward angle. After a while, I started to climb, trying not to make it creak. Once at the top, I started to clamber in the window. I was half-way in and I could hear the man and woman snoring their heads off. I was practically inside by now, head-first, but my legs were still poking out. I couldn't get them in properly. Just then, I felt my feet getting pushed. I couldn't believe it; my stupid brother had come up the ladder and was pushing me in. I tried to signal him to go back down as the ladder might slip. But he took no notice of me and carried on.

I was lucky; I did manage to get through the window and was now on the landing at the top of the stairs. It was deadly quiet. I could still hear the couple in their bedroom sleeping soundly. I tiptoed down the stairs and opened the front door for my brother. We decided to look in the rooms downstairs first. Freddy was at the bottom of the stairs listening to make sure the couple didn't wake up. I opened the front room door and switched the light on, quietly drawing the curtains. I found nothing and turned the lights off and made my way to the back room, which seemed to be a sort of lounge. I put the light on and there, right in front of me, was a bunch of keys, together with a pair of glasses which belonged to him. I remembered him wearing them. I picked up the keys and turned off the lights.

We left, closing the front door quietly and waited outside the house for a few minutes, just to make sure everything was OK. We then went back to the club, and when we arrived, I said to our Freddy that I would go in and that he should wait outside just in case any nosy coppers were about. It was no good both of us getting caught if it came to that. I had the keys ready and I went up to the entrance door of the club.

Once inside, I made my way to the office and quickly found the safe that we had been told about. I went through the bunch of keys and, finding the safe key, put it into the lock. The safe opened, and I helped myself to the money inside.

Once I had done this, I locked everything up, including all the doors of the club, and let myself out. My brother and I ended up sharing the money, which came to about £1,200.00 between us. It was not a bad figure for those days. The man who gave us the information got £200, so everybody was happy, especially me!

After we had done this bit of work, which went off

nicely, I was hooked again as this 'creeping' was a new way of stealing and, providing you were careful, it was very hard to get caught at it.

After doing the job that Saturday, I had a date with my girlfriend, Veronica, on the Sunday evening. We went to our usual pub, a quiet little place in Huyton Village called the Queen's. It was situated by a railway subway. I told Veronica not to go to work on the Monday, but she was scared to take the day off because of her mum. It's hard to imagine, but kids were taught not to take time off work in those days. I did finally persuade her to take the morning off, though, so we had to play truant — not from school, but from work.

On the Monday morning, we both went into town and found a nice jeweller's. Veronica started to look at the rings in the window. She was looking at the £35–£40 range, but I told her to select one for no less than £100. After all, I'd got the money for nothing and, as far as I was concerned, the money was for spending. She was thrilled to bits and, after picking the ring she wanted, we had some lunch and then she went back to work in the afternoon having made arrangements for us to meet up that evening.

I then decided to treat myself to some nice clothes. I went to a shop in London Road called Neville Reed, the top tailor's at the time, as well as other tailors called Brass and Jackson and Eric's in Commutation Row, where I bought myself a beautiful mohair overcoat. I then bought a lovely pair of brown Chelsea boots. I was over the moon with everything. When I met Veronica that evening, we had a lovely meal to celebrate in a quiet restaurant.

Those were magic moments for me. Looking back all

those years ago, I often think about all the money and jewellery I have had over the years (and I mean *lots* of money), the best cars, houses, lavish holidays, cruises round the world, and even now as I am writing this book, I own an expensive house with a swimming pool. But all that means nothing to me compared to those wholly simple years of 1950s and 1960s. I got more out of earning a tenner then than a few grand now. I just can't explain that feeling, no matter how hard I might try.

After pulling that little safe job off at the club, how could I ever go straight again? I was thinking, How could anyone work eight hours a day, six days a week, for the rest of their precious lives on those meagre wages, trying to save and being without nice things? I know there are people that do manage, and are prepared to live without, but not me! I was young and full of ambition, and I knew then I could never work straight again. I was full of dreams. I packed my job in a few weeks later.

The boss of the company tried to persuade me to stay on, but I just couldn't. He was an honourable man who gave me a chance and plenty of help. I made a feeble excuse that I had signed up to join the Navy.

For a few weeks after packing up my job, I pretended to my mother that I was still employed. I'd leave our house in the morning and come home more or less the same time each evening. Our Freddy had moved away from my mother's and had got himself a flat down in Kensington, another area of Liverpool. I was spending most of my time there during the day. We were using the flat as a meeting place where we could plan our robberies.

Anything was going now as far as crime was

concerned. Kieran Oats, our Freddy's mate, was back on the scene, as well as a fella called Sammy Mills, another friend of Freddy's, who was considered a hard-case. Sammy was always involved in all kinds of violence, he was a bit crazy; in fact, he was found dead a few years later after he had murdered somebody in Kirkby, another area of Liverpool. The whole firm seemed mad to me; they would steal money from anywhere and Freddy started to drink heavily.

I decided to pull out from them; they didn't seem organised enough and, besides, they were a lot older than me. After finally breaking away from Freddy, I decided to go back to my old mates. At least we knew what we were doing together and so we formed our own little firm again. Once we were organised, we used to meet in the Eagle and Child pub. Most of the villains in Huyton were in and out of the Eagle. There was only one problem with the Eagle — violence was always around.

Violence was starting to play a big part in my life by now. There were a lot of up-and-coming young tearaways always trying to prove themselves. If someone had a name for being a hard-case, there was always someone else who thought he was harder. What you got then were two fellas having it off — tearing into each other. Anything was used in a street fight — knives, bottles, even guns. It didn't matter as long as someone came out the winner. I had been brought up in a violent area and you had to be able to fight. That was the mentality of it all, especially with most of the gangs in Huyton.

I, though, was always interested in making money, as you didn't get paid for fighting which, I always thought, was a mug's game. By 1961, our firm had been doing all kinds of robberies. After each of these, we would have a pay-off and then it was all back to the Eagle for drinks. The Eagle was like a magnet to everyone who lived around there.

I just didn't know where I was going at that time in my life. I was planning on getting married to my girl, Veronica, and there I was running around with all my mates fighting, drinking and robbing, and all the other kids were joining up with us. Although we were having it bang off regarding money and everything, there just seemed to be no control. I knew deep down in my mind that something bad was going to happen. I knew we just couldn't carry on the way we were. We were all very young and erratic.

I was still living at my mother's house in St David's Road and at the end of our road there was an old building called Hambleton Hall. People used to hire this place out for dances, parties, weddings and other kinds of functions.

All the local kids from Huyton used to go there every Sunday night. All our gang would meet up in the Eagle, and after a few drinks, make our way over to Hambleton Hall. It was the place to be seen at that time.

Hambleton Hall was getting itself a big name in 1962. Kids were coming from different parts of the city just to be seen there, and all kinds of new music and groups were showcasing at the venue. One of those groups was called the Silver Beatles and they were a real crowd-puller. They became very famous worldwide a couple of years later and became known as the Beatles.

On this particular mad Sunday night, my pals and I were there, the hall was packed tight and everyone was having a good time dancing and drinking. I noticed another gang who were on the opposite side to our crowd getting out of order. Every time a girl went past, one or two of them would start grabbing her and cause a nuisance. After a while, one of my mate's girlfriends went past these lads and they started touching her and grabbing her arse. That was it, my mate spotted it all.

The next minute, there was a kick-off which escalated into a big fight. Basically, it was just our gang on to them. Unfortunately for us, we were not only out-numbered by them, they were also armed to the teeth. I saw the hammers and knives coming out. The fight went on for what seemed like ages and, being too few in numbers, we had no option but to get out of there fast. They were giving us all a terrible beating.

I was slashed under my arm by this crazy bastard with a knife. My other mate had his jaw and teeth smashed in with a hammer. When we had all done one, we found out later that one of my pals had been almost kicked to death, and he was lucky to be alive. I wanted revenge straight away.

In this sort of situation, you can't let something like this go — the other gang will think you're soft and weak if you don't retaliate and they'd keep getting you every time you're out with your friends, wives or girlfriends. It wouldn't matter to these types of people, they were like animals. I found out later that it was a put-up job, and that they had deliberately gone out of their way to have us. It was over a bit of work our crowd had done a few weeks earlier. What this meant, of course, was that their firm should have had our job, but the man who had marked our card had told them about it as well. This is what you call 'double card-marking' which is very dangerous, because if too many people know about it and the information reaches the wrong ears, such as a grass, you could be in real trouble. But right now, the way I was feeling, I just wanted to damage those bastards! I wasn't concerned about money or jobs.

About an hour later, we rounded up a lot more of our mates — it was known as a 'call out' — and after a few enquiries we found out where those bastards had gone. Apparently, they had all left for a party at a house somewhere in Huyton. After we had located the house, I fronted up by knocking on the front door. I had a shotgun with me, and my friends were armed to the teeth, too.

After I had knocked on the door, it was opened, to my surprise, by a copper. I couldn't believe it! Here was a copper in front of me and I was pointing a gun at him. I don't know how this copper had the bottle, but he made a lunge at me to try and wrestle the gun from me, but I pulled back and shoved it in his face. I made him lie on the floor and, as he did, everybody scattered, but the policeman just lay there shaking. I thought he would try to grab my legs, so I pointed the gun right at his head and told him to stay where he was. After a couple of minutes or so, I realised the best thing to do was to forget it. I decided to call everything off, especially with the bizzies being on the scene.

I found out later that the copper had been investigating a break-in nextdoor, which had occurred earlier on, and he had just happened to be there at that time. Looking back, I suppose his presence did prevent me from killing someone because of the way I was feeling at that time.

My mates and I decided to wait for another day and

let the heat die down. We split up and went our separate ways home. One of my mates took the gun and all the other weapons we had and planted them in a safe house. I arrived back at my mother's late that night and, after a short while, I went to bed. I had only been asleep for what seemed like a couple of hours, when I was woken up by banging and shouting outside our house. I looked out of my bedroom window and saw a large number of policemen, together with dogs and spotlights, all over our house. They were shouting for me to give myself up and come out unarmed. Obviously, I didn't want my mother and the rest of the family upset and so I fully agreed to do what they wanted. What I couldn't fathom out was how on earth they'd got on to me that quick. I knew I would be OK, or so I thought. The main thing was that there were no weapons in our house; that was always the golden rule with me. Never keep anything, especially guns, at home. As far as I was concerned, they had nothing on me and, besides, there had been nobody injured really, so I thought it would be the usual routine, down to the police station and a grilling for a day and then I would be released on some petty charge. I decided to open our front door and let them in. On doing this, all the police came steaming in and arrested me.

I was taken to Huyton Police Station. What I didn't know at the time was that a lad called Mick D, who had been in our company, had been arrested and released without charge that same night. I found out later that he'd said I was the 'main man' and that I had had the gun. I had always had that sense about Micky D. I knew he would be a wrong one if put under pressure. The bastard had grassed me up good style. I found all this out a couple of years later.

The police charged me with being in possession of a firearm and making use of it, even though I never fired it at anyone, and causing actual bodily harm. I was taken to the Magistrates Court in Prescot and, naturally, was refused bail. They remanded me back to Walton Jail.

While I was on remand, Veronica, my girlfriend, who was pregnant by now, was coming with my family to see me. After a few weeks on remand and through a strong plea of mitigation by my lawyer, I was granted bail. My lawyer mentioned to the court that I was to be married because of Veronica's pregnancy. Both sets of parents were arranging the marriage, our families were Catholics on both sides and, besides, it was the done thing at that time. But I wasn't getting married just because Veronica was pregnant; we were both madly in love. I know the predicament we were in wasn't very promising but we still loved one another.

Chapter Five

It was the beginning of 1963 when I went for trial at Liverpool Crown Court. My trial judge was a man by the name of Openshore, who, incidentally, had prosecuted my older brothers years before, and they had both received long sentences. I pleaded 'not guilty' but I had no chance. The police identified me although a gun was never produced. Some policeman stated that, while I was in custody, I had boasted to him that I had meant to shoot one of them. This was total lies, of course. There were no taped interviews in those days. It was all based on 'verbal', which was one of the most dreaded phrases any villain could wish for in those days. A policeman could state in court that you had told him you had committed the offence and this might have been completely untrue and, no matter how much you protested, they would always take the bizzie's word saying, 'Our police don't tell lies.' Later on, I will be looking at police corruption and exposing a few people. However, I was found guilty and sentenced to three years.

I had been married for six weeks before I was sentenced. Veronica's family were devastated as they knew nothing about all this. With remission, I would serve 24 months. I thought to myself it is no good moaning about it, think positive and get on with it.

Walton Jail in 1963 was full of the dregs of humanity. The place was vastly overcrowded. Three men to a cell at times and everyone dreaded the 'slopping out' conditions. I am not going to go on too much about prison conditions; it was a matter of just getting on with it. All the complaining in the world would not do you any good at all. I will just say that prison had a notorious reputation for some of the prisoners it housed. When I was sentenced, the *Liverpool Echo* highlighted my crime, which was the usual crap: 'Man charged with using guns on the police, violence in street', etc. It was grossly over-exaggerated, as there wasn't one shot fired and nobody got hurt. By the time I entered prison, I had acquired a reputation of being a right nutter, someone you don't fuck about with! I didn't want this sort of image hanging over me but, to be quite honest, ever since I got done for that charge back in 1963, it sort of stuck with me for a long time and, if the truth be known, I never raised my little finger and yet there I was, only just having been banged up, with a massive reputation.

There were quite a few mates of mine already in Walton Prison when I arrived and some of my brothers' friends were there, too. I had only been there a few days when, one night, just as we were all banged up in our cells, my door was suddenly unlocked and a screw was standing there with another prisoner. This con swaggered into my cell as though he owned the place. He said to me, 'Are you Charlie Seiga?'

I told him I was.

He then said, 'Get your gear packed, you are coming with us.'

He then introduced himself — Billy Grimwood. He told me he was a very good friend of my brother's. I was then taken over to 'I' Wing. I could see at once that Billy Grimwood had everything under control; all the cream of the top villains were there. I was introduced to a lot of the cons and offered a drink of anything I wanted. I couldn't believe how it was on 'I' Wing — it was like a little nightclub. 'I One' was like the basement of the wing and most of the cons were selected by Billy. Our cells were left mostly unlocked, and we had a big TV. Remember, this was 1963. It was just incredible!

Billy Grimwood was a real hard-case. He never trained in there like most cons do, he was just a naturally fit person. When fighting, he was so fast, nobody stood a chance with him. Yet the same man would never bully anyone. He was dead fair in his ways. I have seen men who have tried to take him out, but they never could. He was the hardest fella I had ever come across at that time.

Every wing in the prison had what is called its 'Number One'. He is the prisoner who is responsible for controlling the wing, such as cleaners, food orderlies, practically everything. The prison systems do not have anything like that these days. It has all been stamped out, but then it was unbelievable. Providing you were one of the boys, there were all kinds of fiddling going on inside and out. You could have anything you wanted, providing you had the money. Our crowd had everything boxed off in there, through Billy, of course. Don't get me wrong, it wasn't all easy-going, most of the cons were having it terribly hard. I was just fortunate in knowing the right people.

The best way to do bird at that time depended on what job you had. Being a Number One on a wing was one of the best jobs, and there was also a 'red band'. A red band was a trusty prisoner who could go anywhere in the prison. His job was taking mail to the main office and delivering any other messages for the screws or staff. Red bands had a bad name amongst the rest of the prisoners. They were considered grasses which, I suppose, some of them were but without them we couldn't get any bent mail or any of the other things we wanted.

The top job in the prison at that time was the reception wing. There was always one of our pals ready to move into one of these jobs the minute somebody left. Working on the reception was to be my job, thanks to Billy Grimwood, who, as I've said, had plenty of pulling power. The reception wing was separated from the rest of the prison except for the remand prisoners who were on the same wing as us. We worked late hours, sometimes not getting to bed until midnight and then we were up early the next morning. This wasn't so bad, though, as you could always get your head down in the afternoon. However, the rewards were good for all the hours we put in as we would have steaks for our tea. It all depended which screw was on. We would also have the odd bottle of drink. You could do all kinds there, as the amount of contraband that was available was unbelievable. It was always getting through. The remand prisoners had it OK, too. They could have fresh food and clean clothes brought in every day. They were also entitled to half-a-bottle of wine or two bottles of beer every day. All these privileges have ceased now, because of the drug menace.

What I fail to understand is that all these restrictions have not put a stop to drugs getting smuggled in. I have known men go into prison clean as a whistle and come out drug addicts. I think that if the commodity is sought after, it will get in there one way or another.

I worked in the reception wing for just over 12 months and, while I was there, it turned me into something ruthless. I had to be, the way things eventually turned out. There were all kinds of characters coming and going every day of the week. I could see the occasional pal come in and be looked after, or one of the villains we all knew, but then you have got the other side of it — the low-life, the tramps and, worst of all, the sex cases or 'beasts' as they are called. The sex cases got it hard in there; everyone who came in got a bad beating all the time. I was there when one of these beasts came in.

This screw, who was married with kids of his own, hated them. He would always mark our card as to who was a beast. He would even show us what they had done to kids or women as the screws had all the records on them. When we were told one had come in, these filthy beasts would have to have a bath before seeing the prison doctor. After going through this routine, they would be taken to the protection wing for their own safety. One of the screws would tell one of the reception lads which prisoner was a sex case, and then the screw would turn a blind eye while the attack took place. It usually happened in the bathhouse. I have seen some of the terrible hidings these beasts have received. And I have done some bad damage to them myself. When we had been shown what they had done to those little kids, it turned your stomach. Some of the things they had done were beyond belief. You just couldn't imagine that grown men, if you can call them men, could do those filthy things to little children. It was no use the do-gooders on the outside saying these people couldn't help it, they were sick and various other excuses — all I can say to that is that those beasts know right from wrong.

One of the worst cases I knew of was when this cruel bastard had a little girl locked in a room all day and when he returned home, he would go up to that kid's room and torture and abuse her. She was only five or six years old. Can you imagine that poor kid? To be left alone in that room, waiting for that beast to come home each night. The poor child died in the end. Yes, I nearly killed a few of those bastards who came in for child molesting or rape or whatever you want to call it. I don't regret one thing that my pals or I did to them. The odd thing about some of these animals is that they can pull the wool over your eyes.

I remember once this bloke had just come in. He had just been sentenced to six years. He was a very smart-looking fella — he looked and acted like one of the boys. I got talking to him before he went through the reception and he told me he was in for hijacking lorries. He seemed, as I thought, a nice enough fella. When his turn came to go through, the screw in charge called me to one side and told me this so-called lorry hijacker was in for abusing his own little daughter and son. I just couldn't believe it. I said to the screw, 'Are you sure, has there been a mistake about this fella?'

He showed me his charge record which convinced

me. A short time later, when he went for his bath he got boiling water thrown over him, which was justified, as far as I was concerned.

I often witnessed these beasts on visits and their wives who, you would think, would be the first ones to condemn them, actually coming to visit them. It makes you wonder what sort of mothers they were. I can't understand the authorities or the Government who seemed to be so lenient when it came to dishing out sentences to these perverts. They seemed to value money more than a child's life in this country.

Throughout my life, I have had respect for old people, women and children. Civility was drummed into me and yet through the eyes of the police and society, I am down as a bad villain. I won't go on too long about those filthy beasts, only to say that they are on the increase now and yet in prison they are treated better than the ordinary convicts. Why, I don't know, because there is no cure for them, except one — exterminate the bastards. I remember a prison doctor pulling me to one side in reception one night and saying to me, 'Seiga, don't hit any of these sex cases until after I have examined them. They are getting sent into me with black eyes and everything.'

And that's what a prison doctor thought about it all.

The other types of low-life were the winos. They were a different breed altogether. Some of them were funny, though. Week after week you would see the same old faces coming back and, when you think about it, they were all doing a life sentence on the instalment plan. Some of these drunks would get a sentence like 28 days for a measly £5 or £10 fine, which they couldn't pay. It makes you wonder, because keeping a man in prison for 28 days must cost the taxpayer a few hundred pounds and yet his crime was for being drunk or a petty shoplifting charge. I think it would have been more sensible to have made these people do something useful instead, like cleaning the public toilets for a week or so, or maybe washing some hospital floors or something like that. At least he would be working his fine off. I think it would also alleviate the prison population. Yet, who am I to make suggestions? The people who run these establishments are the ones with all the brains, aren't they?

I remember a certain tramp who came in one day. He smelt terrible and his clothes were crawling with lice. He was absolutely filthy! The staff in the reception used to have a long pole with a hook on the end, which was so that you could keep the tramp at bay so you wouldn't get contaminated. The pole was made specially for this purpose. A big old sheet was put down on the floor and the tramps had to stand on it and strip off all their filthy clothes. When they had done this, the clothes or rags were bundled up in the sheet by the tramp and then the bundle would be hung on the end of the pole and taken to be burnt in the incinerator.

However, this particular tramp was coming out of the bath we had for them which was especially for tramps, containing loads of disinfectant. It was like a fumigating bath. This particular tramp was given prison clothes to put on but he wanted his own, filthy clothes back which were by now in the incinerator. But he kept insisting he wanted his own clothes back. We explained what had happened to them and he then went stark raving mad, screaming his head off about all his money. After we had got him under control, the truth came out. He had a fortune sewn into the inside of his jacket. After being told this, me and a couple of pals headed right for the incinerator but we were too late. All the tramp's clothes and his money had gone up in smoke.

*   *   *

It was August 1963 and Veronica had just given birth to our son. We were both elated and we named him Anthony. Veronica, my wife, was a doting mother to our child and she was also very loyal to me; every visit she was there, she never missed once and my mail was always on time. I couldn't have asked for anything better considering the circumstances. My mother was also coping, as both my brothers were earning so I had no real pressures on the outside. My pals were always corresponding with me, filling me in on all the latest news about what was happening on the outside. I was hearing about all the new kids who lived in Huyton and were making a name for themselves. There were lots of changes going on outside and I had only been in prison for 12 months. A lot of the top villains had been discharged from Walton, including my friend Billy Grimwood and some of my other pals. There were still quite a few who remained, though, and one of those I got to know well was a man called Eric Mason. He was a Londoner and had a good reputation.

Eric was considered 'one of the boys' amongst the criminal fraternity. When it was exercise time, which was most days providing it wasn't raining, I used to walk around the yard with him and a few of his pals who were a lot older than me. I gained quite a bit of knowledge from Eric and his pals in 1963. The last time I heard about Eric Mason was when Frankie Fraser, another well-known villain from London, cut Eric's face open with a certain weapon. Now whether Frankie Fraser did or didn't do this, I know that Eric, being the man he was, wouldn't dream of pressing charges or grassing as our principles created a strong bond between villains at that time. That's the way it was. You sorted things out amongst yourselves. There was no such thing as getting a man sent to jail like these so-called 'plastic gangsters' do now. Their type go running to the police if they get severely damaged in a fight or want compensation direct from you so they won't press charges.

I know that a line has to be drawn somewhere. Certainly, we have to have law and order and police on our streets. Nowadays, I believe our mothers and children wouldn't be safe without this. Villains — or so-called villains — of today don't seem to have the same code of conduct as us from the old school. We wouldn't dream of mugging or hurting a woman or child and, as I have stated, there are certain lines that must be drawn.

I read in the newspaper while in prison about a blind man, who was brutally beaten up in his wheelchair for a few lousy pence, and a young girl of 12 who was raped by another animal. To me, those sort of scumbags are not fit to live in society. Like I've stated, I have no love for the police, but then they're a necessary evil in a way.

Another good man who I met in Walton Prison was John McGregor. I had a lot of respect for him and his pal Dickie J. John and Dickie had done a lot of armed robberies on banks, and they were regarded as the 'tops' in Liverpool at that time. I admired them both, not just because they were bank robbers or anything like that but they were very good to a lot of old people, who lived in their neighbourhood. It was a well-known fact that, especially at Christmas time, Dickie J would make sure that all those old people had coal for heating and plenty of food for their tables. Dickie J, I thought, was a very decent man.

John McGregor was a brilliant fella. I was on remand with him when I first came in. My trial started the same time as John's and every day we would be up at the same court house. He would go in one part of the crown court and I would go in another. John was being tried for a big armed wage snatch which took place in Liverpool city centre. It was a very high-profile case named by the press the 'Bowler-Hatted Gangsters', because, apparently, when they were doing the robbery, they were all dressed like city businessmen in pin-striped suits and bowler hats. In the '60s, this is the way many businessmen dressed for work.

It was lunchtime when John and his firm struck and, being dressed as they were, they didn't look out of place mingling with all the white-collar workers. After pulling off the job, they got away with a large amount of cash. It was considered one of the biggest jobs to have been done in Liverpool at that time.

John and I used to come back together from court during our trials and, each night on arriving back at prison, we would be banged up in the same cell. One night, all the lights were switched off and I was half-asleep on the top bunk when John told me to wake up properly. He said he wanted to have a talk to me regarding his trial. Now John McGregor and his firm never revealed anything to outsiders. They were a very tight firm. After I had woken up fully, he said to me, 'Look, Charlie, today in court I was offered a deal.'

He went on to tell me that his own lawyer could guarantee him — providing he pulled up the money and pleaded guilty to being involved in the robbery before the fact — that he would get off with the charge and not be sent to prison. He went on to tell me that it wasn't the police who were bent, but the judge himself. I couldn't believe what I was hearing. He then said to me, 'Look, you're a trustworthy kid,' which I thought to be a great honour, coming from him. 'What do you think?'

I said to him, 'How can I give you advice on something as big as that?'

He kept pacing up and down the cell saying, 'I don't trust the bastards, it's all a trick.'

It's true, many prisoners awaiting their trials get paranoid about who they can or can't trust. They start believing their own lawyers are working with the police sometimes. I myself don't trust most of the cons, because most are scumbags and would sell their own mothers to get out of jail. However, next morning, after walking for most of the night, John and I were both driven to the crown court and, just before we went our own separate ways to court, I said, 'John, take the chance and plead guilty, what have you got to lose?'

That afternoon at my trial, I was found guilty and sentenced to 3 years by courtesy of Mr Justice Kershaw. That same afternoon, John McGregor was fined £1,000 or an alternative of 12 months' imprisonment. The judge who sentenced John was Judge Laskey. Here is a prominent, respected man who had made a pledge to uphold the law, together with a top lawyer, who are both utterly corrupt and the police knew it. When the police at the trial realised what was happening in front of their eyes, they went haywire, but were powerless to do anything about it. Even the local press asked John if he had committed the crime. Obviously, his reply was 'No comment'. When John and I arrived back at Walton, him with his £1,000 fine and me with my 3 years, he told me everything that had gone on in court that day.

He told me he was unsure about pleading guilty at first but his lawyer reassured him and told him not to forget his part of the bargain concerning the money to be paid out to both the judge and himself. I was informed that it was quite a considerable amount. What actually happened was that John McGregor had a recess with his lawyer for ten minutes and then agreed to plead guilty to accessory before the crime. Now the police knew that John McGregor would never plead guilty to anything and, on hearing this, they must have known that something was wrong. When he finally pleaded guilty, the barrister said to the judge, 'My client wishes to change his plea of one of not guilty to guilty.'

The barrister started rattling off mitigating circumstances, saying that John had only played a small part in the firm and that he wasn't the 'Mr Big' or anything like that. He was interrupted by the judge himself saying he would not send this man to prison. 'I will hurt him where it hurts him most. He will be fined £1,000 or 12 months' imprisonment.'

John then told me that, as the judge was speaking,

the barrister turned to him, as though he was shifting his papers around and said, 'John, don't forget your part of the bargain.' The police were so disgusted that they walked out. They were banging doors and throwing their hats around, they were absolutely devastated. They knew what had gone on and they were powerless to do anything about it. Later that same afternoon, while we were still waiting in the reception, John's wife came to the prison and paid the £1,000 fine and he was then released. Before John left, he shook my hand and told me to come and see him when my time was up. I was 22 years old and learning very, very fast.

The Great Train Robbery had just taken place and, not long after, one of the robbers was sent to Walton Prison. His name was James Hussey. I remember me and the rest of the reception workers waiting up late for him to arrive one night. When Jimmy Hussey arrived, he had on a dark blue mac and was carrying a couple of magazines. I was the first con to greet him. I felt dead sorry for him. The sentence they gave him was inhuman. I think it was 25 or 30 years. Here is a man who had done no real harm, never hurt a child, raped a woman or murdered anyone, yet he got a sentence that long — it was just unbelievable. Once again it proves that the people in power — i.e. the Government and even the judges — value money more than life in this country.

I remember giving Jimmy Hussey a cup of tea and trying to console him. In fact, everyone in reception that night was for him. He was OK, though; he stayed strong and never showed any sign of weakness. He had the greatest respect from all the convicts in there at that time and, in fact, he was treated like a sort of hero. I saw quite a lot of Jimmy Hussey while I was there in 1963 and we became very friendly. He finally got transferred to a long-term prison and I never saw him again.

Capital punishment was still in force at that time and I met two men who were to be hanged at Walton Prison. The first was a lad called Joe Masters, who was in the condemned cell waiting for his execution. He had an appeal going on and was hoping to be reprieved by the Home Office. Once a prisoner's appeal has been granted by the Home Office, he is immediately taken, no matter what time of day or night, from the condemned cell down to reception to change his clothes and is then put into another cell in one of the ordinary wings.

Masters did get reprieved. It was midnight and me and my pal had to give him his change of clothes. When he was brought from the condemned cell down to reception, he did nothing but complain and moan because he couldn't have any more free cigarettes. Now here is a man who has just been saved from hanging, and all he was interested in was his disallowance of cigarettes. To me he was a right nutter!

The last man to hang in Walton was in 1964. His surname was Allen. He was charged along with another man, with committing murder of a dairy farmer or milkman. His accomplice was hanged in Strangeways Manchester. When Allen came through reception, it was the usual routine and, after he had been checked over and bathed, he was taken over to the hospital wing.

When Allen's trial started, he was back and forth from court each day. I used to give him his tea most nights and everyone told him that he would not hang as the Home Office was in the process of abolishing capital punishment and, with Masters' reprieve, we all thought that he would get away with it, too. Allen and his accomplice were tried and found guilty and both sentenced to death. When he arrived back after the sentence and before he was put into the condemned cell, I said to him 'You'll be OK, you will win your appeal and get your reprieve,' and that was the last time I saw him alive. The morning of the hanging the whole prison was in an uproar. I remember all of us convicts getting banged up and we were all screaming and banging in our cells. I have never experienced anything like it.

On the morning of the hanging, the prisoners went from uproar to complete silence. We all knew that he was dead. After about an hour, all our cells were unlocked. A pal of mine, who was a cleaner on 'I' Wing, told me he had been ordered to clean out the condemned cell. After he had done this, he said it had been in a terrible mess. There were bloodstains on the wall and some of the furniture was broken. Later on, one of the screws told us that Allen had put up a terrible fight. I believe that what used to happen was that if the condemned man put up a fight, there would be a gang of screws as a back-up and these screws also assisted the hangman.

When a person is given the death sentence, the words spoken by the judge are, 'You will be hanged by your neck until you are dead.' We are all led to believe that being hanged to death is instantaneous. This has been proven to be untrue. A prison doctor is always on hand to pronounce the prisoner dead after he has been executed. There have been cases where it has been proven that the man has actually been strangled to death.

There was a case where this happened, when a man

called Mills was hanged in the late '40s and when he dropped through the trap-door to the cell underneath where the doctor was waiting to pronounce him dead, the doctor tested Mills' heartbeat, and he wrote in his report that the man's heart was beating furiously. He tested the man ten minutes later and he stated again that the prisoner's heart was beating feebly and it was almost 30 minutes later before the doctor could pronounce that the prisoner was at last dead. The doctor wrote in his report, 'As far as I am concerned, this prisoner strangled slowly to death.' It was rumoured that the hangman and his assistant had been known to pull on the prisoner's legs once he had fallen through the trap-door. This was, of course, to hurry his death. Hanging was finally abolished a few months later.

I had just received a letter from my wife telling me my son was ill and working in reception was getting me down. I was feeling very low. The staff had changed around and the screws we had been familiar with had gone to different duties. I think someone had put the bubble in about the good time we had been having in reception. There were also jealous bastards who wouldn't think twice about grassing on us, plus the fact that the sex cases were getting a hard time and constant beatings from us, not to mention all the fiddles we had going, so they started to tighten up and deprive us of our little treats.

One night at about 11.00pm or midnight, I had just finished working and had been up since 6.00am that morning. I went back to my cell to write to my wife, and I was rushing to get it finished as I had to be up early again the next day. Half-way through the letter, my cell light was suddenly switched off from outside, where all the switches were at that time. I shouted through the cell door, 'Could you please put the light back on?'

The screw came back to the spyhole in the door and told me to get my head down. I tried to explain that I wouldn't have time to finish my letter in the morning, and would he please let me have just a few more minutes. He just hurled abuse at me through the door. He was the bastard that we had put up with all day in reception. Every one of the cons detested this screw. Don't get me wrong, there are certain screws who are all right and they show a little compassion, but when you get a bastard, you get a bastard. Anyway, there I was, still arguing with him through the cell door and he was provoking me and that is when I snapped. I went completely mad. I started smashing my cell to bits and the screw ran away. All the frustration and hatred in me came flooding out. I let it all go.

I smashed everything that I could move in my cell. The strange thing about all this was that not one screw came near my cell all this time. After about half-an-hour, I was completely exhausted and that is when they came for me. I knew I was in for a good beating so I got myself prepared. I grabbed a leg from the broken chair and waited in the corner of the cell. When the door opened, I saw a gang of screws with the mattress off a bed in front of them. I had no chance against them. They rushed in and started to beat me. I tried to fight back but it was hopeless. I was overpowered and taken down to the punishment cells and there I was given another beating. You just have to accept this as normal. Let's face it, no one would believe your word against a screw's!

The next morning, I was to face all kinds of charges

— damaging prison property, assault, threatening behaviour. In the light of these charges, I would be looking at a loss of a lot of my remission. The two screws in charge opened the cell and told me to get dressed as I had to be seen by the prison doctor, who in turn asked me my version of what had happened. He then said to me, 'You've had a black-out, haven't you, Seiga?'

I said, 'No.'

He repeated the question and I suddenly realised what he meant and I said, 'Yes, I did.'

This meant that all the charges against me would be dropped. The doctor was well known by us as he was the doctor who worked in reception with us and he remembered me from the times we had beaten up the sex cases. I realised then that he was on my side. Unfortunately, this incident in the cell resulted in me being sacked from my job in reception and I was put to work on one of the wings.

They put me on 'G' Wing and the Number One on there was a man called Peter Lynch. I was introduced to him and we became friends. Peter Lynch was another prisoner who was highly respected and I will always remember him as a man of principle.

Peter Lynch senior had four sons who did a lot of boxing. They are all good businessmen in Liverpool now.

I had been on 'G' Wing a couple of weeks, when one morning my cell door was opened. I was confronted by two screws who told me to get my gear together as I was being transferred. In total, they did the same to 12 prisoners and they told us that we were the ring-leaders and that we were responsible for the near riot over the hanging that had taken place a few weeks earlier. We were to be dispersed to various prisons all over the country. Some were sent to Manchester, some to Leeds, Birmingham and London. I was sent to Leicester.

On arrival, I was met by a crowd of screws who were waiting for me. You would have thought I was a terrorist the way they treated me. I was taken to the punishment block straight away and told that if I caused any trouble, I would be sorted out. After a few days down the block I found out there was a convict down there who worked as a cleaner and was known as a bully. I saw him throwing his weight around to a couple of the other cons. One morning, after I left my cell to 'slop out', he said to me, 'You are one of those Scouse bastards, who think they are hard!' and he started to hurl abuse at me.

I saw the two screws watching and I knew it was a set-up. He was goading me into a fight and, as you can imagine, my temper got the better of me. I got stuck in and he was easy. As I fought him, he was screaming his head off and I knew what was coming next. The screws jumped me and although I was young and fit and could handle myself, I had no chance with all those bastards when they piled in on me. I was put in a strip cell in the hospital wing.

A strip cell was a degrading experience. You were stripped naked and the cell was completely bare. No bed, no chair, nothing! All I was given was a small sheet of canvas. Whenever the cell was unlocked, I was confronted by two screws. They brought my so-called dinner to me in a plastic bowl, which was kicked along the floor by one screw. He was saying, 'Look, here's your dinner, eat it up,' as if I was a dog. I picked up the dinner and threw it all over him. They both threatened me with violence while all I could do was stand in the corner and try to retain my dignity with the piece of canvas. It's funny, when you are in that position and especially when you are naked, you feel very vulnerable and unready to fight. I just told them that the first one of them that came near me I would bite his fucking throat out, and although they would overpower me in the end, I'd get one of them. They just locked the door and fucked off.

There I was thinking, What's happening to me? I'm miles away from home, I can't get any visitors because it is too far for anyone to travel.

My wife and family were up in arms over this. I started thinking, I am going to have to start behaving myself and keep out of trouble. But what can you do — if you are being treated like an animal, you react like one. Every mealtime was the same routine; meals kicked along the floor and each time I would throw them back out. One morning, the cell door opened and instead of the usual screws, a doctor and a man in a civilian suit greeted me.

They told me I was to go and take a bath and put my clothes back on, as they wanted to talk to me. The man in the suit was an outside psychiatrist who then started to ask me questions, some of which were stupid and some very personal. He then just stared at me in stony silence. I just stared back. This went on for some time, then out of the blue he started to tell me that I needed treatment. He went on to tell me that I was suffering from an acute bout of depression which had sparked off a violent disorder. He told me that I would have to agree to treatment or I would quickly deteriorate. He said I had a violent temper and needed some sort of therapy.

I then started to explain that there was nothing wrong with me. It was just a build-up of all the events in Walton and the fact that everything had got out of hand. It was like talking to a brick wall. This psychiatrist didn't seem to be very interested in anything I had to say.

When I think back, I realise the power that these doctors had in these institutions. They can virtually sign your life away on their opinion alone. There is no man on this planet who can read another man's mind. Everyone has their own inner secrets; for instance, a man could be thinking about something ridiculous or something dirty, or even something evil. All these thoughts are locked inside your head and known only to you. No one can say that they know for sure what you are thinking. For instance, you may think you have a very good friend in someone, when, in fact, that so-called friend could be your worst enemy, who is plotting against you by grassing, or even thinking of seducing your wife but you can't say that you know his thoughts because you can't read his mind.

So take it from me, for all their so-called medical knowledge, psychiatrists may have degrees but they are not mind-readers! They can surmise certain things but that only comes to light through the questions they ask and your answers.

So I was to be transferred to Wakefield Prison, which was a 'star prison'. This was if you were a first-timer in prison. I became very apprehensive at first. Another mate told me that Wakefield was a very cushy place. They even had their own football field, a good gym. Television, dining out on the wings and playing pool. He made it sound like a holiday camp. I had eight months left to serve.

I arrived at reception, which was nothing like Walton. It was very quiet and, in fact, I was the only convict to arrive that day. This was because the prison was full, and not many of the convicts left because they were serving long sentences or doing life. Discharges were very few. I used to be embarrassed when another con asked me how long I was doing. How can you tell a man who is serving life, that you are only doing three years and my sentence was nearly finished?

After a few days, I got into the swing of things and met a few Liverpool lads that I knew. As I mentioned earlier, I was sent there for medical attention, so a few days later I was taken to the hospital where I was to see another psychiatrist. After spending a couple of hours with him, he told me that I was going to be given a course of shock treatment and that I would have to sign a consent form. By now I was getting worried as I started to think that there was really something wrong with me.

Wakefield in those days had its fair share of misfits but no one knew who they were. You could be talking to a sex case or a murderer and unless they told you what they were in for, you would never find out from anyone else. No one really revealed what they were in for.

There were some terrible cases in there and some sad ones, too. I remember a lad who was one of our crowd who seemed a decent type. His name was Billy and he was doing life for murder. He had never been in prison before. On the outside, he had been an ordinary, hard-working lad and was completely innocent of the murder. These facts were confirmed.

Apparently, Billy had just finished work one evening and he and his girlfriend were doing a bit of courting. He told me his coat was behind him on the grass bank. A short while later, as the story goes, two men approached him and his girlfriend while they were lying down and one man picked up his jacket and ran off with it. Billy chased them; not only because of his jacket, but his wage packet was in the pocket. He caught the man after a long chase and they started fighting.

By now, the police had been alerted and were on the scene. The man who'd stolen the jacket was arrested and taken to the police station. Billy also had to go to make a statement. Billy stated that while he was at the station, the man who was arrested became aggressive and had to be taken to the cell. He was followed by a number of police officers. Some time later, the police came back to Billy and told him that the man had died in the cell. Billy was later charged with murder. According to Billy, it was the police who had murdered the man and he went on to say that he and the man had only had a scuffle and when he was arrested he had no marks on him, yet when the man was examined his body was covered in bruises and other injuries. Billy appealed, but this was turned down and he just used to walk around in a sort of trance. It was very sad.

My first course of shock treatment had been arranged and little did I know what it involved. Two male nurses arrived to escort me to the hospital wing and get me prepared. I was made to lie down on a long vinyl-like bed and both my wrists were tied. They then put a plastic bit in my mouth, and I had electric devices attached to the temples on my head. This was then followed by my first taste of shock treatment. At first, it was a horrible feeling and then nothing. I didn't know who I was! My memory was a complete blank. I can now sympathise with people who suffer from memory loss; it was so frustrating trying to fathom out who you were. I was left in the ward for a few hours. They told me it would be OK, as my memory would come back to me. Patients in this particular ward were all weird types.

After a few hours, my memory came back and I was returned to the ordinary wing. I made a vow that never again would I go through that! I had a long talk to the doctor and told him I didn't care what he did to me, but I would not have any more shock treatment. He agreed to my request and that was the end of it. After this, I was to have fortnightly sessions with the psychiatrist.

Wakefield was not too bad compared to Walton and Leicester prisons. The facilities were all there — games of football, the gym was OK, as well as a few other privileges. One day, some mates and I were having a kick around with a ball on the exercise yard and just talking about things in general. One of the other lads, a Londoner, who was in for armed robbery asked me whether I knew a lad from Liverpool called Billy Brown. I said I couldn't recall him. He went on to say that he was doing six years in here now. The London guy said he would introduce him to me. A little while later, I recognised some guy walking towards our crowd. The London guy went to greet him with a big smile on his face. He turned to me and said, 'Here, Charlie, I want you to meet a good friend of mine, Brownie.'

When this Brownie recognised who I was, he went white. He was a sex case from Walton, who had been sorted out in the reception there. I exposed the dirty beast there and then. He had pulled the wool over my mate's eyes pretending he was one of the boys. This mate of mine said he would not have believed it. You would not have thought he was like that. I have been told that these days Wakefield is full of beasts now.

There was quite a bit of violence when I was there in 1965. I remember some kid called Dunford who was doing life, who was a good enough kid and did not bother anyone. He just wanted to do his time and get out. He was only about 20 years old. On the same wing as Dunford was a fella called Buckingham, who was a terrible bully and was knocking everyone out for no reason whatsoever. Anyway, he comes over to Dunford. Dunford told him he did not want any trouble and wanted to be left alone. Now, because a man shows a bit of sense and manners does not necessarily mean that he is weak, but some people, especially bullies, take manners to be a sign of weakness. The consequences were inevitable. Buckingham tried it on with Dunford and the big bully ended up stabbed to death. Dunford was tried and found guilty of a second murder and got a life sentence. The authorities branded Dunford a psychopath. I do not know whether Dunford ever got released. I know he would have to have served at least 30 years.

It was 1965 now and I was coming to the end of my sentence. I only had weeks left and I had just been granted one week's home leave. Everything was happening out there in 1965 in Liverpool. Liverpool Football Club had just won the cup against Leeds United. The Beatles were the top group. Liverpool was buzzing. It was the swinging Sixties and I was going home. My wife and son were doing fine and I had a full week to spend out there with them.

I went through all the usual formalities with the prison Governor and he told me what would happen if I did not return back to prison in time. I was finally let out on a Tuesday, I think, and I had to be back the following Monday. My wife and two friends picked me up outside and home I went.

It was a wonderful week. I do not think anybody could appreciate the feeling you have when being released from a prison. My mother and the rest of the family had a home-coming party for me. But it was the fastest week I have ever known and no sooner was I home, it was time to go back. I only had six weeks left. It was the longest six weeks of my life.

I was two hours late getting back from my home leave. I got the train back to Wakefield and got off at the wrong place, which put me back a couple of hours.

When I did eventually arrive back at the prison, I was in for a right grilling. I was put on report to see the Governor the next morning. When I did finally see him, the Governor said to me, 'Seiga, give me one little excuse and I will take your remission from you.'

My remission was up to 12 months.

He went on to say, 'I know you have worked your ticket to get to this prison and I am just waiting for one little slip from you.'

I thought, I have only got five weeks left to do and I'd better watch myself.

A few days later, I was about to sit down and have my dinner. There was a newspaper by me on the table. I picked it up and started to read it when it was snatched out of my hands. I looked up at this con who was staring down at me — he was a right nutter by the name of Harry

King. He was doing life for a double murder. He had shot dead his wife and a policeman. Harry had found out that his wife was having an affair with some policeman. He shot dead his wife and when the police were called they surrounded his house and ordered him to come out and surrender. Harry shouted to the police to send a certain officer in so he could have a talk. The policeman went into the house unaware that Harry knew he was the one who was having the affair with his wife. Harry shot him dead there and then. He then turned the gun on himself. He blew one of his lungs out but survived. Harry was sentenced to hang and got reprieved through diminished responsibility.

So here I am facing this crazy bastard and he had a mate who never left his side. He was a big, gypsy-looking fella, who was also a real lunatic. I said to Harry, 'What is the big idea, snatching the paper? You could have asked me for it.'

He then says it was his paper and I am sitting in his place. His mate threw a punch at me. Now, up until then, I did not want any trouble. I had just been warned by the Governor, but when you are young and erratic and your reputation is at stake — not so much your reputation but your pride — at that moment you forget the Governor and your remission. I was fighting this big mad bastard. A few of the lads gathered around and it was just him and me. Harry kept out of it for the time being. I had a fight on my hands with this fella, but he was too strong for me. I picked up a water jug, which was made of steel, and I smashed his cheek in. I just kept smashing the jug into his face. He was in a terrible mess when I had finished, and was taken over to the prison hospital. The screws came down and I was locked up in a prison cell. Everything was going through my head now. I was thinking, Why couldn't I just have ignored it all? But it is hard to bow down when your pride has been hurt, and it's hard to swallow. I was thinking I have really blown it now. If that fella is in a bad way, I could get five years or more, and once the Court sees my record and what I am in for, that is it. To think I only had a couple of weeks left. I have seen this happen with other cons who have got into a fight and hurt someone badly and the next thing they are doing a long stretch.

After an hour or so, I heard the screws coming for me. I thought, This is it. The cell door was flung open and one of the screws said to me, 'Come on, Seiga, get back to work, you are a lucky bastard.'

The injured con wouldn't grass on me. He told the screws he did not know who it was who had damaged him. Harry King came to see me with a big grin on his face. He told me that he was going to knife me the first chance he got. Now, when you have a nutter on your case, you have to keep watching your back every minute. I was like that for the next few days before I got released.

A few of my mates were also keeping an eye open for me. Some of these maniacs have nothing to lose. Another life means nothing to them. I managed to get released without any come-back from Harry King. I do know those last few days of my sentence were the longest I have ever known. I was finally released in September 1965.

Chapter Six

1965 was a good year for me. I had just served 25 months out of a three-year sentence. I did not realise how time goes so quickly. However, there I was free with a beautiful wife and my son, Anthony, was just two years old. The first few weeks I was out I was just taking things easy getting to know my son and just sort of recuperating. Veronica had got herself a good job. The money I had left her while I was in prison had dried up. Not that there was a lot to start with, but with the baby wanting clothes, a pram and nursery fees it soon goes.

We got ourselves a flat in Huyton. It was a fairly good area at the time and there was a park nearby and I was doing all the usual things a father does, taking my little son for walks and looking after him and being a good husband in general. I was getting restless, though, I wanted to graft again. I needed to start earning money.

A lot of things were changing in Liverpool. New clubs were sprouting up all over the city. A lot of these clubs had been granted gambling licences, which attracted a lot of wealthy people, including villains like us. The Ascot Club in Wood Street was one of the most popular ones, as was the Pink Parrot and the Cabaret in Duke Street. These three clubs were drawing a lot of attention from the celebrities. There was also the Blue Angel in Seel Street which was a favourite of mine and, last but not least, the Cavern in Mathew Street which is still going strong even to this day.

The music has also changed dramatically. Everybody had now heard of the Beatles and the Rolling Stones, but there were a lot of new groups making a big impact. On the music scene there were the Swinging Blue Jeans, Gerry and the Pacemakers, the Merseybeats and Billy J Kramer. There were too many to mention who were coming on strong. In those days, people were calling it the Mersey sound. Liverpool also had the best football team which was top of the league. The whole city was bouncing.

I know that people say that money does not grow on trees, but it did in the '60s. Money was flowing everywhere if you were a robber. There were lots of new faces on the scene in Huyton at this time, and these young lads all wanted a piece of the action. You could not blame them really. My two brothers, Joe and Jimmy, had a mate called Kirmo. Terry Kirmo was a big powerful lad and was a very loyal friend to all my family. He and I became the best of mates. There was nobody in Huyton who could match Kirmo in a fight. He could flatten anybody although he was never a bully; people used to try and use him. I can only say that he had my greatest respect. Then another good mate of mine, a lad called Micky Mac, did some work with me. Micky was always there for you, no matter what. There were also the twins Bobby and Billy Hughes. They were dead game. They would have a go at anything. These were the up-and-coming kids at the time.

However, there I was, out of the nick a few weeks and bang at it again. Some bloke who was always in the clubs had marked my card for a tasty bit of work. In fact, it was his business partner he wanted me to rob. I thought it was deceitful doing that, but I had no conscience whatsoever about it all. They say that principles do not feed you, but it is nice to have one. I would not dream of stealing from my best friends or family, yet some of these card-markers have no scruples. I have witnessed it on many occasions. I have actually seen a bloke who has had all his stash robbed, sitting with his so-called mate who has marked it up, trying to comfort him in a club over a drink.

At the same time, you need reliable information when it comes to good robberies. It is like the bizzies — they find it hard to solve a case without information unless somebody leaves a clue such as fingerprints or some other sort of identification. Without information the bizzies are at a loss.

The job we did was easy. It only took two of us to have it away. It was just a matter of sitting off and waiting outside some flat which this business couple lived in. When they both went out one evening, we just broke in. It was very simple — no alarm on it or anything. He had a small safe in there but it was a decoy, only containing a small amount of loose change. Any robbers who broke in would take the safe thinking they had the prize. We obviously knew there was nothing in the safe. Our prize was underneath the fireplace which had a false hearth. It was removable with an electrical fire on top of it. The hearth was about 3in deep all round and as we took the fire off I just lifted the hearth up which was only made of wood and had a false bottom, and there was the money. We picked up just over £5,000 from that job. £5,000 was a lot of money in the early '60s. A brand-new Rolls-Royce was about £6,000 then and a Mini was £800. We still had to make out that we had stumbled across the money to take away any suspicion from the man who marked our card. I pulled a few drawers open and ransacked the bedroom a little and that was about it.

We had quite a few of those jobs off but some of the graft was not as easy all of the time. Small jobs like burglary only needed three men at the most but if it came to heavy work you might need five or maybe six men with you. We were versatile my pals and I. Anything would go as long as the information was right — anything from a lorry-load of cigarettes to a warehouse full of goods. Now these jobs were all right provided you did not get ripped off by the fence who was taking the goods. Some of those fences were greedy bastards. They were always trying to bargain you down, especially after you'd stuck your neck out. I hated dealing with the bastards. I always call fences 'robbers' ponces'. I preferred doing jobs for cash only. That way it was easy to share out and there weren't any come-backs like waiting to be paid out for this and that.

Our crew was almost mobile now. I had just bought my first new car. It was a 1965 1500cc Cortina and being mobile meant we could now travel further afield out of Liverpool and Huyton. It was like another world altogether. You'd see properties with no security in them.

You could literally drive out to one of these places, break in and come back with a load of goodies. Money was everywhere if you were a robber in those days. I just do not know how today's villains survive with all these sophisticated alarm systems and cameras everywhere. Even the police have it boxed off in certain ways. They have helicopters and armed response teams. I would find it very hard now, but on the other hand villains move with the times. Some of them will find a way to combat this hi-tech equipment whatever the authorities bring out.

I had just turned 25 years of age and everything was going dead sweet for me. I had just bought another car. This was to put on private hire with the other car I had just bought and I started up my own little taxi firm. Taxis were good business then. I also had a Bedford TK truck which I had for scrap metal which was very sought after in the '60s. I hooked up with a pal I knew who worked for BICC cables and my wagon was loaded up every week with a small fortune on it — copper, lead, everything. We used to just have a pay-out every Friday in the pub across the way from BICC cables.

I had also built up a massive fruit round in Huyton. I went round every house in Huyton and asked everyone to buy his or her fruit and veg from me. I had a lad who used to drive my delivery van door to door. He had a couple of young kids working for him. Now when all the expenses were paid out, such as the people I had working for me, my profit margin would be about £300–£400 per week. That was a fortune then. My wife and son had everything. I had a good home and furniture and I always made sure that my mother wanted for nothing.

Having a small business like that kept the police off

my back a bit but, deep down, they had an idea what I was up to. They always do when you have a few grasses to pounce like vultures. There is one good point when you have a front like a legitimate business — you do not become desperate and it keeps the wolf away from the door. Also, I could pick and choose which jobs I wanted to do.

Veronica was very, very happy in those early years. We used to go everywhere together. We had nice clothes, ate in good restaurants and went to all the top shows. I was spending money like there was no tomorrow. The more I was making, the faster it would go. My weakness was having too much of a good time. And the nightclubs I was visiting were starting to play a major part in my life. I think that when you are young in your early twenties and you have nice clothes and women around you, you start to try and impress people. I know it is stupid now, looking back, but at the time I did try and create an image for myself and it was playing a major part in my life. And most of my mates were doing the same thing.

All of this would cause quite a lot of jealousy between different firms. I could be out with my mates having a drink in a club and then there could be another gang in there as well. We would always sort of acknowledge one another, like send a drink over to them and vice versa, but sometimes there could also be a bit of friction. Word might have got out that we had had a good touch or one of our mates had bought a new motor and it might be better than theirs. I know it sounds silly, but this has always caused jealousy and you would always get one silly fucker who would want to kick off. Violence was always lurking around the corner. I also think that when you have acquired a bit of a reputation — not that I wanted a reputation in the first place — some people always want to try it on with you.

This happened to me one night when I was coming out of a club. I was with my mate Terry Kirmo at the time. My name was called out and we were set upon by some fellas. One of these blokes was from a large family of brothers who owned a nightclub in the south end of the city. I was just smashed to the ground for nothing at all. I soon got back on my feet and Terry had already sparked two of them out. I was having it off, one on one, with the fella who had the brothers, when he came at me with a piece of broken bottle and cut the top of my eyebrow. He ended up getting badly injured and being taken to hospital. I was accused of stabbing him a few times in the face. Of course, I denied this. The police wanted him to press charges but he wouldn't do it. He sent me a letter from hospital saying it was all a misunderstanding. I admired him for not pressing charges.

You could understand a man pressing charges if it came to hurting a little child or raping a woman. I would have no scruples against an animal like that, but if it came to just an ordinary fella and he got damaged or he damaged you, you could sort it out amongst yourselves.

The Cabaret club was pulling in the crowds now. All the top shows were held in there and it was the place to be. My pals and I were always in the Cabaret on Saturday nights with our wives and our girlfriends. In Liverpool, it was the done thing to take out your wife or girlfriend, especially on Saturday. You had to take them out otherwise there would be murder. Most Liverpool fellas went drinking on a Friday with their mates and by the time Saturday came to take out your wife, it was a killer, especially if you had a big hangover from the night before. Whenever I would be sitting in a club or pub on a Saturday night with my wife, she would be going on at me about not drinking. I couldn't tell her that I had been drinking and having a good time the night before. I just wished the night was over so I could get back home to bed.

Like most men, we are weak and selfish in many ways. I know villains who are big, hard men who are terrified of their wives or girlfriends, especially if they have been out the night before, and particularly if they have copped off with another girl. I have met many a pal of mine, men who had been on armed robberies with me, or some other heavy work, and yet these same people are petrified of going home to face their wife after being out all night. I have done it myself; I have actually brought a couple of pals home with me to our house the morning after being out all night, having done a bit of business. I have found that one of the hardest things to do is to front up to your wife or girlfriend. Women can't be fooled; men think they are fooling them but Liverpool women, especially, are too 'wide'. They have this uncanny way of finding out if you have been with another woman. Even if it comes down to finding a hair on your clothes or a trace of make-up, or even a smell. They know all right!

I remember coming home very late one night thinking I was very clever. Whenever I went out and ended up with a bit of strange, I always kept a change of clothes in the boot of my car. This particular night, I was changing back into the clothes I had left home in that evening. I was at the side of the road with my boot open putting on my original clothes when, all of a sudden, a cop car pulled up next to me. I had a lot of explaining to do. I had to explain why, at 4.00am, I was changing my clothes. After listening to my explanation, the dirty bastards had phoned my house up and told my wife. I had to face it all when I got home.

I find that most women are good judges of character when it comes to seeing through your friends or mates. The best judge is usually your mother, who can sense if your so-called friend is good or bad. My mother would sometimes say to me, 'Charlie, that mate of yours, there's something about him which doesn't seem right,' and I would always defend them, saying, 'Don't worry, Mam, he's all right,' but most of the time her words would ring true. The same went for my wife. She would meet a certain mate of mine and tell me that he was false and not a true friend.

Looking back, most women I have known have been right in their judgements. There is the old saying, 'Never trust a woman', well, I have put a lot of trust in some of the women I have known. I believe that if a woman loves and trusts her man, she would be willing to die for him. Providing he is truthful and not a liar, she will forgive him for most of the crimes he has committed, even murder! When it comes to her man playing around, though, that is unforgivable!

* * *

I had a phone call from my old friend Billy Grimwood, asking me to meet him for a drink. Some of his friends had come up from London and he wanted me to meet them. I was made up to be going to see him after all the help he gave me when I was a kid in prison. I couldn't wait to have that drink. We decided to meet in the Cabaret club.

I arrived with a couple of mates. Billy greeted us and introduced me to the Nash brothers from London and they seemed nice people. The Nash brothers thought the world of Billy. They had a reputation as villains in London but to me they were respectful and had good manners. I only find people the way they are and the Nash brothers were very nice people. Now, because some villains have good manners and show respect to others, some stupid pricks take that as weakness. I have seen it happen when a man has a reputation and is being polite, you find some silly bastard wanting to have a fight with him and then when they get badly hurt after starting a fight, they start screaming their heads off as per usual.

I was amazed when Billy told me he was running the Cabaret club now, plus some other clubs, too. Gambling was big business in the clubs then and the casinos were attracting a lot of attention from villains especially from London. I don't know why, but Liverpool is a city that is different from any other city in England. There is nobody in this country that has our ways. We talk differently, act differently, we are different.

I have seen a few firms or gangs from other parts of the country come to Liverpool to try it on, wanting to tax people, but it has never worked. I remember some of the Krays' pals coming here. We were all at a boxing event at the Liverpool Stadium. They were sniffing around for a few days but eventually went back to London with their tails between their legs.

I could never imagine any Liverpool man who owns his own club or business ever paying anyone protection money or 'tax' as they call it these days. They would just be told to fuck off. There was protection going on at the clubs and pubs, and it is still going on today, and those 'protectors' are the police. They are the ones who take back-handers. If it is not money, it is free drinks and free meals. I know, because I have had to give them some myself when I was in business. Having a drinks licence is like printing your own money, but a gambling licence in those days was the icing on the cake. The police know how valuable these licences are, and it's up to the police as well as the council to grant them. If the police don't like the look of you and you won't play ball, you have got no chance of obtaining a licence. They have the upper hand at all times.

I have had a few licensed premises in the past, but I could never get a drinks licence in my own name. I had to have someone to front for me, such as my wife or a friend who had a clean record and had never been in trouble. Once you were well thought of by the police, they make sure you don't get raided for drinking after hours, or they always forewarn you if a raid is going to take place. The last business I had was a Chinese restaurant, where I had no problems at all. My friends and customers could drink until five or six in the morning and would never be hassled when they were leaving in the early hours of the morning, not even a ticket on a car outside the restaurant. My partner used to be well in with the police, and sorted out their little perks like meals and drinks.

After our chat with Billy, my pals and I decided to

grab the last hour at the Blue Angel club in Seel Street. The Blue Angel at this time was at its peak. It was one of the trendiest clubs in Liverpool. To gain entry, you had to be well dressed otherwise the doormen wouldn't let you in. Clubbers in those days were smartly dressed. It was only riff-raff or scruffs who would be kept out. The man who owned the Blue Angel at the time was a man called Alan Williams. He was known as the man who gave the Beatles away. The Beatles used to play there for practically nothing. They never did impress me, I was more into Elvis, Ray Charles and Ben E King, who were superb singers at that time. I last saw Alan Williams about two years ago, shuffling down Church Street in Liverpool, still moaning about how he lost the Beatles.

I was becoming sort of nocturnal in my lifestyle. I was living in the fast lane. Although I was still very active when it came to graft, money was coming in from everywhere for me and my mates and I was still doing all right on the business side, too. There was only one problem — my wife. I was starting to neglect her. The lifestyle I had meant that I just couldn't help it. I was staying out all night at parties, never going home and I was messing around with other women. They are hard to resist when they are all around you. I was becoming popular with a lot of people and I found it hard to say 'No' to a party or a beautiful girl. Sometimes, I just couldn't get away. But my family life was suffering, and Veronica was losing her trust in me. She was upset about the late nights and people were telling her tales about me. Liverpool is like a village at times and if somebody who knows you sees you on the town, especially if you are with a strange bird, they can't tell your wife quick enough.

Although Veronica and I were doing all right for money and we had a nice place to live, it wasn't the same. I caught her one night examining my clothes in the bedroom. I thought, Fuck, I'm now living with a forensic policewoman, instead of a wife. I know how loyal she had been to me when I was in prison, but I knew I just couldn't go on lying and being so deceitful to her. She was too proud a woman to accept anything like that. She wanted me to alter my lifestyle and pack everything in. I couldn't — I was in too deep and, to be perfectly honest, I liked my way of life and wouldn't change it for anything.

My two younger brothers, Jimmy and Joe, were starting to dabble a bit in crime now. I was always concerned when it came to them. I knew our Billy was safe; he had been offered a new post in his job in South Africa, so he was well out of it. I had a good talk to our Jimmy and Joe and the truth eventually emerged. Freddy, my older brother, had been filling their heads with all kinds of ideas. He had been telling them about when he was 'at it'. I was furious. They were still living with my parents. Freddy had moved back, too. He had been divorced or something and I didn't want my mother to be upset if anything happened, like the police calling or my younger brothers being arrested.

There was nothing I could do really; they had had a taste for it and, living in an environment like Huyton, they soon became a part of it. Besides, who am I to talk? They had seen my way of life — cars, nice clothes, money — so I suppose they wanted a piece of the action, too.

Our Freddy had done a good job all right. He was a mess and a confirmed alcoholic and it was becoming very embarrassing for all the family. I don't know how a person can become an alcoholic. I know if I have had a few drinks the night before, then I suffered with a hangover for a couple of days. I couldn't bear to look at another drink for a week at least and that's pushing it. I just couldn't forgive our Freddy for corrupting Jimmy and Joe while they were still young. I would never have taught my little brothers to go out and steal.

My other older brother Gerald, or Ged as we called him, was a brilliant brother to me when I was young. He used to bring me all kinds of toys home. I remember when I was about eight or nine, he gave me a box of lead soldiers. He used to take me everywhere with him. There was an American Airforce base not far from where we lived. It was in a place called Bluebell Lane and our Ged used to take me there. All the Yanks used to give us sweets. He never taught me how to steal, he was a good, loyal brother to me. He was also good to my other brother Billy. He used to bring books home for him, which he needed for Grammar school. He was very kind-hearted that way. He became a fine artist. His oil paintings were fantastic. People came from all over Huyton to buy the paintings. It was a well-known fact that most houses in our neighbourhood had one of Ged Seiga's paintings.

It was coming to the end of 1965, and my little business was booming now. My pals and I were making plenty of money. Somebody would always come up with some tasty work for us. By now, our firm was doing a lot outside the Liverpool area. We could be in Birmingham one day and the next it would be Leeds or Manchester. It all depended on what came up. Armed robberies and wage snatches were becoming fairly common amongst villains now.

We got to know a lot of people from different parts of the country. I would get a call from a mate from down south or it could be up north with a tasty bit of work for us. Sometimes, local firms can't do a job on their own doorstep, as they might be under police surveillance. If a job was pulled, they were the first suspects to be picked up by the police. The only way you do have a chance of doing anything in your own area is to leave the town as soon as the job is done, stay low for a few weeks, and then if you do get lifted for it, by then memories have faded a bit and witnesses are hard to find. To have one of these heavy jobs away, they have to be planned meticulously. You have to have the right men with plenty of bottle and not too erratic in their behaviour. By that, I mean if a job doesn't look right when you are about to strike — you get a sixth sense that something is wrong — then it is best to leave it and just walk away. By doing this, you can stay free to thieve another day. It is no good moaning later on if you get nicked saying, 'I should have done this, or that'; you cannot afford to come unstuck on one of these heavy jobs because if you are caught, you are going to go to jail for a very long time. The judge will tell you at your trial, 'You played for high stakes so you must receive a high sentence.' Again, this proves that courts and authorities value money more than life.

Two mates of mine were good family men, good to their wives and kids, men of decency, who would go to the aid of an elderly person who may be getting mugged, or a woman about to be raped, men who wouldn't dream of doing any real harm to anyone. Yet just because there was a large amount of cash involved in the robbery that they committed and of which they were found guilty at their trial in the Crown Court, a certain judge sentenced both of them to 20 years. It is not just their liberty that is taken away, as if that is not enough, they are also deprived of their wives and children, who suffer badly, too. That same judge, in court the very next day, could be dishing out probation to a rapist or child molester. I will never be able to fathom out how this can be called justice.

The element of surprise is crucial when carrying out a wage snatch or money being brought out of a bank. It all depends on what sort of work you are on. I always prefer to see the money in front on me. By that, I mean behind closed doors. I have actually seen money waiting on counters to be picked up by security firms. I have been up on roofs, looking through skylights of sorting offices seeing thousands and thousands being counted and bagged up. This sort of work was more appealing to our team, as we could see what we were getting. Some security vans that carry cash can be dead unreliable at times. They can also become a nightmare when it comes to having one off. Our team was fearless and loyal to one another and, above all, we were determined. However, even with all this tuition, we have had some terrible disasters in the past. I remember — not that it was the first time — a security van we were ambushing nearly came unstuck. One of the guards, who was in possession of one of the bags of cash, was fighting like a lion. My mate Tony, a big powerful lad, couldn't put him down. The guard had the bag chained to his wrist. Another of my mates had the cutters but still couldn't get at the bag.

Time was running out for us and with all the shouting and commotion, we had no alternative but to abandon everything. It was only a matter of minutes before the police were on the scene, and we had only just managed to escape. We put it down to experience; you win some, you lose some. Like I have said before, it takes a lot of planning and possibly quite a bit of time, sometimes a few weeks to have one of these vans away.

I read a book written by a high-profile London villain not so long ago, and he wrote that their firm used to have a security van off once a week. Now to me, that's a load of bollocks. If it were true, he would be a millionaire in a matter of weeks. It would be virtually impossible to do one a week. I know by experience. Time is taken up by surveillance. You need to arrange bent cars, the best escape routes. All this could take a few weeks at least. I do not believe they had one a week.

Sometimes, you had work coming in from all directions — a lorry-load of cigarettes or whisky, a warehouse full of goods — all waiting to be had off. This sort of work needs to be done as soon as possible because if you wait, the chances are it will not be there, especially the lorries, whereas security vans would always be around and they could be sorted any time. And you had to be 100 per cent certain that the job had been planned properly. I believe that any profit at all, no matter how small, is better than no profit. I always liked to have the easy work off first. This way, you were still earning wages while you were planning to have an armed robbery off.

We had just been given a tasty bit of graft, just outside Liverpool. It was a large amount of cash, which was being held in a bank. The bank looked dead easy, it was situated in an ideal spot and the escape route was perfect. The information came from an inside, reliable source. There was only one problem, and it involved my younger brother James. Our Jimmy was a good kid and wanted to come along on the job. I was reluctant at first, but I had no choice really, as it was through Jimmy the information came about and, besides, in the end I was glad we had taken him.

My mates and I did the usual routine — waiting, watching and planning. Let me point out, there were no surveillance cameras in the 1960s. Today, it would be a robber's dream, but in those days, there weren't as many robbers about then and not all of them took to bank jobs. Doing banks was considered 'top of the division', in the same sort of league as safe-blowing years before. Safe-blowers were at the top of the ladder, too. All this rubbish of what was top and why didn't interest me. We could be doing a blag one week and an armed robbery a week later, or we could be robbing a house full of antiques and jewellery. That is giving you an insight into just how versatile our team was. It is funny, one minute I could be robbing a bank which holds thousands of pounds and the next minute I could be stealing for a mere few quid.

This takes me back to the time when I went to buy a new washing machine for my wife. I saw one outside the entrance of a shop. I just literally pushed it away, through the shopping centre and right into the back of my van. Even when supermarkets first became established, I just used to walk in, fill the shopping trolley up with all kinds of the best foods and then just brazenly walk out of the doors with the trolley and load the boot of my car. I never paid a penny for it! Now you might think this was petty. I never did. I put it down to economising on the household bills. I still have certain mates, who have retired from the business and are not short of money, yet still do a bit of pilfering whilst out shopping. I think it is because the survival instinct from when we were always hungry as kids remains within you.

We decided to have the bank away just before Christmas. I had been inside the premises with my mate and weighed it up carefully. The money was exactly where we were told it would be, all bagged up behind the counter at a certain time, before it was picked up by a security firm later in the afternoon. Our plan was to get there a few minutes before the two guards arrived to collect the cash. The information was bang on and everything was looking good. When my mate and I were in the bank days before, I noticed that the double entrance doors had two long brass handles on the inside, which were about a foot long. I thought this was ideal because one of our mates who would be on the door anyway, could wedge a bar of some sort through both handles and prevent anyone coming in from outside, whilst we were carrying out the work.

The staff who worked there looked healthy enough — by that, I mean no old people — and we stipulated, incidentally, that no guns were to be used. We armed ourselves with pick-axe handles, hidden under our coats. I don't want to go into too much detail, but the way we planned it, it seemed that everything would be OK.

Five of us went on the job, each man knowing the part he had to play; one outside with a motor, another on the door and one to jump over the counter to pass the bags over. There were three bags in all. My brother and I were to keep the staff at bay, but they didn't look as though they would offer any resistance or try to be brave. Besides, we didn't want any violence. It was like doing a quick snatch, which would hopefully be all over in a few minutes.

Another good aspect was that the bank was situated on a corner and our escape road was a dead end, which ran to the side of the bank. At the end of the road, there was a walk-through, so it was just a matter of driving at speed to the dead end, leaving the car and going on foot up the walk-through and into the back-up car which was parked there. Only one of our gang was to drive the back-up car away and that would be me! I was to take the money and our working tools and clothing, such as masks and gloves. It looks less suspicious if a tidily-dressed man is driving on his own.

The rest would split up into pairs and make their own way back, usually by taxi or bus. We used this system time after time and never got caught once. I am not saying that we didn't have some very narrow escapes, because we did, such as this bank we once did. We were inside and everyone took up their positions. The man on the door, who we had only just recruited, was called Wee-Wee. His job was to let no one in or out until he got the OK, no matter what happened. Micky, our other mate, was very game and had to pass over the money bags. We had entered the bank a few minutes before it closed and just ahead of the security guards. While this was going off, I had positioned my back to an inside office door. All of a sudden a man, a member of the staff, who we had overlooked came out and grabbed me from behind. He literally wrapped his legs around mine and had hold of me in a headlock. He was screaming to the rest of the staff and then it all happened. Somebody pressed the alarm bell. The noise was deafening. The next thing I knew, Wee-Wee ran out of the door. I knew it was only a couple of minutes before we were on top — caught. Micky came back over with some of the cash, money was dropping everywhere. It was pandemonium now. There was only one thing left to do — escape, but the man holding me was determined not to let me go. He knew the police were on their way.

My brother Jimmy came to my rescue. He hit the man over the head and he let go. We were making our escape in the car but there was no Wee-Wee. As we were driving up the road, half-way along it I spotted Wee-Wee still running and we picked him up. We dumped the car as planned and went our separate ways. I kept Wee-Wee with me. He kept repeating how sorry he was for running out. If he had not run outdoors, we would have had it under control, but with him panicking the staff became brave and pressed the panic button. We ended up with some wages but we lost quite a bit.

I would like to state if you ever read this book, Wee-Wee, me and the boys have never forgiven you for losing your bottle that day. You nearly had us all nicked.

I blame myself for letting him come with us. He was only filling in for one of our mates who was away at the time. Sometimes you get certain types of men who are all talk about what they have and have not done, but when it comes to the nitty-gritty, their arse goes and they become a danger to the firm and you can't afford to give them a second chance on any more work you might have in the future.

*　　　　*　　　　*

It was Christmas 1965. Christmas is a time for celebration and parties when families get together, but it was Christmas every week for our firm the way we lived. There was no shortage of money. We were all doing fairly well for ourselves. My small businesses were booming now the taxis and the other enterprises were bringing in plenty. I was having a good life but I was still living in the fast lane. When I look back, I often wonder where all my energy came from because there were no drugs then. Mind you, I never smoked and I was not one for drinking very heavily.

Talking about drinking, it was Christmas and me and my family were going to have a party. It is funny when you think about it — it takes Christmas or a wedding for families to get together. Some families never see one another for years and yet if somebody dies or gets married then they all seem to congregate together. We were never away from my mother's house, my brothers and I. However, it was the local pub for everyone this Christmas; ours, of course, was the Eagle and Child in Huyton.

I used to hate going into pubs at Christmas time. It was always the same old dance, overcrowded with people making a nuisance of themselves showing off their new Christmas clothes and it was always a foregone conclusion there would be a fight at the end of the night if somebody would start an argument. All these sorts of gatherings used to do my head in. I could not wait until all these occasions were over and everything was back to normal. As daft as it may seem, I would sooner be doing a bit of graft, even though it was Christmas time.

Although it was considered one of the roughest pubs in Huyton, the Eagle always had a good atmosphere about it. Most of the families who drank in there were staunch people. The Dwyers were a big family with a lot of brothers. Tommy was a mate of mine, and Matty and Pat. They were all good lads. Then there was Eddie Cavanagh, another mate of mine who was nicknamed Tit-Head (don't ask me why). Mickey Mac was a good lad and Terry Kirmo. These were people who'd go out of their way to help you especially if the bizzies were trying to arrest you or anyone in there.

You could buy and sell anything in the Eagle and if you needed anything special like a colour telly or a ringer (a stolen car) it would be there for you in no time. They were usually all good loyal people to me, but you would also get the bad ones in there. These were the jealous bastards who begrudged anything you had, like a nice car or clothes. I have seen the way some of these bums perform, always slagging people off who have made a few quid and yet the same pricks will not get off their arses and earn a few quid themselves. They would sooner get rotten drunk and go home and knock fuck out of their wives or girlfriends.

Jealousy creates all kinds of badness, especially grassing. Grassers those days were very few and far between but they were there all right. I have popped into the Eagle on many occasions and I have had a nice suit on and a decent motor outside. I was not deliberately trying to show off or wind anybody up, but you could see the resentful look on some of the faces. I would prefer to socialise in the nightclubs in town where it was all happening. I could not see any enjoyment in a pub drinking buckets of beer all night talking a load of rubbish. I would only be 10 or 15 minutes at the most in the Eagle and that would only be to have a quick drink with one of my old friends or maybe my brothers. They were more or less always there.

On one of these occasions, I was in the Eagle just after New Year's Day 1966. There was a gang standing around the bar causing all kinds of nuisance. I thought this was nothing to do with me and I kept myself to myself. I was just killing a bit of time waiting for my mate to arrive. We were both going into town to the Blue Angel club, where we had a meeting with a couple of businessmen. Now the gang who were standing not too far from me by the bar were bang out of order. One of them threw a glass of beer over some girl who I happened to know. She had a name for being a slag — in fact, most of the lads knew her. After the incident, she came over to me crying. I did not want to get involved, but apparently she had knocked back one of the fellas who was in the gang and he must have got a 'cob on', especially in front of his mates, so I just told the girl to calm down and keep out of their way.

After a few minutes, a glass was flung at me by one of these pricks. One of them shouted over to me, which was very insulting. I immediately recognised him — it was Micky D, the fella who I also suspected of grassing on me when I got arrested and charged for the gun in 1963. There was always bad feeling between him and me. I could never prove that he grassed me, but I had a good idea it was him.

So there I was, waiting to go on a bit of business with a mate of mine and all of a sudden I had all this aggravation to contend with. My suit was in a mess. When the glass and its contents were thrown at me, I went completely mad to think this scumbag was insulting me and then having the nerve to challenge me to fight him. Micky D's favourite party piece was using a broken glass bottle and jamming it into the face of whoever he was fighting. He had made a terrible mess of a fella's face with a glass just a couple of weeks before. He came from over the Alt, which was by the top of Woolfall Heath Avenue. I knew I had a fight on my hands with this bastard and had to be extra careful.

To cut the story short, Micky D and I went outside to have it off in the Eagle car park. By now, a big crowd had gathered round. We had both stipulated it was to be one-on-one and no weapons. So we both kicked off on one another.

Street fighting, as I have mentioned, holds no rules. You use whatever you can — your head, your feet, even as far as pulling an eye out, it does not matter. It is who wins that counts. If you happen to be beaten by the man you are having the fight with, you can always have a straightener next time or whenever you feel up to it.

That was the way it was, or the way it used to be. So we were really getting stuck into one another and neither of us would go down. If you did ever get your opponent down, you would never let him get back up. You have just got to kick fuck out of him and make sure he does not get back up otherwise it could be you. After we had been punching, butting and kicking one another, we both came to a sort of a clinch with our heads close together. The next minute, the bastard sank his teeth into my bottom lip. The pain was killing me and he would not let go, and then I made a mistake. I could not stand the pain much longer, so I punched him right in the balls. He then literally bit my entire bottom lip right off and spat it on the floor. After he realised what he had done, he ran away. I was in a terrible mess.

Somebody had phoned for an ambulance and I was taken to hospital. The paramedics actually took what was left of my lip with them. The hospital doctors or surgeons did their best to try and save my mouth but they could not stitch my lip back. They said it was useless. The surgeon eventually did stitch what was left of my bottom lip together but it looked absolutely hideous. Veronica, who was at the hospital with me, was shocked by it all and I was dreading my son seeing me this way. The doctors reassured me that, in a few months' time, the bottom of my lip would eventually even itself out. I knew I was badly scarred and would be for the rest of my life. I remember saying you should never be frightened of a man with scars on his face — be frightened of the man who gave them to him. I suppose the saying is true to a certain extent but there was no way I was going to let this drop. I wanted to get that animal back and give him a taste of his own medicine.

The police came to see me as news travels fast. They wanted me to make a statement; in other words, to grass, which I obviously refused to do. Had the shoe been on the other foot, the sly bastard Micky D would have had no hesitation about having me nicked. Time was on my side, and now it was just a matter of letting everything die down for a few weeks while I recuperated.

While I was recovering, I was losing a lot of weight through not eating properly. Most of my meals consisted of liquids, as I had to use a straw most of the time. Patience was getting the better of me. I could not chew my food, which was frustrating, and talking was completely out of the question. It was just a matter of time for the healing process to take its course. My pals kept coming round to my place to visit me. I was getting all kinds of offers from them. One mate in particular wanted to go and shoot Micky D. I kept refusing their offers, which I appreciated but I wanted to sort it out myself.

A few weeks later, after my injury had healed a little bit, I went to a place called Wimbourne Road where this animal lived. In fact, I went on a number of occasions to no avail. He was never around. Not that I was surprised; the police found out that I was out to get him. The dirty bastard had got the bizzies to warn me off him. The police came to see me and told me that, if I so much as laid a finger on him, they would arrest me. Now, I never pressed charges on him but just because I wanted a straightener with him, he went and got police protection against me.

To cut a long story short, I did get him back. I had to be extra careful getting my revenge back on him, especially having been previously warned by the bizzies that if I went anywhere near him I would be nicked.

He was a heavy drinker, and lived for his ale more than anything, and especially for his weekend binges. His house only had an outside toilet, and what does a man do before he goes to bed, particularly after a skinful of beer? Obviously, he takes a leak.

It was Saturday night and I knew he would be using

his toilet. I got 'ballied' up (pulled on a balaclava), and then waited in his back garden. I had already seen him in the pub half-an-hour before, and I knew he would be on his way home. I had already taken the lightbulb from its socket in the toilet.

After about 20 minutes, just as I had predicted, he came out of the back of his house to relieve himself. I watched him go into his toilet, fumbling for the light switch. He must have thought in his drunken state that the bulb had gone.

I crept up to the door, which was ajar. I then pulled out the hammer I had in my pocket and started smashing his fucking head in with it. In no time at all, he was lying on the floor of his toilet badly beaten up.

With it being dark, I was just striking wild blows at his face, but my main intention was to smash all his fucking teeth out of his mouth, the teeth that bit my lip off.

When he had passed out, I just crept away into his back garden, climbed over a few fences, and was gone into the night. By the time I arrived back home safely, all forensic evidence on me had been thoroughly eradicated. I also knew there was not one witness who could say it was me, not even the bastard himself!

I did hear over the years that he turned to drink and, even to this day, so I am told, he drinks with a few alcoholics in some old council house in Huyton. He is a confirmed alcoholic now. Mind you, I tormented the scumbag for years.

Chapter Seven

Summertime was just beginning and life to me was so beautiful now. Liverpool was buzzing. The whole city was alive with entertainment. In 1966, the Cavern club in Mathew Street was the place to be every lunchtime. A lot of office workers and businessmen were always in there.

Can you imagine people dancing, eating and drinking in the Cavern during the daytime, while the night time was even better? The music was brilliant. A new singer had just appeared at the top of the hit parade. His name was Percy Sledge and he had a number-one hit with a record called 'When a Man Loves a Woman'. More new clubs had opened; there was the Jacaranda, the Iron Door and a very select club in Bold Street called the Odd Spot. Most of these clubs played a major role in my nocturnal life at that time.

Although I was having a good life and there was plenty of money about, my marriage was still suffering. I did try my best to keep it together but I was not trying hard enough. I just could not give up life in the fast lane. What do they call it — wine, women and song. Quite a few pals of mine were in the same boat. Even now to this day, I have mates who are married living very unhappy lives or living with their girlfriends. Some of them say that they cannot get out of their relationships because of the businesses and the properties they own together. Excuses are made, going even so far as the children. I think once a marriage or a romance is over, it is best just to end it all. It is no good making all kinds of excuses and living in misery for the rest of your life. Pretending to love somebody is one of the hardest things to do. How can you fake a kiss? I would sooner just walk away.

There are villains who have told their wives or girlfriends everything regarding their criminal activities. Now some of them are in deep trouble. It is a sort of blackmail. They are literally terrified of being exposed for deeds they have committed in the past. I am not saying that all women are like that; some women are dead staunch and would not dream of informing on you. In fact, I have known more grasses amongst men than women.

One day, word got back to me that I was under police surveillance, and also my mates who I was working with. It was decided that our team should not be seen socialising together, especially in the nightclubs. I did start to notice that quite frequently plain-clothes bizzies were watching our every move. Plain-clothes police were the CID. You could spot them a mile away. They would always be standing there with cheap crumpled suits drinking half-pints of flat beer. They betrayed their identity, especially when you looked at the hatred in their faces when they stared at you. Mind you, they lead miserable lives really, and I believe there are more divorces and marriage break-ups in the police force than in any other profession.

I was becoming a bit too popular on the club scene and I thought about changing my habits. I did not want bizzies breathing down my neck wherever I went. I started socialising with mates of mine who were not real villains. I thought it would be better to be seen in their company rather than the pals I worked with. Every time a certain job was pulled off, the finger would be pointed at me and our team, so while the police surveillance continued we decided just to chill out for a while.

The police are devious bastards when they want to be. They would think nothing of fitting you up when they think you are at it. There have been lots of cases of police fit-ups which I will cover later.

I remember a mate of mine who lived down Scotland Road called Christy Cummins who was terrible for getting their backs up. He hated the bizzies and every time he had a touch he would always carry a wad of notes on him. He would just go over if some bizzies were in a pub or club and, in front of their eyes, he would drop all his money on the floor. It could be a couple of hundred quid and it would fall right next to them. He would then scoop it up grinning at them and then buy himself a bottle of Moët champagne. He ended up doing quite a lot of bird, not just because of those incidents but for trivial things. Police surveillance does not stay on you too long. If they have not nicked you, after a while they go on to concentrate on other gangs who may be at it.

As a postscript to this story, all through my life I have

been a thief, a robber, a villain or whatever you want to call it. I can now categorically state that since 1958 at the age of 17, I have never been convicted of armed robbery, burglary or fraud or any other illegal way of making money. Please do not misunderstand me; I have been charged on numerous occasions over the years and some of these have been very, very serious allegations indeed, but the police could never get a conviction against me. Now, because I was fairly successful in my line of business, they have hounded me over the years and tried several times to get me, but to no avail. The police in Liverpool and other forces who have charged and arrested me over the years know that they have gone out of their way to nail me on all kinds of jobs but they could never get me bang to rights.

I remember some old copper who is retired now saying to me, 'Charlie, we all used to have bets who could nick you first.' The only way they ever got me was through some cocked-up violence charge and, believe me, I have had quite a few of those in my time.

However, with me taking it easy regarding the club scene and keeping a low profile, my marriage was beginning to look up again for a change. My wife was a bit more relaxed, maybe because I was paying more attention to her and my son. I was still earning good money and both my wife and son wanted for nothing, so in general my life was fairly pleasant. It was now June and Veronica and I decided on a nice holiday. I knew whilst I was away my business would be taken care of. My family were very loyal to me in that way.

It was a beautiful summer that year, 1966, and I was all geared up for what I called a well-deserved holiday. I had just purchased a new car to add to my collection — meaning my taxis, of which I already owned three. Incidentally, a new car is one of the worst investments one can make. The minute you buy one you have lost quite a large amount of money. That's why I always believed in putting the car to work and making it pay for itself.

So there we were, Veronica and me, going on a two-week holiday to the South of France. We had made arrangements with Veronica's parents to look after Anthony as he was far too young to come with us on a long journey. Our intention was to take in a lot of the sights — Paris first, and then on to other places in the South of France. I couldn't wait. We were to depart on the following Monday, and it was now Friday.

My two mates Terry Kirmo and Tommy Dwyer had just come to see me. It was Friday evening. They asked if I would like a drink before I left and I also needed to tie a few things up. At about 8.00pm, all three of us decided to go out in my car and I told my wife that I would be home at about 11.00pm or midnight, as I needed to be up early the next morning.

Saturday was a busy day for me. I had to make sure that all the goods were bought for my fruit and veg business and the taxis were very, very busy as well. I was also responsible for a couple of lorries I had bought which were bringing good money in and every Saturday was pay time.

So my two pals and I went into town having a drink here and there. Nothing too heavy, I was just taking it easy.

But I began to notice wherever we went that Friday

night, whether it was a pub or a club, there always seemed to be three other fellas near us. I said to Terry, 'I am sure they are following us,' as they always seemed to be around where we were. The lads thought I was being paranoid. They couldn't be bizzies.

Later on, we ended up in the Blue Angel club. It must have been about 11.00pm. I thought I'd have an hour and then I would do one. Another lad called Bobby Hughes had joined our company in the Blue Angel. He had a twin brother called Billy. Bobby and Billy Hughes were two smart young kids then. They were villains like us and were getting a reputation.

When leaving the club, we were getting into my car when I spotted the same three fellas who had been there all through the night. I knew there and then I was not mistaken, but I just couldn't figure out what they were up to. The surveillance was off me, so I thought, and I had not been drawing attention to myself. I was puzzled as to why they were tailing me.

On the way out of the city centre towards Huyton, there is a big main road called Edge Lane. About half-way up Edge Lane, there used to be a nightclub called Jokers. It was situated nextdoor to Devonshire House, which is still there now, together with a nightclub called Reds. Anyway, on this particular night somebody suggested that we call into the nightclub called Jokers. By this time it must have been about 1.00am.

The Jokers club was set back off the main road and was a big old Victorian-type house in its own grounds. When we were just about to enter the club, the man on the door who I knew, Danny Jenkins, said to me, 'Charlie, I do not mind you coming in but the other three with you seem as though they have had enough already.'

On hearing this, it was a good excuse to get on home. Just as we were about to go, the three bizzies who'd been on our tail all night turned up. I think it was Tommy or Bobby Hughes who got a bit annoyed about not being allowed into the club. And the three plain-clothes coppers got involved, too, and that was it. Somebody threw a punch and there was a kick-off. A few punches were dished out here and there and, of course, two of the bizzies ran back into the club and one ran down the road out of the way. After a few minutes, it was all over and no weapons were used in the fight and everyone split up. I thought the way things had gone, I am not going to get home now.

The four of us got into my car and at last we were on our way home. We were driving through a place called Old Swan, when my car was rammed by a police jeep and the four of us were ambushed. There were police jeeps and cars everywhere. There must have been about 20 coppers and they all steamed into us. The bastards used truncheons and they worked us over good and proper. They handcuffed us all and took us all in separate vehicles. I was dragged into a Police Land Rover.

The four of us were taken to Eaton Road Police Station. The next morning, Saturday, all four of us appeared before Dale Street Magistrates. Myself, Terry Kirmo, Tommy Dwyer and Bobby Hughes were charged with grievous bodily harm with intent and using an offensive weapon — which, by the way, was a car jack and was in my car — on three officers outside the Jokers nightclub.

None of us could believe the charges. There we

were, the four of us, in front of the magistrate covered in bruises and black eyes. They said that one officer was treated in hospital and his injuries were extremely severe. It turned out that the said officer, and I quote, 'had one stitch on his finger'. These were the terrible injuries he'd received from us four. What a joke.

Terry Kirmo, Bobby Hughes and Tommy Dwyer were all granted bail at Liverpool Magistrates the following morning. I, naturally, was refused bail. The police told the court they wanted me remanded in custody pending further enquiries and more serious charges were to follow. Of course, this was to keep me for as long as possible. There were no other charges they could bring against me.

Most magistrates are just puppets in a court. Some of them don't even understand the law properly. The magistrates' work varies when they are not sitting on the bench. In fact, I've known a certain magistrate to be working behind a supermarket counter and another in a pet shop. One was even a retired school teacher.

The majority of these people don't know the first thing about the law and yet they have the power to deprive you of your liberty, even if you are innocent.

But, like I said, it's the police who pull the strings. They are all just kangaroo courts and they will never change. Even to this day, it is still going on, and I believe it's going on more than ever before.

I was taken to Risley Remand Centre in Warrington. It was a new place at the time and I thought I'd most probably get bail in a couple of weeks. Well, there goes my holiday to France, I thought. It would just have to be put off until a later date. Obviously, my wife and family were distraught over it all. But then what's new? My young life at the time was so unpredictable that nothing came as a surprise. One day I could be planning and dreaming with my wife over our holiday in the South of France, the next I was banged up in jail.

My solicitor at the time told me I'd more than likely get bail after a week or two and the charges would be reduced to the lesser one of assault. So, in the meantime, I ended up with a 'lie down' in jail and what a glorious summer it was that year!

It was the usual routine in prison. On remand, up and down to courts every other week, prisoners hoping they would be granted bail and awaiting sentence.

While in there, I met a few familiar faces I knew from the outside, which wasn't unusual. Also, the police had started to play head games with me. It seemed that every time I went to court, which was once a week then, my bail kept getting refused. I knew then that I stood no chance of getting bail and I was eventually, after a few weeks, given a date for my trial at Liverpool Crown Court.

Together with my mates, I was pleading not guilty and I thought things weren't as bad as they seemed, especially when our side of the story was heard.

I had been in Risley for about seven to eight weeks by now and the news had just come over the radio that three police officers had been shot dead. It happened down South somewhere. Then the following week, another policeman was killed up North. By now, the media and public were screaming for blood. The police mounted one of the biggest manhunts of all time and the papers were full of stories about the police murders, such as 'Our police must be protected from these villains!'

This couldn't have happened at a worse time for me.

I was up in the Crown Court the following week to face a judge and jury on a charge of serious. violence against three police officers. My three mates and I pleaded not guilty. We were up in front of the Right Honourable Judge Youds. The four of us stood no chance the way the case was conducted by the prosecution and the police. The jury obviously believed the police's version, especially after what had been going on in the press about the three police shootings.

The judge in his summing up said to the jury, 'The police say they were badly beaten up by these four men. The four men — Seiga, Kirmo, Dwyer and Hughes — have denied it. It is up to you, the jury, to decide.' Then in the next breath he said, 'I know who I'd believe, members of the jury!' Talk about influencing the jury, because that is what he did.

We were all found guilty. Bobby Hughes and Tommy Dwyer were given a Borstal sentence. Terry got two years and, when it came to my turn, the judge said, 'Because of people like you, our police officers are not safe on the streets. Some have been killed doing their duty because of your kind!'

My wife Veronica pleaded with the judge. He then paused for a moment and said, 'I feel sorry for your wife. You will go to prison for three years.' I thought I was going to get at least five to seven years the way that judge was talking to me. He must have had a change of heart. The police in court were jubilant. They were grinning at us and actually shaking hands with each other.

Well, I was truly fitted up and for one stitch on a policeman's finger, the so-called serious injury. So I went to prison for three years.

That same year, a man called Harry Roberts, along with two others, were charged and found guilty of the murder of the three police officers. Now, whether Harry Roberts actually shot these three coppers, I wouldn't know. Because of what I have experienced over the years regarding police corruption, I have no faith in the judicial system whatsoever. Even to this day, I would not put anything past them. As I have previously stated, they would have no hesitation in fitting you up, given the chance. Obviously, my opinion on police corruption is based on past and present experiences.

Law and order is essential to our society. Our mothers, sisters and children wouldn't be able to walk the streets freely if we didn't have law and order. Not that our streets are very safe now! The law must be enforced in a proper manner if we, the public, are to uphold and respect the very community it is controlled by.

Just after I had received the three-year sentence, two young mates of mine at that time both got four years from the same judge. The Merseyside Police started jumping on the bandwagon, totally taking advantage, and they started arresting all kinds of villains on charges of violence against the police.

The two lads had played no part in the violence they were charged with. The bizzies knew this was an ideal way of nailing any villain because of the publicity at the time. The bizzies must have been in their element. All they had to do was be in a fight with some villains and charge whoever they arrested with GBH on the police. This went on for quite a while. They rounded up a good few boys that year. 'Cleaning our city up of crime,' they called it.

I had done about six months of my sentence when Veronica filed for divorce. I was disappointed with her over it at the time. I thought she could have been more loyal to me, especially now, when I needed her. I know she waited for me throughout my last sentence, but I think her mind was being poisoned by her family. Anyway, what was the point of trying to save my marriage, when it was already in tatters?

I never contested the divorce and I never asked her for anything back which belonged to me at the time. I received a letter from her saying she still loved me but couldn't go on living this way. She finally ended up in America with my son, who still resides there to this day.

During my confinement at Walton Prison from 1966–68, I experienced quite a few incidents there and met quite a few characters, too. First, I was assigned to my old wing, 'I' Wing. I was told by a friend of mine who was also on that wing that I was going to get done in by Davey Fitz, who was the number-one cleaner in there. Davey was a big, strong, powerful lad who could handle himself. He was the brother of a man I was accused of stabbing while outside.

Apparently, some fella by the name of Benny, who came from Stoke, was putting in the 'mix' (stirring up trouble for me). This Benny fella had always wanted to be one of the boys and was creeping around anyone who had a reputation. I was told that he was a nobody in his home city of Stoke. I did know a few villains from Stoke myself, one being Larry Parks, a good staunch lad. I served my last sentence with him in 1963. Larry was one of the boys at that time.

After some time, Davey Fitz and I fronted up to one

another. We had both seen sense over what had gone on with all the mixing and agreed to shake hands and let it drop. Now, by not fighting with one another, it doesn't mean that either one of us was scared. It was just seen as sensible and not letting the other pricks have the benefit of us going down the block. Davey Fitz did tell me it was this Benny who was the mixer and he had been stirring it for other lads in there, too. My intention was to have a little meeting with this Benny fella as soon as I got the first opportunity.

When Davey's time was up in Walton, I promised I would look him up when I got out, for us to have a drink together. We became good friends over the years. The last time I saw Davey Fitz was at his cousin's funeral. His cousin, Davey Ungi, had been ambushed and shot dead by a gang of young villains.

I was having a drink with Davey Ungi only the week before he was killed. I remember it was in a pub called Cheers — I think the pub was his local. He very kindly gave me and a girlfriend a lift into town later on that evening.

Davey Ungi was a true gentleman; in fact, all the Ungi family are decent people in my opinion. It was so sad the way Davey Ungi was gunned down. My heart went out to Davey's brothers, Tony and Joey, and the rest of their family. This senseless killing started all the gun wars off in Liverpool, not that it had anything to do with the Ungi family. Other villains were 'potting' one another off, settling old grudges.

The bizzies were up the wall, they didn't know where the next shooting was coming from. It was almost an everyday occurrence, but it finally settled down.

After about three or four months of my sentence in Walton, a new workshop opened. It was called the Tailors. It was to be my place of work for the next 15 months or so.

I met a few of the old school in there. John McGregor was finishing off a sentence for a platinum and gold job. Another mate of mine, John Cummings, was framed for an armed robbery. What a liberty the police took with him!

John Cummings was driving a friend's car doing a bit of shopping one Saturday in broad daylight. After he had done his messages, he then gave the car back to the lad who he had borrowed it from. That evening, someone stole the car, unknown to John. The men who stole it used it for a robbery. When the car was recovered by the police, it had John's fingerprints all over it. Now John Cummings is a sensible lad and I couldn't see him doing a robbery in a straight car but with no gloves on. It was just a liberty; everyone in the city knew he hadn't done it.

There was this fella called Baxter, who used to knock about with some fella from Birkenhead. The two of them used to walk around the workshop sticking their chests out and both wore their shirt sleeves rolled up so they could show off their muscles and tattoos. I then discovered the reason why they were posing so much. It was because there was a black lad in there who was gay, whose name was Eddie Davies but everyone used to call him Shirley Bassey.

Now I've got nothing against gays, as long as they don't try anything on with me. I think that once they see you are straight and you're not interested in anything like that, then they don't bother you. It's the other kind that I've got no time for, the ones who are supposed to be men. I've actually seen cons who have wives and girlfriends on the outside and the same cons who are only doing a short sentence, going out of their way to cop off with a fella. To me, that is absolutely disgusting.

One day I was coming along 'I' Wing when I saw this con who looked sick. He was shuffling along towards me and when he got close to me, I couldn't believe who it was. It was our old friend Kieran Oats, my elder brother Freddy's mate. To see a man deteriorate so much was a shock to me. He looked absolutely terrible. I knew he had finished his seven years, but he got another ten not long after. It was really sad to see him like that. I can remember being a kid when he used to call at our house years before, and he was always dead smart and carefree. It looked like he had turned into an old man before his time. Years later, he hanged himself and he only had a few months left of his sentence.

But that is the way prison gets to some people. What I couldn't understand was why he had waited so long to do himself in, having served all those years and then only having a few months left.

There was another character in there at the time called Knobby Hanlon. He was a right nutter! He would think nothing of throwing himself over the landing to land on the nets, which were fixed across the landings for that very purpose.

Knobby had a fight one day on 'I' Wing with another con, over a bit of snout (tobacco). When the fight got broken up, Knobby was locked in his cell and an hour after the fight the con who he had been fighting with came along to have a talk to Knobby. With Knobby's cell being locked, the con started to talk to him through the spyhole, which had no glass in it. After a few minutes of talking to each other, they decided to be mates. Obviously, they couldn't shake hands with the cell door being locked, so they each decided to put a little finger through the hole. Knobby sank his teeth into the bloke's finger and bit the tip of it right off.

Knobby eventually achieved his ambition a while later, not long after his release. He gave a woman a severe beating (he was always beating women up) and eventually he committed suicide by throwing himself from a high building not far from where he lived in Liverpool. I think that was the best thing that could have happened to him. At least he couldn't harm any more inoffensive people.

The fact that I was a non-smoker stood me in good stead while serving time in those days. Tobacco was the sought-after commodity. I could afford certain types of food with the tobacco I purchased from the prison canteen. Some weeks I would buy one ounce or maybe one-and-a-half ounces. It would just depend, then I would make a large amount of rolled-up cigarettes, which I would roll out to be about half the size of a civilian one. Now that was a generous size compared to the average prison roll-ups, because the majority of the other cigarettes in there were like match sticks.

Every week, each prisoner was entitled to fresh fruit, according to the strict diet sheet that was laid down. The fruit consisted of one apple or orange every week per man. In regional prisons — in other words, local prisons — a lot of old tramps and down-and-outs made up the majority of the prison population. These types of low-life would sell their souls for a cigarette. I did not want their souls, just their weekly fruit supply. After all, a lot of them couldn't even bite into an apple, simply because they were old and had lost their teeth. They were more content with a couple of rollies. In the end, I used to have them all queuing up outside my cell, to swap their fruit for a smoke. It was great; I used to get a couple of dozen pieces of fruit each week. They were happy with the deal and so was I.

Tobacco would enable you to get anything. I even had my cell cleaned out every day by one of the cons who was the landing cleaner on our wing. I also had somebody boxed off in the prison kitchen and got a meat or cheese sandwich every evening. All these privileges, just because of a smoke.

Prison was like a jungle — you had to be fit and strong to survive. All the time I was in there, serving my sentence from 1966–68, I trained every day in my cell. I was only 25 years old then and I would keep thinking positive and stay clean and healthy. Some prisoners would crack up and go under. I've seen it happen on many occasions. Men I knew and who I thought were strong ended up physical and mental wrecks. In fact, as I'm writing this book on Category A wing in Strangeways Prison, Manchester, a prisoner two cells away from me just tried to cut his own throat and, the week before, another guy from London mutilated himself. He was in a right mess. Now these people haven't even been up for trial yet! Once a criminal is put on Category A it is usually a known fact that there is no chance of you being found not guilty at your trial, because the evidence against you was supposed to be so overwhelming. The charges you face are the highest in the land, such as murder or armed robbery, and it would be a threat to the public if you ever escaped (and that in itself is virtually impossible). Being on a Cat A wing, you are in a cage inside a prison. Towards the end of this book I will elaborate on what it is really like in a Cat A wing and knowing what your fate is going to be.

However, Walton Prison in the '60s was vastly different to the way prison life is now. I think as far as prisons go, it was a lot better then than it is now. First, the wings were not all segregated; a prisoner could move freely from wing to wing and whatever wing you were allocated to, you always had your own landing screw. He would know everything about you, such as your behaviour, where you worked in prison and whatever else you happened to get up to. To sum it up, he was supposed to keep a watchful eye over you. Some wing screws were utter bastards, yet others were all right. I suppose it's like everyone else — you get good and bad in everyone. Every wing had five landings and our landing screw on 'I3' wing was an OK bloke. If you were on a good landing, which I was, life was a bit easier.

Most of my pals were on the same landing as me and we all used to stick together. Every weekend there was always a bucket of hooch (home-made beer) going for our crowd, and most of the landing screws turned a blind eye to it all. The landing screw we had certainly did; in fact, he actually sampled a drink on many occasions. There was always somebody who had a guitar and, if the right screw was on duty, he would let three or four of us get banked up together in one of our cells. With the home-made hooch and the guitar we would all have a good drink and a sing-song. This went on most weekends over the time I was there in the '60s.

I know to the reader this may sound like being in a holiday camp rather than prison but, believe me, most of the cons in prison at that time were having it very hard. Our crowd were just fortunate as to who we were and how we did our bird. The other poor bastards were not so fortunate. They were on a 23-hour-a-day bang-up. Imagine three men sharing a cell and only being let out for one hour a day and that's, of course, if it wasn't raining on the exercise yard. Otherwise, you didn't get out of your cell, unless you were a cleaner on the wing or you had some other form of work to do. But believe me, for those who never had jobs, which were hard to come by and still are to this day, it was a living hell. I've seen many cons taken out of their cells with their wrists slashed open. Some even went as far as hanging themselves. Think about it — three men being banged up day after day, for months or possibly years. There were no facilities in their cells, such as toilets or showers, like there are nowadays. No wonder men cracked up. They say 'familiarity breeds contempt', but you couldn't get more contemptuous than that. Some prisoners would go to any extreme to acquire a single cell.

There are still prisoners who prefer to have a cell of their own. I know I do, because you can keep yourself clean and tidy. Imagine living in a cell with somebody day in, day out, especially if the other person has filthy habits. I remember being on remand in Walton Prison when I was charged with murder in November 1997, and they put a prisoner in with me. This guy was riddled with needle marks in his arms and legs. He was a smack-head (heroin addict) and he was dead filthy, too. The next day I told the screw either to get him moved away from me or I would rather go down the block, where at least I'd be guaranteed to be on my own. The screw told me just to get on with it and refused to move him. I caused all kinds of protests. I even went as far as telling the screws I would end up killing this prisoner if they didn't get him moved from my cell. The screws knew I was already on a murder charge, so in the end they took my advice and moved him. I know you, the reader, may think, Well, what do you expect? After all, you are in prison for some crime you have committed, whatever it may be.

Yes, but a man losing his freedom is bad enough, without losing his dignity as well.

Chapter Eight

Time soon passes by in prison, at least that is one thing I know to be certain: I had done over half my sentence by now, and it was already the beginning of 1968 and so my release date which was for that coming August was getting nearer. While I was serving this sentence, I had my usual ups and downs like the odd fight, but I managed to stay lucky — by that I mean by not getting caught for any misdemeanours or being put on report, so far anyway. But you can ask anyone who has ever been in nick about the pettiness that occurs, especially where the screws are concerned. They fucking love to take any little bit of authority they have to the extreme.

Take an incident, for example, where I was caught bang to rights in my cell and the charge was 'being in possession of civilian food and cooking utensils'. And these so-called cooking utensils consisted of an old enamel plate and the lid of an old tin can.

This all came about because a mate of mine was

detailed to work outside the prison on a farm. Every evening he had to return back to the prison and be accounted for. He was brilliant at smuggling absolutely anything into the prison. All kinds of contraband would come in, and particularly fresh eggs. When you are outside and free, fresh eggs mean nothing, but in a prison they were considered to be pure luxury at that time in the '60s. We were only allowed one hard-boiled egg a week.

This mate of mine used to deliver a couple of eggs to me every other day or so. One of these days, after having just been locked up in my cell for the night, I decided to make myself two scrambled eggs for my tea. I did my usual cooking routine, placing the tin lid on the floor with a little scrap of torn cloth dabbed in a little bit of paint thinner, which I acquired from the workshop. I used to hold the old enamel plate with a little margarine in it slightly tilted in one hand, letting the margarine melt after I'd lit the cloth in the tin underneath the plate. Once this was done, it only took a few seconds for the plate to heat up. I would then crack the eggs in the hot margarine and my scrambled eggs were cooked.

Just as I was about to settle down and enjoy my little feast, my cell door was suddenly thrust open and standing there were two horrible screws; their faces were fucking smirking all over with delight.

'You're on Governor's report, Seiga,' they said, quickly confiscating the evidence — plate, tin and even the cooked eggs.

I wasn't worried about the punishment that I was going to receive the next morning from the Governor. But what did worry me was that I would lose my cell. I was almost certain to receive seven days' bread and water in one of the punishment cells or, even worse, lose some remission from my sentence. I had been in the same cell for the past 20 months on 'I' Wing with our little firm and this wrecked my head being moved from my mates.

Oh well, I thought, fuck it, I'm nicked, and there is nothing I can do about it.

The next morning, the two screws came for me, packed my bedroll and bits of belongings and I was taken down the block. There I was put in a punishment cell along with three or four other prisoners who had been charged with other various offences such as fighting, or possessing illegal contraband. While we were all waiting for the Governor to arrive, the screws outside were putting together a makeshift court. This consisted of a table and a couple of chairs where the Governor sat together with the prison chief and sometimes the prison chaplain would be there as well. Every prisoner was supposed to get a fair trial; this, of course, was a joke. No prisoner is ever found not guilty, and a screw's word is always accepted before a prisoner's and that is final.

When the Governor finally arrived, the cell door was opened and the first prisoner was called in. We could hear what was being said; it was the same old story of the prisoner denying his charge and the screws giving their version. Five prisoners went in front of the Governor that morning and were all found guilty. Some were sentenced to a period of bread and water and lost remission. I was the last to be called, and when I was facing the Governor, I was flanked at either side by two screws just in case I kicked off. While I had been listening outside, I noticed that the other prisoners in there giving evidence stood no chance. I'd also been told that this Governor was tough, especially if you had extra food which had been pilfered.

So there I was listening to the screws telling their story about the scrambled eggs and producing the evidence on a plate. When the so-called trial was over, I was asked whether I had anything to say before sentence was passed. I replied, 'Yes.' I then gave them a cock-and-bull story.

I said first of all I would like to apologise for all of the inconvenience I had caused, but I added, 'I would like you to try and understand my situation. I have been in prison almost two years and when I was approached by a certain inmate who offered me two fresh eggs, I found the temptation too strong to resist. Well, Sir, I am guilty and understand that I have to be punished accordingly.'

This came as a surprise to the Governor. I don't think any prisoner had admitted their guilt before and also made an apology on top of it all.

The Governor then looked straight at me and said, 'Well, Seiga, I take into account that you have not denied committing this serious offence, and you have also shown some sort of remorse. You will be fined two weeks' loss of earnings, but don't be tempted to buy any more stolen eggs again.'

I couldn't believe it. I had got off very leniently. No remission and no chokey. This meant I'd be going back to my old cell and mates on 'I' Wing.

When I got back to my cell, it was approaching dinnertime, so it was too late to go to the workshop. Our landing screw told me to help the orderlies by carrying some of the food up from the kitchen and back into our wing. We all had different types of 'scran' to bring back up, such as potatotes and bread. Ironically, I was given a big tray of eggs to carry.

Every dinner and teatime, the Governor and Chief would always stand on what was called 'the centre', which nearly everybody had to cross to get to whichever wing they were on. Our wing orderlies were just coming across the centre carrying the food, and I was at the back of the queue carrying this tray of eggs and, just as I was passing the Governor, he looked at me and the eggs I was holding. He must have thought, What the fuck is happening here? I've just given this inmate a walkover half-an-hour ago and here he is still in the egg business. I just carried on walking past, laughing my bollocks off.

There are two ways of doing bird — the hard way or, let's say, the more bearable way. I always tried to make it a bit easier if I could. Maybe it would be a different matter if I was doing a long stretch, like ten years or maybe life, then you wouldn't know how your mind would react, especially if there was no hope of you ever being free again. I do know there are men in prison who just want to get on with their sentence and get out. Some of these men I have met and know personally are very hard lads who can handle themselves and who just want to keep out of trouble and get on with it. Yet there are others who have started off with a small sentence but will not bow down and will end up doing a longer time.

You also see a man's true character in prison and how far his loyalties will go, especially if he has a friend or two but, believe me, there's not many of them. I saw a con with some friends walking on the exercise yard one day and he got into an argument with a screw. The con hit the screw and they started fighting. The next thing a panic button had been pressed and there is a gang of screws all knocking fuck out of one man. Now I never saw any of his mates pile in and help him. When it comes to being loyal and sticking together with your fellow inmates, believe me, there's not very much of that around.

Take Frankie Fraser or 'Mad Frankie' as he is known, and all the beatings he has had. I know he dished out a few himself but I bet not many cons, if any, came to his aid when he was being beaten by a gang of screws. Jimmy Boyle, who wrote *A Sense of Freedom*, got some terrible beatings from them. I bet you he'd tell you nobody tried to help him either. As I was pointing out, you can do bird the easy way or the hard way. It all depends entirely on the individual.

* * *

Prisoners are entitled to a change of labour if they put an application in to the wing officer. It's sort of like changing your job on the outside. So who should walk into our workshop one day but the Benny fella from Stoke, my arch enemy. This sly bastard had been stirring up trouble for too long; he was also a bully in his own right, picking on lads who were not fighters or abusive. I thought, He's got to go, but I'd have to be extra careful and make sure I don't get nicked for this slimy rat. Incidentally, I found out he was the one who had informed the screws about the stolen eggs I had in my cell, which got me put on report for a couple of weeks.

A few days later, my chance came. We all had our own work table in the shop, and I had a mate who worked alongside me. His name was Ron Blackhurst, a good kid. He would always back you if he had to. The barber would come into the shop and he always had the barber's chair next to some wash basins. These were always a slippy mess with water and soap suds all over the place. The rat Benny was sitting in this barber's chair one day waiting for his hair to be cut.

The barber had been told to go and take a piss in the toilet for a few minutes, which he did. A few of my mates knew what was going to happen. I said to Blackie, 'I am going to stab this fucker. You make out you've slipped by the wash basin and bang into me. I will then stab him.'

The plan worked. Blackie bumped into me then I lunged at the Benny fella with a pair of industrial scissors in my hand. I tried to cut his ear off with them, but his ear must have been hard as leather, so it all got a bit messy. There was blood everywhere and he was screaming his head off.

By now, the whole workshop was up on their feet. The screws came running over. Luckily, they never saw what was going on. A few of my mates had blocked out their view. I kept insisting to the screws it was all an accident. Benny knew different. I told him to keep his fucking mouth shut or I would kill him next time. Blackie and a few of the lads backed me up and said it was an accident. Benny was rushed away for treatment. Although I wasn't charged, the screws had a good idea what had gone on, so I was taken out of the workshop and sacked from my job!

I was put to work the next day brushing around the prison yard and picking up any bits of litter. This was considered a lowly job inside. They thought I would be sick of the job but I was made up. It was summertime and

I was out in the fresh air. Also, my release date was drawing near. I only had a few weeks to do and there I was getting a bronzie on my face. Every day I would walk around the nick with the yard brush following the sun and avoiding all the big old shady buildings.

My day finally arrived and I walked out of HMP Walton in August 1968. It was a warm, sunny morning outside. I was greeted by my brother, Ged, and a good loyal mate of mine called Tony Woods. I got into Tony's car and the radio was playing 'Hey, Jude'. It was Paul McCartney's number-one hit at the time. I felt terrific and to me the world was beautiful once again.

After my release from Walton Prison and after celebrating with my family and friends, exactly one week later, I was bang at it again. I wanted to recover those lost two years in prison. Once you have tasted the good life, it's very hard to let go. There were all kinds of firms sprouting up in Liverpool now and all were very versatile in their own way. Some were into heavy stuff like armed robberies, others were into burglary, lorry hijacking and so on. There was one firm in particular which was making a big impact on the Liverpool criminal fraternity in the late '60s. Two of them were mates of mine, one was called Frank C and the other 'Whitey' Mac. I went to work with them for a couple of years and I was glad to do so, as we all made a fortune together. The robberies we did and the amount of cash and jewels we stole was incredible. It was mostly houses we targeted.

Now, you, the reader, may think, houses — that's a bit petty! But let me tell you these were the big, wealthy homes of people who could afford to lose a bit of money. Rich people who owned all kinds of businesses and properties. When you come to think about it, these rich people were all fucking the tax man anyway, and so our little firm were just relieving them of the tax man's money.

People used to ask me what I did for a living in those days — I used to tell them I was in the light removal business. We only ever took cash or jewellery unless, of course, there was a safe in one of the houses we were stealing from and we came across plenty of those at times. Sometimes we would carry a safe out of one of these premises and get all the way home only to find fuck all inside them, but then there were other safes we stole which had thousands of pounds and jewels in them. We worked all over the country at that time down from the south coast to the North. We just used to follow the bonnet of our car and whichever part of the country we'd be in we would find money. I think out of all the stealing I every did throughout my life, those rich houses we stole from were the easiest.

I will give you an insight as to how simple it all really was. First, we would make sure there were no bells or alarms on the premises, and as I've already mentioned, people those days weren't security-minded compared to now. Obviously, we had to have the right house we were going to break into, that part was easy. We would only have to go to the local library and obtain the voters' list, then we would have the person's name, address and phone number. Having done this, it was just a matter of sitting off the premises, usually in a little van we had purchased from a motor auction under a phony name, that we called the 'grafting car'. Most businesspeople were nearly always punctual when it came to leaving for work, whether it was a factory they owned or a couple of shops. When we would see these businesspeople leave their houses, normally in the morning, we would then follow them to their business premises and actually see them open up. Having secured all this, it was back to their house. Sometimes their wives would still be at home but that did not deter us in any way. We knew they would eventually go out shopping, or to the hairdresser, and we'd wait. It was always the front door we would break into; this was the simplest way, especially if the door was just on a Yale lock. It was usually three of us who went in; because one of us would pull a chair up and sit by the front window keeping a watchful eye out on the front path just in case anyone was to call or come back. The other two would do the searching. The upstairs would be the first to be turned over. Sometimes we could be in a house for hours, it all depended how soon we would find the prize; at other times it could be a matter of minutes before the stash was discovered. All the time, the ones who were doing the searching upstairs would also be listening out for the man downstairs, who was keeping an eye on the window just in case it came on top. Our main priority was to always keep the back door open as our escape route. There have actually been times when we have been going through the back door as the owners have been coming through the front door. It was very rare that this happened to us because we were good at our work and we also knew most of the owners were still at their businesses until 5.00pm. Don't get me wrong, it wasn't all smooth going, we did have our moments.

I remember on one of these occasions we were inside some big luxury detached property. It was night time, about 9.00pm and it came on top. One of my mates who

p: My beautiful mother, pictured here in 1954 with my grandmother
d our Billy.

set: Me with my little daughter, Britt and her friend. Britt is the one
th her hair in plaits.

ttom: Some of our gang of Teddy boys and girls jiving in 1956 –
ı in the crowd there somewhere.

Top left: In the days when beers were cheap! Me in 1956 aged 16, with my mate 'Brim' Furlong.

Top right: A young 20-year-old in his prime.

Bottom left: Aged 25, just before I was sent to prison for three years.

Bottom right: Having fun with a girl I met on holiday.

Top: Myself and some of the boys in 1968.

Middle left: One of my best mates, Joey Doyle (pictured right).

Above: Me in 1985, at a party with my friends. We were all slightly the worse for wear!

Left: Relaxing with a lady friend on a Mediterranean cruise in 1972.

Top left: Me with my 1970s hair, relaxing at the seaside.

Top right: My gorgeous daughter, Britt, on holiday in Spain.

Bottom: Me with Gary and Click, a couple of the boys, in 1978.

ese two pictures were both taken in restaurants of mine. *Above*:
ı just visible behind Mr T himself and, *below*, I am pictured with
m O'Connor and Joan.

Top: Having fun with my friends in 1982.

Bottom: Myself (far right), with (left to right) Tony, Tom O'Connor and Eddie Kidd.

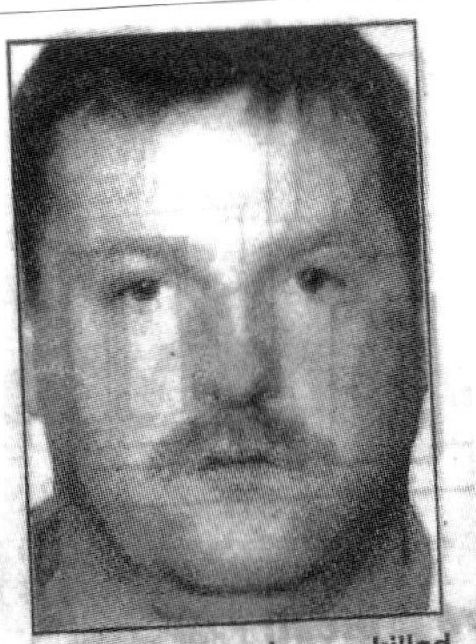

● George Bromley . . . killed by a mystery gunman

Bromley was an evil criminal who dealt in fear and terror.

He had aspirations of promotion from a lowly contraband crook to a Premier League gangster.

But his dreams of ruling the underworld roost came to an abrupt end in Charlie Seiga's kitchen.

His activities and dealings were so known to detectives he was once called in to a police station and warned his life was in danger.

But with all the arrogance and bravado of a seasoned Don, Bromley just shrugged his shoulders and walked away.

By Paul Kennedy

8 Liverpool Echo, Tuesday, October 27, 1998

SOAP STAR GUEST AT DEATH HOUSE

By Harry Dean

A BROOKSIDE star told a court he was a party guest at a house less than 48 hours before a man was murdered there.

George Wilson, who played Little Jimmy Corkhill, was called as a character witness by the defence in the trial where Charles Seiga, 58, denies murdering George Bromley.

Mr Bromley, 33, of Alvanley Road, West Derby, was shot dead by a mystery gunman at Seiga's home in Valescourt Road, West Derby.

Richard Henriques QC, prosecuting at Liverpool Crown Court, claimed Seiga played a part in the alleged contract killing by allowing the unknown gunman in to his house.

Mr Wilson, whose Brookside character was murdered, said he got to know Seiga in 1992 when he frequented the restaurant Seiga formerly owned in West Derby.

Mr Wilson, formerly of Barnfield Drive, West Derby, said he became more friendly with Seiga because they drank at the same pub in West Derby.

Two nights before the shooting Mr Wilson said he was in the pub when Seiga invited him and about six other people back to his home for a drink.

Mr Wilson said Seiga was a good cook and generous host.

He said they arrived at Seiga's home at 11.30pm and he left about 3am.

(Proceeding)

Chef in murder trial refuses to name friend who called at home

MY MYSTERY GIRL

By Harry Dean

RMER restaurant ner Charles Seiga, who ies murdering a "ca- criminal", today sed to name a mys- girlfriend.

he woman called at his e a few hours before the der.

orge Bromley, 33, was n the head by three bul- fired by an unknown nan at Seiga's home in scourt Road, West y, just before 6pm on ember 18 last year.

ga, 58, denies murder.

Bromley, of nearby anley Road, West Derby, had gone round to Seiga's home for a meal on the day of the killing.

Giving evidence at Liverpool Crown Court today, former chef Seiga said he would not name the woman because he did not want to get her into trouble.

Reveal

Richard Henriques QC, prosecuting, said: "This is a very serious matter. You are standing trial for murder. Any woman you name will not get into trouble."

Seiga replied: "I am an innocent man on trial for murder. I am not going to reveal her name. I don't care what you do to me. I am not going to say who she is.

"I am not prepared to name her. You can go on and on and keep me here for a week but I am not going to name her. She has nothing to do with the murder. I am quite clear about that."

Mr Henriques said if Seiga gave her name it would be treated discreetly. Seiga could write the woman's name on a piece of paper so members of the public and press would not know her identity.

But Seiga said he would not even write down her name.

Confess

He said: "I am an innocent man. I should not be here and the police know that."

In a further clash with the prosecutor, Seiga said: "What do you want me to do, confess to a murder I haven't done?"

(Proceeding)

● Charles Seiga . . . "I'm innocent"

rious press cuttings about the murder of George Bromley, for which as tried and found not guilty. The one at the bottom of the page tells how I refused to reveal the identity of the woman who had been at house, as she was a TV star and I wanted to protect her.

GUN DRAMA

● POLICE GUARD . . . armed police watch over a handcuffed suspect in Town Row, West Derby, this morning. Exclusive *ECHO picture: FRANK LOUGHLIN*

Four held in swoop by armed Mersey police

EXCLUSIVE by Val Woan and Paula Wright

FOUR people were arrested today in a swoop by armed police on a Liverpool house.

They were held just a few hundred yards from where club doors boss George Bromley was blasted to death.

The *ECHO* captured the moment when one man was handcuffed and ordered to sit on the ground as an armed officer stood guard over him.

Officers armed with Heckler and Koch semi-automatics searched the large detached house in Town Row, West Derby, and a car parked outside, as other officers sealed off the road and a police helicopter hovered overhead.

Police refused to confirm whether or not the drama was connected with the murder of 33-year-old Mr Bromley on Tuesday. He was shot three times in the head as he sat in the kitchen of a friend's house in Valescourt Road a quarter of a mile away.

His own home in Alvanley Road is just around the corner.

● Turn to Page 2

Left: A newspap report detailing the police armec swoop in which myself and two others were arrested in connection with the Bromley murder.

Below: Entertaining at my home. I'm th one in the open-necked shirt.

was keeping look-out on the window shouted, 'Let's go, the police are outside.' We all ran out of the back door of the house and down a big lawned garden, which seemed to go on for ever. When we got to the bottom of the garden, there was a big high wall. We all started to climb over (I was behind the others), when a copper ran up to me just as I was nearly over the wall, grabbed hold of my ankle and tried to pull me back down. I would not let go of the top of the wall. I thought, I'm nicked here, and then in desperation I shouted, 'Pass me the fuckin' gun while I shoot this bastard.' On hearing this, the copper let go of my ankle and ran back down the garden. Of course, there was nobody there who I was shouting to, my mates had long gone. I was just bluffing my way out. I got over the wall and ran as fast as I could, making good my escape.

The money we were getting and the times we were having those years were unbelievable. Frank and I spent money like there was no tomorrow. He would always buy top-of-the-range cars. I remember we had just had a big 'pay-off' and we both went out and bought a new car each. Frank picked a white S-type Jag and I brought a Morgan sports car. That's the way our young lives were — fast cars, clubs, women.

I remember once we were invited to a big show in Blackpool. The Bachelors were playing there; they were fairly big in the '60s. Freddie Starr was also billed on their show. Freddie was just trying to make the grade at that time, and wasn't really well known. I had a mate, John Stewart, who was Freddy's road manager, and they had been friends as teenagers in the '50s. Frank and I and the rest of our firm were invited to see the show and were then invited back to a party with them.

The night before we went to see Freddie Starr and John Stewart, a good piece of work had cropped up for our firm, and we decided to have it away. It consisted of a lot of jewellery which was in a penthouse flat near the city centre. There was only one problem — the penthouse was several storeys high, so we had to climb up the back of a building nextdoor to it and then jump across the roof to the penthouse. It was a bit risky but we had a go anyway. Frank and this other fella was with our firm at the time. To save his embarrassment, I won't mention this other lad's name. We told the other lad to stay where he was and keep watch, and then Frank and I jumped across the roof. We broke into the penthouse and, after turning it over, we came away well pleased.

The next night, we went to Freddie Starr's party. When we arrived, my mate John Stewart said to me, 'Look, Charlie, do me a favour. I want you to make out you are three businessmen to these show people I'll be introducing you to.'

Obviously, we weren't going to mention we were, in fact, three villains. Everything was going great, the show was very good and once it was over we were all invited back to the party, which was being held in some house in the suburbs of Blackpool.

Back at the house, the party was in full swing; all the Tiller Girls from the London Palladium were there. I copped off with one of the girls. She was a fine dancer. Now, up until then all these theatre people thought we were honest business gents. The next morning, most of the guests were milling around drinking coffee and the lad who'd been on the roof with us the night before started having a fit in front of everybody. Frank and I tried to restrain him on the lounge floor but he just went stark raving mad. All the guests in the house were deeply shocked. The lad then got to his feet and he ran to the front lounge window and shouted to me and Frank, 'Come on, it's on top, the police are after us.' He then crashed through the window and ran down the driveway foaming at the mouth.

Frank, John Stewart and I felt dead embarrassed over it all. We apologised to the guests. We then found it very hard to convince them that we were honest business gents. The horror on some of the guests' faces, especially the Tiller Girls, was unbelievable. They were all in deep shock. Frank and I went to try and find him, driving around the area in Frank's car, but to no avail. It was a Saturday morning and we just didn't have a clue were he had gone. Some time later, he did manage to get himself home. How, we will never know. To think he was up on a very high building the night before with us! I dread to think what might have happened if he had had a fit then. I never did any more work with him after that. In fact, it was only a short time later when the rest of us all split up. Whitey had invested all his money wisely and, after finishing with crime, settled down and became a successful businessman. Frank's doing OK these days. We still keep in touch.

* * *

It was coming to the end of the '60s and two mates of mine from jail, George A and Gerry Foster, gave me a call. They told me they had a bit of tasty work to be had and would I be interested. They were professional cat burglars, always selecting country pubs and hotels mostly in Wales. I had never worked in Wales before — or with cat burglars for that matter — but little did I know I would spend years working and sometimes living there. We always robbed these pubs and hotels at night, preferably at the weekends as they were always the busiest times. Looking back it was all so easy then. We would select these country premises to rob when we'd found out a couple was running them. You could tell that when you went inside — you would always see the husband working in the bar and the wife in the lounge or vice versa. Then George or myself would take up our positions, with either me in the bar and George in the lounge, or vice versa.

Gerry would break into the living quarters from the outside; he could climb like a cat, almost silently. George and I would know if something ever went wrong. If we saw the landlord or his wife go up the stairs to their quarters for something or other, and come running down with a shocked look on their faces, then we would both know it was on top, but that was very rare, and even then we wouldn't panic. George would casually walk out of the pub, and I'd follow him once I'd finished my shandy or lemonade. We always stipulated no drinking while working. We would get into our car and pick Gerry up — assuming, of course, he had got out of the upstairs fast. Gerry always carried a small torch with him and he would wait in a country lane which would be the pre-appointed pick-up point. We always knew where he'd be hiding because of his flashing torch when he saw our car coming along. It was then just a matter of picking him up and getting out of the area fast. As I said, that very rarely happened because he was too good at his job, a true professional.

I remember a big country hotel we screwed once. It was our usual routine — taking our positions up, one in the bar and one in the lounge, keeping a watchful eye on him and her. There were also quite a few young barmaids working on this particular night. It was a Friday or Saturday, and very busy. After George and I had been in the place for a while, I spotted the landlord going upstairs to his rooms. I thought, This could come on top, because obviously Gerry was already up there. I thought any minute now the landlord is going to come running down. I looked across at George who was in the lounge as if to say, 'Get ready'. We knew Gerry was safe because he would be out of a window in no time. George and I waited in anticipation. We could do nothing until the landlord came back down — but nothing happened. The landlord was still up there. By now, ten minutes had passed and I'm thinking, What's going on up there?

A few minutes later, our landlord came down with a smile on his face and carried on with his work happily chatting to his customers.

Not long after all that, Gerry briefly appeared in the pub doorway and gave us the nod. He always just used to show his face from the entrance door to me and George after he had done his work upstairs. Sometimes he could be up there in one of these places for ages, depending on how quickly he would come across the goodies. On this occasion, when George and I made our way out of the hotel pub, Gerry was already sitting in the car grinning all over. I was not pleased at all and said, 'What the fuck's been going on up there?'

He then told me he'd heard the landlord coming up the stairs so he dived under the bed and stayed quiet. He said he hadn't disturbed anything but he could smell plenty of money there. He thought the landlord was just going to pick something up and go back down. Then he said a barmaid came into the bedroom and that the landlord and the barmaid started having a quick jump on top of the bed with Gerry underneath. When they had finished shagging, he heard the landlord say to the girl, 'Come on, we'd better get back down to work, I don't want my wife to get too suspicious.' After they had both left the bedroom, Gerry, as cool as ever, carried on with his work. We got quite a large amount of cash and jewellery out of that place that night.

Throughout my time with those two cat burglars, Gerry and George, we never came unstuck once and we were doing two or three pubs a week. The money we made was incredible. We were wining and dining in some of the best hotels. The summertime was no good for that type of work. The nights were too light. When the summer came, George and Gerry would take it easy, like going on a good holiday and relaxing. I myself never really socialised with Gerry and George, one of the reasons being they were very fond of drink and horses. George was the worst, particularly when he was under the influence.

I remember being in Southport with them once. I think it was about 1970, and George had just bought a new Ford Anglia for his wife. He'd had a drink and he wanted to go on the beach while the tide was out. So what did George do? He drove on to the beach in his wife's new car. After a while, he went for another drink and left the car where it was parked. When he went back to fetch it, the tide had come in. I said to him, 'Come on, let's try and save the car.'

All he said was, 'Fuck it. I can always go and buy her another one.'

That was George when he had had too many. After a while I decided to move on. We split in good faith.

I liked the idea of grafting in Wales. The people at that time were still a bit gullible when it came to crime and the pickings were rich out there, too. I knew an antiques dealer who lived in Prestatyn, North Wales. His name was Frank Duce and he had put me on to a nice piece of work. It was a big old warehouse full of thousands of pounds' worth of antiques. I took my brother, Jimmy, with me on it and also a mate of his. I asked our Jimmy to go and hire a big van to do this antique job.

We did the warehouse and loaded the van up with all kinds of antiques — grandfather clocks, ornaments, silverware and oil paintings. The van was loaded to the brim. After coming away from the warehouse with Jimmy and his mate driving the van, I was to follow behind them in my car, just in case.

We'd been driving for quite a while on the main coast road out of Rhyl when I spotted a police car just sitting in a side-road. As we drove past, I glanced in my rear mirror and, just as I'd suspected, the cop car started following us. I just had this feeling the police were going to pull the van over. We only had a couple of miles to go before we got to Prestatyn and to our friend, the antiques dealer's garage. I thought, Fuck this. I had no intention of losing our hard-earned goods. So I acted. I started swerving a bit in the road behind the van, making out I was drunk to the police car that wasn't far behind me. I then put my foot down and overtook the van. Our Jimmy knew what I was up to. The next minute, the cop car started chasing me. I had not long bought my new MGB sports and it could move pretty fast. I thought that when the police finally caught me, our Jimmy and his mate would be long gone and so, too, would the goods.

There I was, screeching around corners in my sports car in Rhyl. After a short while, I managed to lose the police and parked up in a hotel car park. I switched my car lights off and decided to take a little walk around just in case the police caught me, but then what could they charge me with anyway? I hadn't been drinking, the car wasn't stolen. I would most probably get done for a speeding charge, which is fuck all. It was about 10.30pm now, and a lot of these holiday resorts in winter time are very quiet. There aren't many places open. I thought, I've got to get my head down just in case I happen to bump into any coppers who may be lurking around. As I was walking, I saw a café. I thought, I'll stay in there for half-an-hour or so until the heat dies down a bit. Just as I entered the café, a girl was cleaning up the tables. I asked for a coffee and she said, 'Sorry, we are just about to close.'

I said, 'Go on, give us a cup and I promise I'll drink it up fast. I'll buy you one, too.'

A few minutes later, we were both sitting having a coffee together, talking and having a laugh. She looked a right stunner — mini skirt, boots, long dark hair. Twenty minutes later, she packed her job in and was with me in my sports car driving to fuck knows where. She told me her name, Thelma, she was 19 and she lived in St Asaph but was bored and wanted to get away. So there I was with a beautiful young girl at my side driving deeper into Wales. This was the sort of life I always lived, not knowing what was going to happen next.

We both ended up in a small hotel that night in a place called Bangor. The next morning, I took Thelma shopping. She had run away with me in what she stood up in so she needed a change of clothes and essentials. I also phoned my antiques friend, Frank, in Prestatyn, and he told me everything was sorted. There was a nice package of money waiting for me. I told him I would pick it up some time when I was passing through. Jimmy and his mate had done OK for themselves out of it so they were happy, too.

Thelma and I had a meal that evening in some little restaurant in Bangor. After our meal, we took a stroll around the town. Bangor was a very small, quiet place — well, it was in those days. There was only one main street passing through it and everything seemed to be along that street — a few pubs, stores, shops and so on. Half-way down the street, I came across a jewellery shop. I couldn't believe what I was seeing; it didn't have an alarm on it, and the display had no bandit grille on it. It was all lit up and it was full of gold. There were all types of rings, sovereigns, bracelets, chains and the rest. There must have been a nice few grands' worth on show there. It was an old-fashioned building like all the others in that street.

I stood up against the window peering in. The bottom part of the window was fairly high up from the pavement, roughly about 4ft. I said to myself, I've got to have this, it's fucking talking to me. I noticed that none of the other shops seemed to be alarmed either. This was real virgin territory. You'd never see anything like that in Liverpool.

The next morning, I was up bright and early. I went and located one of these old DIY stores and bought a glass cutter, a small lump hammer and a roll of sticky tape and a pair of scissors. Thelma, by now, had a good idea how I lived. I mean, let's face it, what person wouldn't? I had a new sports car, clothes and money on me. Those days, people were not as well off as they are now. I came clean to her to a certain extent. I didn't really know her and I didn't want to put the girl in any jeopardy, so I spoke dead blunt to her. I asked her if she'd stand at my side while I broke that shop window and took the jewellery. She turned to me with an excited look on her face and said she'd love to. That was it. It was going. I told her to go and buy the biggest handbag she could find.

That night, at around 11.00pm, me and Thelma were walking down the high street arm in arm. We stopped at the shop and made out we were just admiring the jewellery on display in the window. I looked up and down the street. There were a couple of people going home. It was fairly quiet. I made sure nobody was looking and I got out the glass-cutter and scored the bottom corner of the window, which had the tape on it. A smack and it broke first time hardly making any noise. It never shattered because the plastic tape was all over it. I then picked the glass out of the way and there was a hole big enough to get my whole arm in. I started helping myself to the gold pieces and putting them in the bag Thelma was holding. I got quite a considerable amount. There were some pieces I couldn't reach but I was happy with what I got. All this took a few minutes. There was still nobody around. We then just turned and walked away arm in arm.

When we got back to the hotel, I decided we should get right off because the minute that job was discovered, the police would be looking for any strangers in town and, with it being a small place, you'd never know what might happen. We left Bangor at 11.30pm that night putting all the gold under the passenger seat of the car. I decided to go to Chester that night because I knew a good jewellery fence. I thought, So far, so good, but then again things can go a little bit wrong.

After driving for a while, I realised I had taken the wrong route and we found ourselves driving through Wrexham. Then it happened — the car ran out of petrol. As if that wasn't bad enough, we had conked out a few yards away from the main police station. It was so quiet, it was like a ghost town. I said to Thelma, 'Look, we have got to bluff our way out of here. We will go inside the police station and give them a story.'

One thing about Thelma, she was cool and calm. We both looked reasonably dressed. I said to her, 'Let me do the talking. You just agree or nod to what I have to say.'

When we went into the police station there was a big red-faced Welsh copper sitting behind the desk. I said, 'Excuse me, Officer,' trying to disguise my Liverpool accent at the same time, 'my girlfriend and I are two medical students from the University and we're on our way to Chester but unfortunately our car has run out of petrol. Could you please help us in any way?' I already knew main police stations have their own petrol supplies.

I added, 'We will pay you, Officer, if you could oblige us with some petrol.'

He said, 'I'm sorry, son, but our patrol driver is out at the moment and he has the key to the petrol pump. I don't know how long he's going to be out for — it could be an hour or so.'

He then came round from his desk and asked me where the car was. I showed him where it was, parked only a few yards away. He then suggested we both push it into the police compound and when the other policeman got back he would get him to give us some juice. I thanked the officer for all his help and everything.

After we had got the car into the compound, I said to the copper that my girlfriend and I would sit in the car and wait. He nodded and went back into the police station. It must have been about 2.00am by now and Thelma and I were sort of dozing off in the car. All of a sudden, I heard a knock on the window — it was the big red-faced copper. I thought he'd sussed us out or something had gone drastically wrong. There we were, sitting on thousands of pounds of stolen jewellery and I'm thinking, We're nicked.

I wound the window down and there he was holding mugs of hot cocoa in his hands and a blanket under his arm.

'Here you are,' he said, 'that should keep you two young people warm.' Then he said the other officer shouldn't be too long.

I couldn't thank him enough. What a lovely big Welsh copper! If he only knew.

We did eventually get our petrol and got to Chester without any more problems. I had a meeting that same day with the fence and disposed of the gold jewellery. To me, it was just another bag of money which I got for nothing and to spend silly.

I decided to stay around Chester for a few days so Thelma and I booked into the Grosvenor Hotel. After a bit of wining and dining, I took Thelma to Liverpool with me. I introduced her to friends and some of my family. We stayed together for a few weeks and then I had to let her go. That's the way I was. Women just used to come and go with me and that's the way I wanted it.

Chapter Nine

It was the beginning of the '70s now and I was into every type of villainy within reason. No matter what sort of work came along, I would get involved, as long as the rewards were good. I had started to hang about with two brothers who came from the south end of the city who were well known in Liverpool around that time. They were very heavy, very fit and could handle themselves. The youngest one was very game when it came to having a go at anything. I remember these two brothers and I, along with a few more of our crew, were called out to do somebody a favour in Manchester.

A businessman, George Downey from Liverpool, was getting a bit of hassle. He was refused his membership card from the Playboy club. The Playboy at that time was the place to be seen in, and no expense had been spared, having been lavishly decked out, boasting a big casino and, above all, oozing with class. All the top celebrities frequented the place.

George Downey was a ruthless gambler and was

winning lots of money most nights in the casino. Sometimes he would win thousands and because of this they would not renew his membership. That's where we came in. Our crowd were fairly heavy and I was tooled up as usual. When we arrived at the club, all the staff, doormen and managers listened very sensibly to what we had to say and, after a nice little talk, George was reinstated. After this was all sorted out, we were all invited to the Midland Hotel to a party with the number-one footballer at that time, Georgie Best. He was with Marjorie Wallace, a tall, young Texan girl, who had just won the Miss World title. Everyone was talking about football to George when I got into conversation with him and Marjorie Wallace. I said to George that I knew fuck all about football. That was it; the guy was made up with me. After a short while, George and I, together with Marjorie Wallace, had a little drink on our own. George got bladdered some time later on and I ended up with Miss World that night for company. She was beautiful and we had a nice time.

Although I was making plenty of money having a good time with the clubs and the parties and so on, the people I was involved with weren't as versatile as me when it came to doing graft. Like I've mentioned before, some firms just stick to the line of business they know best. Me, I was open to offers for any good work that was put to me. If it was heavy like an armed robbery, I would select the right men to come with me. If it was a burglary, I would select different men, men who were not into violence.

I won't go into too much detail about every robbery I have committed throughout my life. There are so many, if I were to mention them all I would never get this book finished. This I do know and so do the police — I have never done a prison sentence, except when I was sent to Borstal for safe-blowing in 1957, for any of these robberies I have carried out. People have often said to me, 'Charlie, you have got some bottle.' I always told them it wasn't bottle, any fool can have that, it's just plain common sense and how you plan and execute your work.

The police had started playing their games with me again by putting surveillance back on me. They were literally breathing down my neck at times. Most of the time, I lived at my mother's house. I mean, let's face it, the old lady is the best person to live with, isn't she? All that home cooking, always washing and ironing your shirts for you. My ma used to pamper me soft. Mind you, I always had my own flat to take a bird back to now and again. I could never bring a woman to sleep back in my mother's. There would be murder. It was the same with the rest of my brothers. It just wasn't allowed.

I always had my car parked on my mother's front driveway and when the bizzies were on my case they used to wait 'til I drove down our road and then they'd give me a tug. It would be all the usual rubbish. They would come out with, 'Is this your car? ... Have you got a licence?' and so on.

I was just pulling away from my mother's driveway one day, when I spotted them waiting at the end of our road to pull me. I was in an E-type Jag which I had only just bought. I quickly did a U-turn half-way down our road and went the other way. The cop car came after me. I drove in the middle of the main Liverpool road leading into town. I switched off the engine, locked the doors and sat inside with the radio on full blast. The bizzies were all around the car, knocking on the windows trying to get me to open the doors. A big crowd started to gather, traffic was jamming up the road and I just reclined my seat and shut my eyes and would not speak to them. In the end, they left me alone and fucked off.

I decided I had had just about enough of them bizzies on my case again. I also decided to get away for a bit and have a holiday. What do they call it — 'out of sight, out of mind'? I had a few friends in different parts of the world — Spain, Africa and the States. I'd always fancied going on a cruise. To me, it seemed more appealing than flying to a holiday resort for two weeks or so and flying back again. There is nothing you can take in on one of those holidays. I have been on quite a few of them in my time and, to me, they are a load of rubbish. I would sooner travel and stop off at different places, so this cruise and the couple of others I went on really suited me.

The first cruise boat I sailed on was called the *Edinburgh Castle* and we sailed out of Southampton. No expense had been spared on this boat, it had every amenity you could wish for — swimming pool, cabaret, casino, and so on. It was a good all-round boat. First port of call was Madeira, a beautiful place, then on to Las Palmas, then to South Africa and finally to the Seychelles. We stopped and visited all these lovely places and it was absolutely brilliant.

The first port we docked at in South Africa was Cape Town, where the passengers were allowed ashore for six hours or so. Before we went ashore, we were told to be very careful and conform to the South African laws. Apartheid was still in force in 1973, so 'when in Rome, do as the Romans do'. I didn't! I broke the law as usual.

When I got off the ship in Cape Town, there was a long queue of taxis waiting to take you anywhere you wished to go. All the taxi drivers were black. I got into one of these taxis and the driver said to me, 'Where do you want to go to, boss?'

I said, 'I've only got a few hours ashore before the ship sails, so where's it all happening then?'

He rattled off a few restaurants, museums and theatres.

I said to him, 'They're out of the question for me, mate. Take me to a bar or something or, better still, take me to one of your clubs.'

He said, 'I can't do that because of the apartheid.'

I said, 'Fuck the apartheid, take me to one of them.'

He ended up taking me to some black club and I asked him to join me for a drink inside and show me around. These people were on meagre wages at that time so I slipped him a few quid and when we got inside the place, it went all quiet. It was just full of blacks. I was the only white fella in there and that wasn't allowed by South African law, but after a couple of minutes or so everything became normal again.

There were some black girls looking over at me all the time and the taxi driver asked if I would like to go with one of them. I said yes. He said I'd have to be discreet because of the law and it was a jail sentence right away.

To cut a long story short, there I was in the taxi and this black girl was lying down on the floor so as not to be seen with a white person and the driver took us to fuck knows where. He finally pulled up after a few miles and we were out of the taxi. The driver sort of winked at me and said he'd call back in half-an-hour or so.

This girl just sort of laid down on the grass. I sat down with her and just as I was about to get comfortable I heard a funny noise in the grass not far away from us. I froze a bit. It sounded like a hissing noise. I thought this might be a snake and I hate snakes. I said to her, 'Did you hear that?'

She said, 'Oh, it's nothing, don't worry.'

I was just about to settle down again, when the next moment I heard an animal, like a roar or a grunting noise. I jumped up. We were almost on the edge of a jungle. I thought, I hope there's no loose lions around here. I wouldn't have minded if I had had a gun or some other kind of weapon to defend myself, but I didn't even have a penknife on me. I said to the girl, 'Come on, let's go, I've had enough.'

She kept insisting everything would be all right, that there weren't any snakes or anything.

I said, 'I'm taking no chances, I'm going,' and with that she burst out laughing. She must have thought I was another soft Englishman. The taxi lad finally arrived to pick us both up and she told him what had gone on. They both laughed their heads off on the way back. I could see the funny side of it eventually — I mean, some of these people actually walk through the grass in their bare feet, don't they?

When I arrived back on the boat a few hours later,

the South African coast was included in the cruise and so the next port of call was Durban. The ship was berthed this time for slightly longer — 48 hours. I had relatives in Johannesburg and, before sailing to the Seychelles, I decided to pay them a visit. My brother Billy lived out there and I had a niece, Angela, who also lived there. Billy had done well for himself — honestly, of course. He owned his own business and some property.

In South Africa, they have a special train called the Blue train, which has all the luxuries you could wish for. It's a little like the Orient Express. I thought, I'm having some of this, so there I was travelling through Africa on this beautiful train. The scenery was magnificent. When I arrived in Johannesburg, I was greeted by my brother, our Angela and her husband Mike with the rest of the family. They held a party for me that night in a place called Hillbrow. I met a girl at the party who was a South African actress called Anna. We hit it off together. She took me around showing me the sights and, because I was so busy with her having a good time, I missed the ship for the Seychelles. When I realised what I had done, I made a few enquiries the next day. I was told the boat would be returning back to Durban in a few days' time and I could join up with it again. A couple of days later, I was on my way back to Durban coast on the luxury Blue train with Anna.

When we got to the coast, we wined and dined together in some beautiful bars and restaurants. When it was time to set sail again, I promised Anna I would keep in touch and everything. I remember holding her hand in this beautiful restaurant which was situated on the water front, saying my last goodbyes ready to board the ship. All of a sudden, the restaurant doors were noisily opened. Two fellas were standing there, a little drunk. They then shouted, 'Charlie, Charlie Seiga.' It was two fellas I knew back in Liverpool. Henry Santamaria and Robby Brown, both from the Scotty Road area. They were also the crew working on the boat I was to sail back on. I finally said my last goodbyes to Anna and boarded the cruise ship.

It was another 12 days' sailing and visiting other beautiful places before I got back to England. It's funny, when you've been away from home on holiday you can't get back quick enough, especially if you're from Liverpool like me. Throughout my life, I've been abroad to all kinds of different places but when I'm away I always get homesick. I love Liverpool. It's like a magnet. It draws you back all the time.

When I finally arrived back home in Liverpool, a letter had been posted to me. It was an invitation to a new club called the Chauffeurs. A friend of mine, Charlie Scott, had just opened it. It turned out to be one of the trendiest clubs in Liverpool at that time. I became quite a regular there. Charlie Scott was always a good host to his clients who attended there. I always thought it was nice to walk into a place and be greeted with courtesy. Most of the club owners were like that in Liverpool in the '70s, but you always got some horrible pricks who didn't like to be acknowledged in a nice way. The same sort would, as I've mentioned before, take manners as a weakness and then the bullying game would start. I've seen some of these dogs actually terrorising some of the club owners. This happened one

Friday night when I was out on the town with a mate of mine.

We had done the usual round of the club scene, generally having a good time. We decided to go and see a club owner who was a friend of our crowd. His name was Jim Island. He was the owner of a club called the Beachcomber, which was located in Seel Street. We all used to call it the 'Beachy'. Jim Island was one of the old, elegant-looking types. He was always dressed immaculately. When my friend and I arrived at the club door, Jim was standing there looking very frightened and the two doormen were trembling with fright. One of the doormen I knew, a big fella called Frank, said to me, 'Charlie, he's in here, he's fucking kicking off with some of the customers.'

I said to him, 'What do you want me to do about it? You're getting paid for this type of work, aren't you? What's the matter with you?'

It was no use, they were all petrified of this man who was inside the club. I told them I'd go and try to reason with him. I won't call him a man — this person was a fucking animal, and even that's too good a word for him. His name was Eddie Palmer, one of the biggest headaches in Liverpool at that time, and he was the worst bully anyone could ever meet. Bully or no bully, Eddie Palmer was big, fit and strong and, above all, he could fight. Club owners hated him. He was always extracting money and free drinks from them. Some taxi drivers were scared stiff of him, too. I believe when he called a taxi from home to go out clubbing, the poor taxi driver would have to chauffeur him from club to club and not get paid at the end of the night. He used to drag people back to his house in the early hours of the morning. He lived with his mother and I believe he would drag his poor mother out of her bed and make her start cooking breakfast for him and his drunken guest. I don't know what makes a person like that; it's beyond me. In my opinion, anybody like that wants putting down.

I walked into the club and there by the bar stood this fucking animal annoying everybody. He had hold of some young girl by the hand, squeezing her fingers back and trying to force her to go home with him. I heard him say to her, 'You're fucking coming with me now.'

The poor kid could only have been about 17 or 18 and was absolutely terrified. Now, by then nobody was doing anything about it all. I couldn't help myself. I walked over to him and said, 'All right, Eddie, how are you doing?'

He looked at me as if to say, 'Where have you come from?'

I took hold of his and the girl's hands and said, 'Come on, Eddie, mate, leave her alone. She's only a kid.'

He let go of the girl's hand and I gave her a look as if to say, 'Get out of his way.'

He had had a few drinks to make matters worse. Then he started on me, not physically first just verbally.

'Who the fuck do you think you are?' he shouted, then carried on with all kinds of verbal abuse at me.

He insulted me that much that if I had been tooled up at that time, I would have given it to him there and then. I used a bit of sense and stayed calm. I turned away and said to my mate, 'I'm going to kill this animal.'

I made an excuse to leave for a few minutes. I then went outside to where my car was parked. I opened the boot of my car and pulled out a commando bayonet, which is designed for one purpose only and that's to kill. I also kept a pair of gloves in there as well.

A few moments later, I went back into the club with the bayonet concealed under my suit coat. I intended to stab Palmer with a glove on. The bayonet was down to nobody. I had to be very careful the way I was going to do this, as I wouldn't want to be seen by any witnesses. Once the knife was in him, I would just sort of stand back. The place was crowded and fairly dimly lit. If it was carried out in the right manner, nobody would have a clue who'd done it.

I thought, Fuck it, he's got to go, then I saw the back of him a few yards away. You couldn't miss him really, being the size he was. I had started to edge slowly over to him by now. He still hadn't seen me. I had the bayonet in my gloved hand down my side. I was right behind him now. He had a neck on him like a bull. I quickly put my left arm around his neck from behind in a sort of head lock and then I brought the bayonet up and plunged it upwards into his back. For a brief second he didn't move. I pulled the bayonet out of his back and I stabbed him again. This time it was good and hard. The bayonet went right in up to the hilt. He dropped on the floor and he sort of started spinning on his side going around like a cartwheel. Blood was pumping out of him one way and piss was coming out of him the other. Then I heard my name being shouted out.

'No, Charlie, no, you've killed him.'

I couldn't believe what I was hearing. This was

coming from one of the punters who had obviously recognised me. I went cold. Incidentally, after hearing that, I was never to trust anybody again. I lost a lot of faith in human nature after that night.

There was only one thing left to do — get out of there fast. I had made a major mistake by stabbing him twice. I should have kept to my plan and stabbed him once and then mingled in with the crowd. And my name getting shouted out didn't help — I was now identified. A few minutes later, I was driving out of the city towards Huyton. I finally arrived at a safe house I knew and made contact with my brother Joe. Our Joe came as quick as he could. I could always rely on Joe or our Jimmy and the rest of my family for that matter. We were all very loyal to one another and still are. My clothes were all disposed of and the car was taken away. I had to sit tight in his house. I was holding up ready for my next move. News bulletins had come over on the TV and radio describing how a man was in a serious condition and might not last the night. All through that night, I was kept informed how Palmer was doing. The news was broadcast every hour. I was then told a priest had been called to give him his last rites, so he wasn't going to make it.

The police had started a big manhunt for me. I was wanted by every police force now. They were checking the docks, airports and stations. They had put stories about such as 'Don't tackle this man ... If you see him, he's a very dangerous person and must be caught.'

Some time later, a little bit of luck came my way. I had been told Palmer had made it through the night and the next morning the medics had him under control.

Apparently, the hospital had only just acquired new blood transfusion equipment and because of this, his life, for what it was worth, was saved. At least, I thought, I wouldn't be on a murder charge now, but if caught I could still go to prison for a very long time.

After a couple of weeks or so, Palmer was allowed home from hospital to recuperate. I had arranged a meeting with a few loyal friends of mine, including Terry Kirmo. We all got around the table and discussed what was to be done about Palmer. He had made a statement naming me. Terry and our Joe and the rest of my mates paid Eddie Palmer a visit and in no time at all he had gone to my solicitors and had retracted his statement. There was also the club manager and a couple of barmaids who had made statements, but not directly naming me. After all this was sorted, I was to put myself about in the town and just act normally, as though I'd done nothing wrong. So I decided to walk into the lions' den, a pub called the Bowring Park, not too far from where I lived.

The Bowring Park pub was frequented by a lot of bizzies, and at that time they were never out of the place. Before I threw myself in, I had one more important thing to do — pay my last respects to my beautiful sister, Delia, who was dying in hospital. She didn't have long to go. It was cancer.

My friends and my brother-in-law Joe drove me to the hospital where I had my last visit with her, knowing I would never see her again. It makes you wonder, doesn't it? Here is a beautiful lady who has worked hard all her life, has never done anybody any harm, brought three lovely daughters up, and she's dying with the worst death anybody could wish for. She was also very religious and yet, if there's a God, He lets her die like that while, on the other hand, He lets an animal like Eddie Palmer live.

I walked into the Bowring Park pub and within minutes I was pounced on. There were bizzies everywhere. I was cautioned and one of the coppers said to me, 'Charles Seiga, I am arresting you for the attempted murder of Edward Gerard Palmer.'

I was taken to the main police station and, after the usual two days of routine questions and trying to make me admit to the offence, I was eventually remanded to HMP Risley Remand Centre, Warrington.

My brother Joe and Terry Kirmo came to visit me the next day and, when they walked in to see me, their faces were very glum-looking.

'What's wrong,' I asked, 'is everything OK?'

And then they hit me with it — Palmer had made a fresh statement saying he'd been intimidated into making the retraction and it was me who'd tried to kill him. Palmer had to be talked to again, but this time with a guarantee.

After a few weeks, I was eventually sent to the committal court. When the court was in process the first witness to be called was, of course, Edward Palmer. The barrister who was defending me, Alex Kennedy, asked Palmer one question when he went into the witness box to give evidence.

'Mr Palmer, is the person present in this court who gave you those horrific injuries?'

Palmer then turned and looked over at me for a few seconds. He then replied, 'No.'

That was the end of the case and I walked. There was no reprisal from Palmer. He knew best not to fuck with me. Some time later he got knifed in the throat whilst sitting in a car. He died as he lived; violently. He finally got his just desserts.

Nobody ever did get sentenced to life for that cold-blooded murder. I wonder why?

Chapter Ten

1975 had arrived and little did I realise but that year would start to change my life. Well, to a certain extent. By that I mean I would still be involved with crime, but I was choosing my work more carefully now.

I had been courting a young woman by the name of Joan and she became pregnant by me. When the baby arrived, it was a beautiful little girl and we called her Britt. She was to be my fifth child. My first child was with Veronica, who I married in 1963 and sadly divorced in 1967. We had a fine son and named him Anthony. Then in 1968 I was courting a girl named Marie and she had a lovely little girl who we called Jean. My relationship with Marie didn't last long so we parted. In 1969, on one of my travels I met a girl from Wales called Pat. We were courting for some time and she, too, became pregnant. She had a pretty little girl called Hayley. Then in 1972 I had been going out with a girl called Jean. After a while, she became pregnant by me and had a baby boy. Jean, under pressure from her family, had the child adopted.

Out of everyone, sadly I never got to know Jean's child. Each and every one of my children's mothers were all clean and decent ladies. They were also very loyal to me. Some of the relationships I had with them were short, and some were a lot longer, years in fact. I have always believed that a man should be willing to assume responsibilities when it comes to his children. But then there is another side to the coin. I don't mean to phrase this in a bad way, but what gives the person the right to have a child without consulting her partner? Maybe the partner is not quite ready to want to have a child just yet. I have always believed that if two people are in a relationship they should share everything together. I don't think it's fair if one plans to do something without telling the other, and particularly when it is revealed a pregnancy is involved. And sometimes by then a few months have gone by and then it's definitely too late to change one's mind. I certainly have never said to any woman in my life, 'I would like you to have my child' — if I did, I think she has the right to say 'No'. I don't mean all this to sound clinical.

Sometimes a person can think they are in love when they first meet but, after a while, the magic can die and it's pointless going on when that happens. It's no use pretending still to be in love, it will just bring unhappiness in the end for both sides. I always believed true love is for sharing with one another and to dream together. Sadly I never found that with any of my children's mothers, except one. I know it all seems very selfish on my part, but being me and the life I lived I just couldn't settle down. I still keep in touch with some of my ex-partners. They all seem to be doing OK for themselves and they know I've always appreciated their loyalties to me. I will always be there for them if I can help them in any way.

* * *

Most of my mates had been buying their own houses and properties and putting their money into legitimate businesses. I was now 35 years of age and I thought I, too, had better start doing something myself with what stash I had. It's all very well taking it out of the pot and not putting anything back into it. Money soon goes if you are not careful, particularly the way I had been spending over the years on cars, holidays and the club scene. I had nothing to show for it all.

I decided to buy some property and start a legitimate business up at the same time. I fancied living out in the country for a while, not too far from Liverpool, though. I bought myself a beautiful traditional Welsh cottage. It was magnificent. Inside, it had all the original oak beams on the ceiling and a big old-fashioned fire grate, which was lovely when lit with wooden logs. There was a big farmhouse back kitchen and, to top it all, there was almost an acre of land together with a stable — it was a dream. I thought, This is the life for me. No more bizzies breathing down my neck.

I got in touch with an antiques dealer I knew, Frank Duce, from Prestatyn. He'd always been a good fence and had bought quite a lot of stuff off me over the years. When I met him again, we got our heads together. I gave him a considerable amount of cash and became his business partner. We bought some property together. One was an old warehouse for storage purposes and the other was an antiques shop. This was great because, although I was still active in crime, it was also a good front for me. Here I was in the antiques business and doing all right for myself, too. And it gets better — my mates started paying me a visit from Liverpool and, in the '70s, good antiques were a highly sought-after commodity. Then the inevitable happened — Wales took a battering over the next couple of years. There were literally hundreds of thousands of pounds' worth of jewellery and antiques stolen from there. After all these goings-on, the Welsh Police paid me a few visits. It doesn't take them long to put two and two together to find out who you are and where you're from. They told me they believed it was me who was behind all these antique robberies and threatened me. They would have me in the end.

Now I have lived with these threats from the police ever since I was a kid, so it was nothing new to me. It was true I did make a lot of money when I lived in Wales. I mean I had a legitimate antiques business, didn't I? I do remember one job that stands out vividly in my mind even to the present day. I still think about it.

It all began when my partner Frank called to my cottage one day. A Rolls-Bentley pulled up outside my place and out stepped Frank and this very wealthy jeweller who was from Manchester. Frank introduced me to him and we all went inside my cottage for a chat. They both came right to the point. The jeweller said that he'd heard a lot about me and I had come strongly recommended. Frank then butted in and said, 'Look, Charlie, we've got a job for you, one of the biggest you have ever done.'

The jeweller then offered me a million quid if I would

get him a certain item from some big wealthy house which he knew about. He asked me if I was interested and I told him I was more than interested. I mean, it is these sorts of jobs a robber dreams about.

They then both told me the score on it all. Apparently, millions of pounds' worth of gold, diamonds, paintings and other priceless works of art were smuggled out of Russia just before the Revolution began in 1917. The place I was supposed to break into was where a lot of these treasures were stashed.

After we had discussed it a bit more and come to an agreement, they took me to show me where the premises were. After driving for a while, we finally pulled into the driveway of a big, old Victorian-type house. It didn't look that impressive to me but then they never do. They say 'never judge a book by its cover'.

The jeweller told me that, once we went inside the house, we should let him do all of the talking, as he knew the owner quite well and did a lot of business with her. He also said he would point out the article he wanted me to get and to take that and nothing else.

We went up to the door and the jeweller rang the bell. It was answered by an elderly lady — I thought she looked a bit eccentric — who instantly recognised the jeweller. He explained to her that Frank and I were both dealers and interested in buying.

She then beckoned us into the hallway which was like a long corridor with rooms on both sides. I noticed that the door to every room had a big old key in it.

The woman then began to open each door to the rooms so that we could view the contents. We all went inside the first room and I couldn't believe my eyes —

there were priceless oil paintings everywhere.

Then we were led to each individual room and every one of them contained unbelievable treasures. One room alone was full of priceless silver and gold antique ornaments. The jeweller said to me, 'Have a look at the brooch she's wearing, it's worth thousands.'

The brooch was pinned to an old cardigan she had on and it was full of big diamonds. In one room we entered, I noticed a small safe just lying underneath a window. It was one of those little carry-out safes. The jeweller told me to ignore that and to concentrate on the prize he wanted me to get for him. We eventually came to the room where my million quids' worth was hiding, but when he showed me what it was, I couldn't believe it. It was a small antique cabinet with a glass front. You couldn't see what was inside it, as it had soiled white cloths on the inside of the doors.

After a while, we eventually came away from the house promising the lady we would be purchasing some antiques at a later date. Frank was an expert on antiques so he fobbed her off by saying he did a lot of export to America. We eventually arrived back at my place and the jeweller asked if he could rely on me 100 per cent not to fuck anything up. I told him it was dead easy and not to worry. He then said, 'Look, just get me the cabinet with its contents intact and there's a million quid waiting for you.'

I thought if he was going to pay me a million quid for doing this, what must the contents be worth inside the cabinet? The three of us then went over a few more plans, and said our goodbyes. I did reassure both of them that I would get it sorted.

This was the sort of work that only comes along once in a lifetime — one million, and that amount in the '70s was a *lot* of money. I decided to keep this one in the family. My brother, Joe, was coming on it and my nephew Paul. He was my brother Ged's son. Paul was just starting to find his feet. He was only young but very game and intelligent with it.

Once I had put the work to them, they were obviously both delighted and very keen. The way I had it planned out, I stipulated to them that there was to be no violence on the lady.

The next day, Joe and I went to a motor auction where I bought a Volvo estate car. It had a roof-rack on it which was all the better. Whenever we had to buy a working car in those days it was always from an auction because we used a phony name and it was never down to anybody. I then went and bought a set of old antique-looking chairs. I tied them on to the roof-rack of the Volvo and they looked very convincing to bluff my way into that big old house. It was a late Friday afternoon by the time I'd got everything arranged and with the weekend on top of us we decided to put it off until the following Monday morning, because then we wouldn't look suspicious, especially when we drove up her long driveway and she saw the antique chairs on the roof-rack. We knew the lady would open her door, particularly when she saw that we were just more antiques dealers calling on her. I told our Joe and Paul that when we called on the Monday, I didn't want anything out of place and I insisted we all looked reasonably dressed. One was to stay in the car just in case someone else turned up at the house while the two of us were inside it.

So the plan was that when we drove up the driveway the one who was to stay in the car would lie low in the back seat and only sit up after the two of us had entered the house. His job was to blow the horn if anyone arrived. I knew all this would only take five minutes for what we had to do. It was dead easy, really. As soon as she walked into the first room I would just back-pedal and lock the door on her as all the doors had a key in them. We would just go to the other room where the cabinet was kept, and after a little bit of manoeuvring we'd be in the car and away. It was all that simple. After we had left the premises and got safely back to our destination, which would only take about 20 minutes, I would then phone the police or fire brigade and briefly explain there had been an accident. A lady had been locked in a room. She would only be in there for 20 minutes or so and I would reassure her before I left that everything would be OK. Well, that's how easy it all was. Only two more days and I would be a fairly rich man. I started relaxing over the weekend and counted my chickens before they hatched.

On the Sunday, I saw through my cottage window Frank Duce pulling into my drive. I thought he most probably wanted to go over a few more things regarding the job I was pulling off the next morning or how much he would want for his cut. When I opened my front door, he just stood there with a long face on him.

'Is everything OK?' I asked.

'Why did you fuck the job up, Charlie?' he said.

I asked him what he was talking about. He then told me he'd got a phone call from the jeweller in Manchester and he said that the house had been burgled last night and that a small safe had been stolen. He also said the woman hadn't reported it to the police.

I said to Frank, 'Well, if that's the case it can still be done,' but he said it was too risky and, besides, he was still convinced it was me who had done the job. We had a big argument over it all and he just fucked off sulking. I was absolutely gutted. I couldn't believe what had happened and to think we were having it the following morning.

A couple of weeks later, a man was charged with stealing a safe from the same house. The truth as to what had happened emerged in the end. Two sneak thieves were sniffing around that neighbourhood on the prowl looking through the window of the house, the very one we were going to break into. It just so happened they'd seen the very small safe that I'd previously looked at a few days before. Then one of these sneak thieves had been pulled in over a petty charge in Liverpool and he wanted bail. He had not long been out of prison and he was scared of losing his girlfriend if he didn't get bail so the soft prick goes and tells the Liverpool bizzies who had him about a job he'd done over in Wales. The safe was full of gold, Fabergé, Russian icons and gold coins. There must have been a fortune alone in that safe. Never mind the cabinet I was supposed to take. The police didn't even know the house had been robbed until this soft prick told them about it. I never did get to know what really happened when the police called at that wealthy house in Wales. I'm almost certain they would have advised the woman to put all those treasures in a bank of some sort. I just wouldn't know. What I do know is I lost a million quid all because of a fluke by those two petty sneak thieves.

Frank Duce came to see me with his tail between his legs. He couldn't apologise enough to me.

After that episode, it was back to the drawing board again. You win some, you lose some. I thought, I'm a lucky person, really. I have a nice house, a good business giving me a decent income and I'm still making plenty as far as crime goes and, above all, I have a beautiful little daughter who is only a few months old and who is growing on me more and more.

I remember one winter's night it was very cold and my little daughter Britt used to sleep in a little cot at the side of our bed. I heard her whimpering that night and I got out of bed to see if she was all right. Her mother was fast asleep. When I bent down to Britt, her little hands were cold so I picked her up and got her into bed between me and Joan, her mam. Joan was awake by now and said, 'Charlie, she might get crushed by the two of us.'

I said, 'There's no chance of that happening.'

With that I put my arm around my little daughter. She snuggled into me getting nice and warm. That's when I knew I was really hooked on her. It's called a 'tender trap'. I had never brought up a child before, as all my other children were brought up by their mothers. I just can't imagine how some parents can harm or abuse the children. They're so helpless when they're first born and solely dependent on their parents. This is when a true mother would die for her young. I would have no hesitation whatsoever killing anybody if they harmed my child in any way. And that takes me back.

I had been a couple of hundred miles away from my cottage looking at a nice bit of graft with my mates. I remember getting home late this particular night and Joan and the baby were sound asleep in bed. After I had gone up myself, it must have been about 3.00am when I heard my guard dog Ali, a big-boned German Shepherd, growling downstairs. He was a good look-out. I used to chain him to the back kitchen door of a night time. I got up out of bed and went downstairs to investigate. I then heard a loud bang. Something had been thrown at my front door. I opened my front door and outside down the pathway was a gang of about six or more gypsies shouting for me to come out. Before I went out to them, I armed myself with an antique sword and a hatchet which I had put down my belt. I said, 'What the fuck do you lot want?'

They said a safe had been stolen from them. I was responsible for it. They also said the police told them it was most probably me as I was the only villain who lived around these parts. I tried to reason with them but to no avail. They were all screaming and threatening to come into my home and smash it up, me with it. One of them had a wooden pick-axe handle and he made a swing at me with it. It didn't connect. That's when I lost my head, not just to protect myself but my little daughter and Joan. I kicked off on the fucking lot of them.

I went mad, swinging the sword at them all, and they started running away. One shouted that they'd be back 'with a gun to shoot me'.

I managed to get one of them, putting the sword across his neck and telling him, 'I'll cut your fucking throat open if you come back here.' He was terrified. He told me the police had blamed me for robbing them. After I had let him go, about ten minutes later the police called to see me. I was taken to the local station and so, too, were some of these gypsies.

Apparently, somebody must have called the police or the police themselves already knew what was going on because it was the bizzies who had set it up. It's a good job they never caught me with the sword and the axe.

We all got summonsed to appear in court but I refused to go and I heard no more about it. They must have dropped the charge against me. It was in all the Welsh papers a couple of days later, describing how a man came running out of his house with a sword and axe. I was willing to die that night rather than let that crazy gang of gypsies get into my home and upset or hurt my child. I would have almost certainly killed some of them before they got into my home. But there again, that's the police for you. They caused all that trouble by spreading malicious rumours about me without any proof whatsoever. I knew then that the police wanted me out of Wales.

When I lived there in the '70s, I was their number-one target. I bought a very fast car so I could avoid them when I was going about my business. The car I bought was a Jensen CV8, one of the fastest cars at the time. When leaving my cottage; I would take all the back country roads to lose them as the police were on my tail quite a lot then. Another reason why I needed a very fast car was because the motorways were opening up all over the country at the time which was great for our line of business. When my friends and I would arrange a meeting, I could be there in no time at all.

I remember having one of those get-togethers in a flat somewhere in New Brighton. There was a fellow from

Leeds in the flat who had come to see us all over a big job he knew about up North. It was a place where gold and platinum was stored. There were two guards who were on the premises at all times and had to be taken care of. The job was discussed and planned as to how it could be done. There was only one problem — I didn't like a certain person who was among this crew. He seemed to want to take over everything and I didn't like the way it was being planned either. I had never done any work with this firm before. I was just invited along, but nevertheless I said I could be counted in on it. We had all agreed to hit it the following week. My part in the robbery was to sort the two guards out using a sort of frightening method, which was easy, really, especially if you carried a shooter. Nobody's going to argue with a sawn-off shotgun.

Doing armed robberies in those days, I always preferred to have a gun with me. The main reason was that it was a deterrent, and by that I mean people wouldn't get brave and have a go when a gun was pointing at them. I can honestly say that in all the armed robberies I have ever done, I have never had to shoot one person, simply because by shouting loudly and acting in an aggressive manner it's enough to make them realise you mean business. It has always worked for me. I might have blown a hole in a ceiling or fired at a door at times, but sensible people don't want to argue with a gun, unless, of course, they are stupid enough to try.

Once the meeting was over and we had all dispersed, I went back to my cottage and carried on as normal, working the antiques business and playing at home with my little daughter. When the following week came round,

I was all geared up and waiting but nothing happened. Nobody made contact with me. I thought, Well, maybe there's been a delay for some reason or other. Sometimes these things do happen.

After a couple of days had gone by, I more or less forgot about it all. I thought it must have been called off. I wasn't too keen on the people I was going to do it with anyway. They weren't the usual lads I worked with as I'd only been invited along by somebody.

After two weekends had passed, it must have been at about 6.00am on a Monday morning, while I was in bed with Joan and my little girl who was sound asleep, that I heard my front door getting smashed in. The noise was terrible at that time in the morning. Joan had woken up and was screaming and so, too, was the baby. I had almost got out of bed when I was pounced on by the police. I don't know how many there were, but it seemed as though my cottage was full of bodies. They dragged me on to the floor and had me spread-eagled. They then handcuffed me from behind. They also made Joan get out of bed. Then a frenzied rampage followed. They turned the cottage over looking for guns and gold. It was the Leeds police hit squad. They told me where they were from and that they were arresting me for an armed robbery that had taken place in Leeds. After they had ransacked my home, leaving my daughter and her mother hysterical, they frog-marched me into a police car still handcuffed from behind. I was taken to the local police station in Prestatyn to be interrogated. I knew then that the gold job had gone off without me.

I was seething now; it wasn't that I'd been left out of going on the graft, but the pricks who'd done it had never warned me and, above all, how had my name been thrown in?

In the interview room, the head games had started. They wanted to know where I'd been on the Saturday before between the hours of 8.00pm and 10.00pm that evening. Now being in a situation like that it's not very easy to think straight, because of the psychological techniques they use on you. For example, steaming in on you in the early hours of the morning, smashing your home and, on top of it all, being abusive to your wife. Nobody's mind is focusing properly when this happens and the police know this only too well.

I wouldn't answer any of the questions they put to me, because in a situation like that you might say something you could regret later on. The right to remain silent was still in force then. And there were no taped interviews with a solicitor at your side like there are nowadays. They tried the 'frightening' tactics with me, banging furniture and pushing me around. They said two people had been brutally beaten up and a large amount of gold had been stolen. I still remained silent, asking only for a solicitor. They told me I was to be taken to Leeds and the interviews would continue up there, seeing as how I wouldn't tell them where I'd been. They said I was to go on an ID parade. They wanted me to speak certain words in my own accent. I knew then what they were up to. Verbal evidence was still accepted by the local magistrates court at that time. It was the most dreaded thing they could use against you, a criminal's nightmare. What chance would I have? First, they would make sure I was identified; second, my voice would be recognised; and last, the verbal.

I couldn't think straight and, to tell you the truth, I couldn't have told them where I'd been two Saturdays before at those times. I wanted to avoid going on that journey to Leeds and to be fitted up. I then said to them, 'Look, before you take me, can I make a phone call to my girlfriend?'

'Certainly,' they said.

Oh yes, they would let me make a phone call to my girlfriend but if it had been to a solicitor they might well have refused.

I knew when I made that phone call one of them would listen in on the conversation in another room. I got through to Joan who was still very distraught at the cottage but she was also clever in her own way. I said, 'Joan, these police officers are about to take me to Leeds. They want to know where I was last Saturday between the hours of eight and ten.' Then I added, priming her, 'I know where I was and you know where I was, don't you?'

She paused and then said what I wanted to hear.

'Wasn't that the night we had a drink in the cottage with my mother and sister and also your Billy, who was home from America with his wife?'

I then said, 'Yes, that's very true,' which it was because I had never gone on that robbery.

Joan's family and my brother and his wife were all of an impeccable character. You couldn't get better alibi witnesses than that. The police then had to go and interview our witnesses after several hours had passed. The police had turned the other way now and the dismayed look on some of those coppers' faces when they came back into the room made me feel relieved.

The copper who was in charge then said to me, 'All right, Charlie, we know you haven't been on this job now, but you do know about it. Your name has been thrown in the hat and we know you knew who's done that job.'

I then said to them, 'Can I ask you one question?'

He nodded.

'Am I being charged with anything?'

'No.'

That was it, I just told them that I was leaving the police station now. They tried to act all nice to me then, and offered me a lift back to my cottage, but I refused.

When I arrived back home, Joan was still distraught over it all, especially the way she was made to get out of bed in front of all those policemen. I said to her, 'It's a good job you could recall about that Saturday night.'

Then she hit me with the truth. 'It was the Friday night we were all having a drink in the cottage, not Saturday.'

'Are you sure?' I asked. 'Why did you tell me it was Saturday?' I was getting very apprehensive by now, just in case those bizzies had changed their minds and decided to call back and charge me.

Joan said, 'After you've had a good night's drink you suffer with a terrible hangover the next day and you always stay at home.'

This was quite true. The truth then dawned on me. I was at home that Saturday with Joan and the baby. Now if I would have told the truth to those Leeds police do you think for one minute that they would have believed me? Would they fuck. What court would believe Joan, my only witness, because my little daughter couldn't verify anything for me. She was only a few months old at the time. Yes, I would have been truly fitted up even though I would have been telling the truth.

* * *

I had lived in Wales a couple of years by now and I knew it was time for me to move on. My good instincts told me it would only be a matter of time before the police would have me. I had, in fact, heard from a good source that I was the North Wales police number-one target by now so, with that stigma attached to me, I moved back to Liverpool.

I owned a big old Victorian house in Liverpool. It had eight bedrooms, three bathrooms and a wine cellar. It also had a big walled garden. It was previously owned by a big wealthy family called Babcock, who were wealthy corn merchants in the old days. I'd paid around £18,000 for it in the early '70s. The same house in London would probably have been worth a couple of million.

It's crazy when you think about house prices. I read an article in the paper not so long ago saying a small double garage went for half a million quid in London. Where they get these prices from beats me.

As I was saying, I had outstayed my welcome in the Welsh hillsides and I decided to move into this house of mine. It was funny living there at times. After all, there were only three of us. Sometimes I'd be shouting to Joan a few rooms away, the house was so big. It did have its good points, though. It was brilliant for entertaining and I did quite a lot of that in those days. I would have the best food and wine and our family and friends would visit for parties. Money was never a problem. It was still rolling in.

It was approaching 1980 now; I was pushing 40 and I was still bang at it. I had made myself a vow that, by the time I reached 40, I would retire and go straight, but how could I possibly do that? Money was still growing on trees. Well, it wasn't as fruitful as years before, but the pickings were still there. Times were changing fast. People were getting more security conscious now but the secured premises were still not as sophisticated as they are today. Cameras were still very few and far between and large amounts of cash were still being carried around, especially in post office vans. We used to call these vans the 'red devils'. Our team hit quite a few of those post office vans. They were a bit risky.

It was the usual routine — planning properly, hitting fast and making sure we had a good escape route. Every time we did one of these post office vans the pay-out always varied. Sometimes we could get £20,000 and at other times it could be as much as £80,000 or so. But all the time I was into these armed robberies at the age of 40 I was sticking my neck out a bit. I knew if I was ever captured I would get 10 or 15 years. I began to realise the amount of money involved in these post office vans especially if there were four or five men on the job. The pay-out wasn't very high, plus the fact they were getting harder to hit.

We were all in our house one day. My mates and I were planning out some graft when we heard about another gang of armed robbers who we knew getting captured on a post office van. While this gang was on remand in prison, a mate of ours who was involved with them showed the charge sheets and deposition papers on a visit and it actually revealed where the cash that the post office vans carried came from — it was a sorting office. Why hadn't we thought of this before? I should have realised that's where the big money was kept, sorting offices.

It was like years before when I was a kid doing smash-and-grabs on electrical shops, when I remember saying to my pals if we could do electrical shops, why not jewellery shops? They're bigger and better. That was it for our team now. Fuck the post office vans, let's have the sorting offices, or SOs as we called them.

First, there were three ways they could be had. Number one, believe it or not, was sneaking them.

I remember the first one we had. Two of us had climbed on to the roof of this old sorting office. Most SOs would be in ideal positions, such as right next to railway stations in Victorian-type buildings. They were always away from residential areas because of the volume of PO vans coming and going at unsociable hours, and the noise of the mail trains. So my pal and I were actually peering through a sky-light watching the SO staff sorting out money bags, putting them into pigeon holes. While we were on the roof casing all this, the staff all ceased work and went to the far end of the building for their tea break. There wasn't a single person down there below us guarding that money. We stayed on the roof and waited and, after a good half-hour, the staff were back and carried on with their work. I looked at my mate who was next to me and said, 'Are you thinking the same as me?' and he nodded. The skylight had metal bars but that was no big problem.

The following week we were back at the same time,

same place. It was the same routine as the week before. The staff had gone for their break again. Once this happened, we wasted no time. We literally sawed through the metal bars in the skylight but not completely. We left a fraction of an inch on each bar so as not to arouse suspicion if anyone looked up. We had completed the job just before the staff came back.

All the time this was going on, our other two pals were on the ground with walkie-talkies listening and watching at all times just in case, but everything was OK. Nothing was out of place.

One week later, we were back watching and waiting. The minute the staff had gone for their tea, I went down on a good strong rope. The drop wasn't very far. I stood on top of a long bench table, and a thin rope was also lowered from the skylight with a large laundry bag attached to it. I went for bags I thought had money in. The first bag I got hold of I knew was money instinctively. I could tell by the feel and it also contained coins as well as notes. I put as many bags as I could into the laundry bag and my pal on the roof hoisted it up. I had to be quick and fairly quiet just in case one of the staff came back, but everything went OK.

When we all finally got back to our destination, the money was chopped up four ways. We got just over £200,000; not bad wages 20 years ago and for just a simple sneak.

The other two ways of doing those SOs was either by steaming in with shooters and tying the staff up or burglary. We all agreed on burglary. Sneaking them was out of the question by then. I don't think any of the staff would have left the money unattended again. This information would have been passed on to most of the SO staff by now. Before we ever attempted to burgle one of these SOs, we always located one that was the most likely. They are usually, as I mentioned before, situated in isolated places. The next important part was to make sure the cash was there. They closed on a Saturday usually at 1.00pm and opened on Sunday evening at 9.00pm. That meant we had all Saturday to case the place thoroughly. Winter nights were the best; when it goes dark at about 4.00pm. Our main target was to locate a safe or vault and, believe me, it didn't take very long to accomplish this. What was amazing about all this was that the silly fuckers would leave the lights switched on where the safes and vaults would be. They must have thought by doing this it would deter any thieves and if the police were prowling around they could see that the safes were still intact.

Once the safes or vaults were located by us on the Saturday evening, we would always go back on the Sunday night with binoculars and sit off watching the movements, especially if there was any activity around the safes or vaults and spotting when they were opened. Inside the premises, there would be high-value parcels (HVPs) and it would always be the manager who would open them up to sort them for the different delivery vans. Each van could and would carry anything from £50,000 to £100,000. So let's say the sorting office had four vans. You could safely say there could be £200,000–£400,000 inside that vault.

The robbery would have to be done using diamond-drilling equipment. We actually employed another man in our team for this drilling job. He was worth his weight in gold, absolutely brilliant at his job. He would wait outside until we had made the entry and got everything set up. Then he'd come in using his expertise. The actual weight of the tools we used could weigh as much as 200kg. This would consist of the actual drill itself, which would have a 10in diamond bit alone. To give you an insight into the other tools we used and how heavy it could all be, here's an inventory:

1. High-powered drill for raw bolts to mount drill on to wall
2. Transformer (about 5kg)
3. Extension leads
4. Water hose, at least 100ft
5. Water pump. This was used to feed water to the cutter to keep it cool and speed up the cutting. It also kept the noise down a bit.
6. Crow-bars for gaining entry, and also for ripping alarm bells off walls
7. Hacksaws for cutting phone cables
8. Screw drivers, spare fuses (for breakages) and spares such as cutters, etc.

All this equipment alone cost quite a few bob but they were our working tools and were essential to us all. Before we gained entry, we would locate the MANWEB grid which was always outside somewhere. Then the electrical wires would be cut. It was then a game of patience. We would all sit off the place with our scanners on for a good hour, listening and watching. After this was done we would go and put the alarm bells out of action and sit off for another hour and, if it was all OK, we would then go in with our tools. It all went well and we had success. We would move out early Sunday morning mingling with the traffic, church-goers, car boot sale people and so on.

That was big money for me. Those years we made plenty together, but there weren't just us at it, there were other firms hitting SOs as well. Now, because of all this, it started bringing a lot of jealousy and resentment among the villain fraternity, especially in Liverpool. Some firms were blaming others for stepping on their toes doing what was supposed to be theirs and vice versa. Terrible, malicious rumours were put around, especially if you were out having a drink on the club scene.

There was one firm in particular at that time in Liverpool and they were very good at their work. In fact, I'll go as far as saying they were the best. They had several nightclubs which were very successful and I had respect for that firm, like they did for me. Their names were the Hughes brothers and I've known them since we were young kids. They were very smart lads at that time and they came from Huyton like me. There was only one problem — they socialised with a certain person whose nickname was 'The Dog' and, believe me, that's just what he was, a fucking dog. In fact, it's too good a word for him. I've met some terrible people in my life, but the one with the worst personality was this 'Dog' prick.

I was having a drink one night in a club called the Hollywood in Duke Street, Liverpool city centre. Who should walk in that night but The Dog. He came over to me after a short while and asked if I wanted a drink, which I accepted. I began to sense something odd as I knew deep down he didn't really like me. I thought, He's up to something, that's for sure. We got into conversation and he kept asking me where a certain mate of mine was. I told him I'd be seeing him shortly in another club called Chauffeurs in Hope Street. After a while, I ended up in the club with The Dog and this mate of mine who The Dog was anxious to meet. After a bit of chit-chat, The Dog went to the bar for a round of drinks. While he was gone, my pal said to me that the prick wanted him to get around the table with the Hughes brothers and let certain things drop.

Apparently the Hughes had had a falling out with this mate of mine who was very heavy at the time. He said he would not make friends with any of the Hughes, he just wanted to do them in. I tried to persuade him to forget it all and make up. After all, it was down to the gossip-mongers spreading rumours around, but he wasn't having any of it. He said he was still going to do them in.

When The Dog came back with the drinks, he started getting sarcastic with me and was really getting bang out of order. Little did The Dog realise but I myself was trying to get this mate to make friends with the Hughes as well. Then he said another sarcastic remark to me but I wasn't having any of it. We both started arguing. I ended up kicking off on him. I smashed him up and he ended up on the floor out cold.

I sort of apologised to the owner of the club, Charlie Scott, and some of the customers nearby. I really didn't want this but I'd been left with no choice. It was either him or me.

A few days later, my young nephew, Paul, was attacked. The people who'd done it told our Paul that they were looking for me. One of the men who'd attacked him was a Londoner and he said he was going to shoot me. I always take things like that with a pinch of salt because anybody with a bit of sense who really was going to shoot you wouldn't let anybody know they were going to do it. I knew that that slimy Dog was behind all this. I knew also he had gone back to the Hughes brothers and twisted the story around, spreading malicious rumours about me. Well, I thought, nobody's going to hunt me. I'll go and hunt them.

I called out my three brothers and my nephew Paul to come with me. We were all dead loyal and I knew in my heart we would all die for one another. That weekend we got tooled up and bought a van and went looking for them. I wanted to try and place them when they were all together. Every night we were out looking for them, and then a few nights later we had good information that they were all in a pub in Huyton called the Yew Tree.

We drove to the Yew Tree pub and, before we went in, I made sure we were all armed to the teeth. I had three weapons on me — a knife, a hammer and a meat cleaver, the handle of which I had strapped to my wrist. There's nothing worse when you're going to be in a bloodbath fight than losing or dropping your weapon. Before we steamed into this crowd, I just made double sure none of us would come unstuck.

I remembered a few months before, a fella I know (who doesn't want to be named) went into a club in town to shoot somebody. He had a double-barrelled shotgun with him. He did shoot the person he was after, then he made a major mistake. He fired the other shot into the ceiling as he was leaving the club. He was quickly pounced on by a few villains before he could reload the gun. The gang who jumped him cut him to pieces with a Stanley knife.

I was just making sure I wasn't going to make a mistake like that. We were going to go in there fast, do the business and get out fast.

The person who'd given us the information came out of the pub to meet us and told us they were all together at the centre of the bar. I said to my brothers, 'Come on, let's do it.'

We all walked in quickly and headed straight for the bar. The place was fairly crowded with customers but we spotted them. I walked right up to them and it all kicked off. The tools came out. There was blood everywhere. It got messy, there were people screaming their heads off. Two of the people had their hands hanging off. It didn't take long and I was out of there fast.

The next day, it was headline news. Two men were in hospital with their hands nearly chopped off. One of them was The Dog. While they were both in hospital, a girl I knew had a sister who worked as a nurse there, and she was looking after the two men who had been butchered. Whenever the police questioned the two men, the nurse would listen to what was being said and it would get relayed back to me.

A few days later, I was arrested by the heavy mob, who came in force for me. I was taken to Eaton Road Police Station and charged with wounding with intent to kill. After being in the police cells for a couple of days, I was remanded in custody to HMP Risley.

When I arrived at Risley, I was in remand prison clothes. The police had taken my civilian clothes from me for forensic testing. Remand prisoners had to wear brown jackets and trousers and cons wore blue. There was always a pecking order in remand prisons at that time. If a prisoner was wearing his own clothes, which was allowed for remand prisoners, he was classed as 'one of the boys' by the rest of the cons, but if a prisoner wore the prison brown, he was frowned upon by some of his fellow inmates. Only the tramps and the low-life wore the prison clothes because their own torn, dirty clothes wouldn't be fit to wear.

The next morning, after a sleepless night and realising where I was, saying to myself, 'What the fuck am I doing in here?' I queued up for breakfast with the rest of the cons. I was starving after having been in the police cells for two days. I wouldn't eat anything from them.

Now, because you won't play ball or make a statement, the bizzies have been known to spit and piss on your food before they bring it to you. I wasn't taking any chances so I had just done without for a couple of days. I knew my family would be visiting me that day with a clean set of clothes and some decent food would be brought in for me, but right now I was famished.

When it came to my turn in the breakfast queue, it was beans on the menu, a couple of rounds of bread and a mug of tea. I held my tray out and the prisoner who was dishing out the beans gave me a very small portion just about a spoonful. I said, 'Give us a bit more, will you, mate?'

Now, don't forget, I was dressed in prison brown and I hadn't had a shave for a few days. He looked at me with contempt and said, 'Fuck off, you tramp.'

I just went fucking mad. The tray I was holding was

made of stainless steel, so I started smashing his fucking head in with it. Then all hell broke loose. A few screws grabbed me and took me down the block. After a couple of hours, I was released and taken back on to the wing — still hungry. Some of the lads I knew in there got the con who I'd battered to drop the charges against me. One of the lads who helped was Rusy Jones from Kirkby. He was a good friend of mine at the time. And the con who I'd smashed came over to me to apologise. I spat in his face and told him to fuck off. That's what you get in prisons — prisoners doing a screw's job, who think they're screws themselves.

After a few weeks on remand, with bail being refused, I was finally taken to the committal courts in Liverpool. The police had a witness against me. I knew Bobby Hughes would never in a million years grass on me. He and his brothers were very staunch that way. The witness the police had was a barmaid, but when it came to her giving evidence in court she changed her mind. Not that she was scared of me or anything. The police were putting pressure on her, but she wouldn't budge. (If you ever read this book, Caroline, thanks a million.) I was finally set free through lack of evidence.

Some time later, I think it was a couple of weeks, I was in my car with a lady friend. We had just come out of the Adelphi Hotel. We decided to go to the Knightsbridge club in Duke Street. While we were both in my car on our way to the club, it was suddenly rammed. A gang of the fellas got out of the other car and came at me. A knife was pulled and I was stabbed in the top of my leg. The other one pulled a gun and shot at me. I felt the bullet graze my stomach, just taking a layer of skin off. It all happened so fast. One of them was shouting, 'You haven't got your hatchet now, have you?' They all seemed as if they were panicking. One of them kept shouting, 'Let's go.' They all fucked off as quick as they'd come.

I had good information a few days later that somebody had paid a so-called hit-man by the name of Roy Grantham, who, incidentally, is now dead. He was from London. He must have needed glasses if it was him who'd tried to kill me. A good contract killer would put one in your head, not down below. The ones that aim for your legs just haven't got it in them to go all the way.

Billy and Bobby Hughes and myself got around the table and had a good talk. They knew who was responsible for stirring all this trouble up and putting the mix in. We agreed it was pointless going on with this family feud and we all parted on good terms. I still class Bobby Hughes as one of my good friends. In fact, the whole Hughes family are all staunch people.

Not long after the senseless trouble we had with one another, the Hughes brothers and their firm came unstuck on some sorting office out of town. The armed police were lying in wait for them. When they all steamed in to have the place off, the police opened fire on them. One of the firm (who doesn't want his name mentioned, and I will respect that) got shot by the armed police. He was very lucky he lived. The bullet came out of his chest. I couldn't understand why Bobby was on that blag. He was a very wealthy man, and he certainly didn't need the money. I remember him telling me years later, 'Charlie, if you had been with us we would never have got caught.' I was always gifted with that extra sense, somehow, and if something wasn't right I would always stipulate, 'Don't do it.' They all ended up with lengthy sentences. Our team stayed with what we knew was the best method — having these SOs burgled and using our drilling equipment.

Chapter Eleven

It was now the mid '80s and times were changing rapidly now for, shall we say, the 'good' robber. Through technological progress, the police now had all the best and most sophisticated tools to combat crime. The helicopter had started playing a vital role for them; cameras were everywhere; and money wasn't being left lying around like years before. There was a new type of commodity that was very sought after and, with it, a very different breed of criminal had also emerged — the drug dealer. Who would have thought that the guttersnipe would have his turn to make money; in fact, a lot more money than we robbers made. I was approached on many occasions to get involved with that game, but I refused. One fellow said to me, 'Charlie, it's like you're throwing a few million quid in the River Mersey.'

But my wild days of plundering and robbery were coming to an end. I was in my forties now. I had made a nice few quid over the years and keeping my liberty was very precious to me. So I was ready to go legit. Well, sort of!

I had bought a new detached house near West Derby village for my daughter's benefit, really, as she was attending the village school at that time. I had also heard through the grapevine that a nice piece of property was up for sale together with a business. It was in a good residential area in a place called Eaton Road, Liverpool 12. Apparently, the owner of the premises, a man called O'Shea, had shot dead a young man not far from the building. While he was in jail, his wife was negotiating a deal to sell the property. I believe the place had been booming up until the shooting. Bill Shankley and most of the Liverpool footballers frequented the establishment quite a lot but, because of the murder, they had all boycotted the place. I thought I'd take the chance and buy it. I've always liked a challenge. It was a nice freehold property with a house attached to it. Little did I know that it was going to be my place of work and home for the next few years.

I turned it into a nice restaurant bar called the Sandfield, and it was a success right from the start. I started getting all the local businessmen wining and dining with their family and friends. There was one character in particular who was often in the place, Trevor Scot, also known as Scotty. He was very popular with the Liverpool football team and he'd come in with Bruce Grobbelaar and Graham Souness. They became regulars there. Once it was up and running, I bought another restaurant bar in the city centre and that, too, was a success. So there I was now, semi-retired from the other 'business' and making a good living the honest way for a change.

One night, just as the Sandfield was closing, a couple of Mercs pulled up outside and a mate of mine, Tony Finnigan, got out of one of them. He asked me whether it was all right if the TV personality Tom O'Connor came in. He was with all his entourage, and Eddie Kidd was with him and some other theatrical people.

Tony Finnigan was a good businessman himself. He owned several properties in Liverpool and also had a club, but he was also a minder for Tom O'Connor. After that night — and what a night; the party must have gone on until the next day — with me having everything under control, Tom and his entourage were well pleased. He became quite a regular at my place, knowing nobody would give him any hassle. He brought lots of stars in there. All the *Brookside* cast were coming in, and they even filmed a scene for an episode. Footballers were also visiting.

I even had Mr T from *The A Team* in one night. He was decked out in all his gold necklaces. He couldn't believe how warm Liverpool people were, and I ended up taking him to a few local pubs, but I told him to keep his gold behind in case he got mugged. Only joking, of course. He got himself a bit rotten. He was made up with all the birds who were all over him.

I ended up socialising a lot with Tom O'Connor and Tony Finnigan. I was never away from the shows and all the parties we used to have. I remember one night Tom asked me to accompany him to some club he was performing at somewhere in Birkenhead. He was a bit apprehensive about the audience. I think he thought they were all going to kick off. The place had a bit of a bad name. I got a few of the boys to come with me to give him some support.

Everything went OK and just after the show had finished a young girl approached me. She said, 'You're Charlie Seiga, aren't you? I am a friend of your daughter's.'

She introduced herself to me and her name was Clare. I won't mention her full name because she is a well-known TV personality now. She is also a brilliant singer as well as an actress, but at the time I met her she wasn't famous then and was struggling a bit. After we'd talked for some time, I had a word with Tom O'Connor and he got her on a show. She then went on to cabaret after that touring around the world. We became good friends, Clare and I. When she was away, she often used to write to me and when she was at home she would call round to my house or my restaurant. We would have a meal together and a laugh. One thing I will say about her — she never forgot herself.

I remember I was in some nightclub in town just before I was charged with a murder. She was in the company of a lot of TV stars but she broke away from them and came right over to me and gave me a big hug. Keep it up, Clare. I always told you with your talent you would be famous one day.

So this was what my lifestyle was like. Still clubbing it and partying, only this time I'm above board and it keeps the bizzies from breathing down my neck for a change. Talking about bizzies, whenever I bought a nice car I was always tormented by them but now it's different as I can prove where my income comes from and because of this I went out and bought a 500 SL Mercedes convertible sports car. I thought the bizzies might start hounding me but they never did. Maybe it's because I'm legit now. Well, sort of.

A lot of my mates who were villains always called in to my restaurant to have the odd drink with me. On one of these occasions, the restaurant had closed for the night. It's funny; during the course of the evening I'd have all straight punters in, but when I closed up I'd have my own crowd in. I would have all the blinds pulled down, lock all the doors and have what we'd call a 'lock-out'. Then we would have our own entertainment. I used to make sure everything was under control. There was never any rowdiness or anything like that.

However, on this particular night my mates and I were all around the table. We had just purchased a big plot of land. It was situated on the main Liverpool Road and through good information we knew Sainsbury's wanted to build a big supermarket on it. But how could we, of all people, negotiate with Sainsbury's? We were villains. Their directors would never entertain the likes of us. So we brought a friend of ours in to do the deal. His name was Derek Hatton.

Now, Derek wasn't a bad fella. The stories people have spread about him is a load of rubbish. What I know of him, he's only ever tried to help people. There is one good thing he did for Liverpool — he got a lot of new council houses built for the poor people. OK, maybe some of those people abused it all, but he was always there to help. I respect Derek and he's still a good friend of mine.

Anyway, the deal was nearly sorted with Sainsbury's, coming to about £1.5 million. Not a bad profit considering it was only bought for £80,000. While this was going on, the press had got to know about it. There were all kinds of stories going round saying gangsters in their big flash cars were doing a deal with Sainsbury's. That fucked everything up, and Sainsbury's pulled out. Private houses were built on the site in the end.

After that episode, I made arrangements over another restaurant. I turned it into a Chinese. Most people in Liverpool love Chinese food. I was the first Englishman to open a Chinese restaurant in Liverpool at that time and that, too, was an instant success. At that time, it seemed as if I couldn't go wrong. Everything I touched turned to money. I had a nice detached house with a swimming pool, a successful business with a good income, my daughter was going to a top private school, everything was going sweet for me but I was still dabbling with crime. When I say crime, I don't mean it in its old-fashioned sense. The old criminal world had changed dramatically. Scams (fraud) were on the increase. A lot of snide (fakes) was playing a big part in the criminal fraternity now — counterfeit money and passports, clothes, alcohol, whisky, you name it. All this was highly sought after. I would get visits from certain people and they would put something to me; sometimes it would be to finance these scams or sometimes it would be for a bit of advice as to which was the best method of doing it. I don't know why these young villains came to me and I still don't know why. Maybe it's because of my past experiences. I would get involved if some of this work sounded promising.

On one of these occasions, a man and woman came to see me one night. His name was Freddy. He was a nice enough fella and he came with good credentials; the woman he brought with him was called Flo. After the three of us had had a good chat together, with me weighing up the pros and cons, I agreed to join them in their enterprise. It was manufacturing high-grade spirits — whisky, vodka, brandy and so on.

I didn't realise the vast profits that could be made on this illegal booze. To produce top-quality scotch — and I mean top-quality — we had a bloke, known as the Chef, who actually put it together and was employed by us. He knew his job perfectly. He'd worked in a Scottish distillery before joining our little firm. I didn't know how simple it all was to make first-class spirits. Every spirit such as whisky, vodka and brandy all come from one ingredient, and that is pure alcohol. The secret is what it contains afterwards. For instance, he could put some special ingredient in the alcohol to make scotch and then a different type of ingredient to make brandy, and so on. The man was a professional. Obviously, he had had years of experience.

The couple who I was involved with had already acquired a big unit on an industrial estate. Our front was that it was down on paper as being a detergent factory. We purchased cartons of soap powder, lots of containers with diluted bleach and various other kinds of detergents. It did cost us quite a few grand to set up this place. We also had to purchase some other equipment such as vats which contained the booze, pallets of bottles imported from France, crimping machines for the bottle tops, various shower units, labels had to be printed and various other apparatus acquired. We also had to buy a large quantity of sugar and yeast.

After investing this money, the return on profits was

phenomenal. Even to this day, it would cost a legalised distillery in the region of 50p–60p to manufacture one bottle of scotch whisky. It's the government tax that makes it expensive. So if the ordinary man in the street was to buy a £10 bottle of scotch, there would be at least £9 tax on it. I thought, Well, we're only fucking the tax man, and on the other hand we're giving Joe Public a cheap drink.

Once we got started, we just couldn't make enough of the stuff. My main role was distributing it. I know a lot of people in the pub and club trade so there was no shortage of customers. One man alone — a very wealthy businessman — put an order in for a couple of thousand bottles with his own label printed on it. I could see this business expanding so rapidly we started looking for bigger premises, preferably out of Liverpool. I knew that we would have to have a different way of selling the gear because it would only be a matter of time before the other crowd, Customs and Excise and the police, would have heard of it. I had a good talk to my partners about how careful we would have to be. I said that instead of selling so many cases to Joe Bloggs here and there, let's stop all that because we could come unstuck. I then suggested we make £100 grands' worth at a time and I can sell it all to one buyer. Once we sold that amount we would make another £100 grands' worth, and so on. I knew I would have no problems getting shot of it all with the contacts I had, most of whom were out of Liverpool anyway. And, of course, this would minimise the risk of coming unstuck.

They just wouldn't listen to me. They wanted to keep selling it in dribs and drabs — 20 cases here, 30 cases there or whatever.

After a year or so, just as I had predicted, it came on top but, as luck would have it, we were tipped off before the raid took place. Where our unit was situated there were other units also conducting various businesses of their own. There was a sort of odd-job man who would go around asking the people who owned or rented these units if they needed any work doing. Well, this particular day the odd-job man had seen a couple of men doing some painting on a unit opposite ours. He then said to the manager of the unit, 'I thought you would always give me any work you wanted doing.' Apparently, he must have had some sort of an agreement with him. The manager then said to him that those men he was on about weren't painters but Customs officers keeping watch on the detergent factory opposite — ours.

The odd-job man, out of the goodness of his heart, came discreetly over to our unit and warned the staff they were being watched. Once we had had our card marked, the staff (two young lads and a woman) were ordered to destroy and dismantle everything inside the place. They carried it out efficiently. We were always prepared for anything like this. Inside the still, we had a small incinerator. That was for destroying any labels and other paperwork. We also had a large waste grid in the centre of the floor where the staff could wash away anything incriminating. Part of our equipment was also removed, tell-tale stuff that could get us nicked. We had a big, steel roll-shutter door that our vans used to back up to for loading purposes, as, naturally, everything was done behind closed doors. The staff loaded all the suspicious equipment into one of the vans, and it was all driven away right under the Customs and Excise noses, even with our precious chef inside. A few more adjustments were made inside the place to leave no tell-tale signs. Then all the detergents were packed out on shelves; containers of diluted bleach and other various detergents were put on show.

In no time at all it was transformed into a legitimate wholesale detergent warehouse. When the knock did come from the Customs and police, I thought it was so funny. The staff had to sit it out and keep their mouths shut. They had been well vetted before being employed by us. The Customs and police couldn't find one bottle of scotch or any other incriminating evidence, and they were absolutely gutted. They did arrest the staff but as long as they stuck to their guns and kept their mouths shut, I knew they would be OK. On hearing this, my partners and the whisky chef disappeared for a while on my advice. I told them to keep out of the way and the staff and I would do the fronting up.

The following day I, too, was arrested, but I was prepared. To be brief about all this, I ended up in court along with the staff and a number of other people who were also arrested and charged. These were people who had purchased some of the contraband. The evidence was very weak against us all. I remember at one point in court I was called a 'modern-day bootlegger', but after a lot of debating with the crown prosecution, the charges were eventually dropped against us and we were all discharged. That was the end of my bootlegging days — or so it seemed.

A loophole was found some time later and with the right finance you could buy containers full of export contraband before it had left the country, so some firms were making fortunes again fucking the tax man.

I think out of all those scams I was involved with, there was no comparison when it came to the real thing. Well, nearly the real thing — counterfeit money. It took quite a few grand to finance the lay-out of this golden opportunity. I can't mention names of the people I was grafting with on this enterprise, as it wasn't very long ago and I wouldn't put them in any sort of jeopardy. One of the men who was involved with us was a wizard in his own right. He did all the printing of the money and it was as good as the real thing.

As a brief insight into how this operated, we first had to obtain a Canon CLC 500 laser copier. It weighed about 200kg and the cost of one of those machines in 1990 was £28,000. It actually copied money in any form of currency. It was a magic machine to us. One of our customers I had gone to meet was a businessman in Manchester, originally from Pakistan. He wanted £1 million quids' worth in Pakistani currency from us. And, of course, we supplied it to him with pleasure. In sterling, we would only print £5 and £10 notes, stipulating that no £20 or £50 notes would be printed. The small notes were easier to move and didn't arouse suspicion. I have actually seen a £100 grands' worth printed in less than an hour, so this can give you an insight into how much we could really forge.

Everything was going along smoothly until technology stepped in the way as it usually does. The ultraviolet light was brought out to detect forgeries and, not long after that, the Government had chips put in all the CLCs to detect notes of any currency and that fucked a good job up. Prior to this enterprise, we had had a good run and had made a nice few quid each.

Well, there I was making plenty out of these scams and at the same time earning a good living from my legitimate businesses, too.

* * *

My wine bar/restaurant in the city centre was drawing a lot of interest, in so far as several people wanted to buy it. It was in a densely populated area and all kinds of new pubs and bars were opening up there. Two businesswomen had been making a lot of enquiries with a view to buying it, so I arranged a meeting with them. One of these ladies was very keen to buy, but her partner became a bit apprehensive. The two buyers were not from Liverpool and were put off a bit by the name that the city of Liverpool has and everything they had heard about it. After I had talked to the more reluctant one for a while, and put her at ease about Liverpool, telling her there is good and bad everywhere, it just depended where you went. I convinced her there were some lovely areas and the atmosphere in some of the pubs and clubs was brilliant. I told here I would take her round the pub and club scene to prove how right I was and how friendly people were.

We arranged a date and I booked a table in the Continental club. The Continental was one of the top clubs at that time and all the stars and celebrities were always in there. The restaurant was run by Franco, a friend of our crowd. He was a good host and always made a fuss of you.

So there I was in the company of a pretty businesswoman trying to impress her and convince her about Liverpool not being a bad place. When we arrived at the Conty, the commissionaire on the door, Alan, always showed me respect whenever I visited the place. I was a regular there, and so far so good. The restaurant was upstairs inside the club and had a balcony overlooking the ground floor. We were escorted to our table and sat down to a nice bottle of champagne which Franco had brought over. After we had had a couple of glasses, I said to her, 'How do you feel now? You'll never get any trouble in these sort of places.'

Just as I got her nice and relaxed, I heard a bit of rowdiness from behind me. There were four fellas drinking out of bottles leaning over the balcony making a nuisance of themselves. One was spitting his beer down on to some of the customers who were on the dance floor below. I thought I'd move tables and keep out of their way. This was one thing I could do without, having promised this lady it was a select club. Just then, the waitress came across with some more champagne and at the same time my friend's daughter and her friend came over to say hello. I invited them both to sit down and have a glass of bubbly.

Now, all of a sudden, the rowdy fellas who were behind me had gone very quiet and I said to myself, 'Thank fuck for that.' The waitress then came back to move us to a different table out of their way. She then told me they had been making a nuisance of themselves all night and that they were some of the Everton football team.

A minute later, I was tapped on the shoulder from

behind and it was one of these Everton players. He said I was sitting in his chair and he wanted it back. I told him to go away and behave himself. I said, 'You know quite well it's not your chair,' and told him to stop being stupid. He then went back to his football mates. What was really getting their backs up was that they were footballers and nobody was paying them any attention.

These footballers had seen me come into the place, I'd been made a fuss of and I was sitting in the company of three beautiful-looking birds, who weren't giving a fuck for them either.

A couple of minutes later, this prick was back again. He said, 'If you don't get off my chair, I'll knock you off it.'

Now, I was trying to show this lady a pleasant time and now I've got this nuisance to contend with. I stood up and the prick smirked at me. He must have thought I was going to give him the chair. I just lost control and got stuck into him. The next minute, all four of them were trying to kick fuck out of me. I was going down. I couldn't handle four of them — I'm not making excuses for myself or anything, but I was touching 50 years of age.

Just as I was about to get done in, a young mate of mine, Peter L, came running over and sparked two of them out. The arses went out of the other two and Peter and I did them in. The doormen arrived and carried them into the restaurant kitchen to bring them round.

My potential buyer had obviously disappeared. My suit was practically ripped off my back and my watch was smashed to pieces. I was fuming. My mate Peter and I waited outside for them. When they came out, the fighting kicked off all over again. One of them literally ran across the roofs of a line of parked cars to get away and the others legged it as well. We had no chance at all of catching them. After all, they were all fit footballers, weren't they?

I found out later the names of two of them. The following Monday morning, I got tooled up and went down to the training ground to cop for them but I was told they wouldn't come in to train as they knew I wanted them. This went on for a few days and I had all kinds of Everton supporters asking me in a nice way to lay off them as it was fucking all the training up. I was still determined to get them.

Then I had a call from their manager, Howard Kendal, and he begged me to ease off. I told him I would chop their fucking legs off. They wouldn't play football again after I had finished with them. In the end, I did let it go on one condition — I wanted my gold watch and suit sorted as well as an apology. Howard Kendal reassured me this would be taken care of.

By the way, if that businesswoman I was with that night ever reads this book, please accept my sincere apologies for that terrible incident in the Continental restaurant and I will still maintain not all Liverpool people are bad!

* * *

These days, I look back now and think how times and people have changed, especially after that last episode took place in the Continental. I would never have thought four fit young men would attack one man who was twice their age. That would never have happened when I was in my youth. If I was ever out having a drink in a pub or club with my mates and a man came in with a lady, even if she had a skirt on up to her arse, not one of us would dare get out of line. That's the way we were. We all had manners and a bit of respect.

I don't know why, but I still get a lot of young and up-and-coming villains who come and want to have a drink and talk to me in my restaurant. I notice most of them seem to have a completely different attitude towards life now. The villains I knew in the past had good principles. They say principles don't feed you, but I always believed in having respect and values. These days, there just seems to be none of that left. It's like dog eat dog. I think the drug game is playing a big part in it all, too. I've seen all the back-stabbing going on and all the rip-offs happening. There just doesn't seem to be any trust left at all. Not long ago, a woman came to see me. She was broken-hearted over her teenage daughter. I think the girl was about 17 or 18. It appears she had been set up on a drug deal. Apparently some drug dealer had sent her to Holland to pick up a kilo of weed and to bring it through Customs. Don't ask me how these people persuade young girls to do this for them. Maybe they have a hold on them somehow. Anyway, on the same return flight, the dealer also had another girl, only this one was carrying 1kg of coke, a lot more valuable than the weed. Incidentally, neither girls knew each other. When they finally arrived back in England, the girl carrying the weed was informed on, and captured by Customs. Basically, this prick had used her as a decoy so that the other girl could get through with the coke.

A few months after this incident, the scumbag dealer

was found dead in the flat where he lived. He had overdosed on the very shit he was peddling. It was rumoured he never took drugs himself. He must have tried some out and gone too far.

As I was saying, times have changed considerably. I've often been asked whether I had any regrets about my life and whether I would have swapped my villainous ways. My answer to that is 'No', simply because I would never have tasted or sampled the good things out of life. If I'd never become a villain, a robber, a gangster or whatever you want to call me, I might have ended up clocking on in Ford's or some other factory for the rest of my life waiting for my gold watch. I don't suggest for one moment that anyone should follow in my footsteps. That is up to each individual. But the criminal of today just isn't the same breed as we were.

* * *

It was now coming to the end of 1996, one of my daughter's birthdays was drawing near. She wanted to change her car for a new model. She asked me, as they always do when birthdays come around, could I help her out? I took her to a man I knew who had one of the biggest car businesses in Liverpool — Georgeson's Motor World. I knew the manager who worked there very well. His name was Eddie Kelly and he and his wife used to dine in my restaurant quite a lot. When I arrived at the car place, Eddie came right over to me. He was always a pleasant fella. I'd had good car deals with him before and I knew he would take care of my daughter.

After I had been there for ten minutes or so, a very

hard, fit-looking fella about thirtyish came over to me. He said, 'Are you Charlie Seiga?' He went on to say, 'I've heard about you. I'm George Bromley.' I had heard a lot about him, some of which was not very pleasant, but quite ruthless. Although two of a different kind, we were to do some business together. Little did I realise a few months later that I would be charged with his murder, allegedly having pumped three bullets into his head in a contract killing.

Chapter Twelve

After George Bromley and I had introduced ourselves to one another, about a week later he called to my house as he had moved to the same neighbourhood as me — West Derby, a suburban area of Liverpool 12. We both had a good talk and after a while it was agreed that I would unload a large consignment of contraband spirits that he had in his possession and could I also give him some ideas about some property he had, such as houses and flats. I think he was ready for the off at the time. He did reveal to me he was selling everything he owned and was going to live abroad — Portugal, I think he said it was. He was a fairly wealthy man in his own right, but then I discovered later on where his wealth had come from. He was a ruthless tax man who extracted money from other criminals, mostly drug dealers. I will elaborate more about this later on.

He always seemed to have plenty of gear around him that he wanted moving such as cigarettes and spirits. I will say, though, he never once approached me over drugs. I think he knew that I wasn't into that game and, to be honest, I don't think he was — it was just never mentioned.

After a couple of months had gone by, I decided to sell my house. It was far too big for me now that I lived on my own. My youngest daughter Britt, who was the last to live with me, had moved to university. She was studying law and her ambition was to become a barrister. It was a fairly decent home I lived in, detached with all the trimmings, a heated swimming pool and all the mod cons. George Bromley fell in love with it and wanted to buy it right away. He had all kinds of ideas for it, and building a gym and a sauna was his top priority.

Over the next few weeks, he started concentrating on my house and began calling more often. He also started bringing some of his firm with him when he called. I think he was trying to impress them by showing them around the house and how he was going to build his gym and everything. One of his mates who came around regularly with him was called Kevin Maguire. He was a keep-fit fanatic who was to help him design the gym, but he was shot to death some time later, ironically whilst working out in a gym, of all places. Kevin Maguire was in the same business as Bromley. So we had agreed on a price for my house and we both shook hands on the deal. After this was done, Bromley wanted to celebrate a bit so we both decided to have a meal and a drink in town.

Now up until then, I hadn't really been out socialising with George Bromley. I had heard all kinds of ruthless moves he had been getting up to and carrying out. Other villains I knew started pulling me up and saying, 'Charlie, what the fuck are you doing knocking around with him for?' I was told he was a dog, a grass, who had shot and stabbed and cut people up. I always thought if a person gives you respect and has done no harm to you, your family and friends, and especially if you don't know if the rumours are true or not, then you should give them a chance. After all, I myself have damaged quite a number of people in the past. And why haven't any of these people he was supposed to have hurt done anything about it? Still, as the saying goes, 'there's no smoke without fire', and if the truth be known, I was getting a bit wary so I put myself on guard.

It was a Saturday, 27 September 1997, when we both went out for our night on the town. Just before we left his house, George Bromley told me that the serious crime squad had warned him that they had reliable information he was going to be killed. In other words, a contract had been put out on him. George told me it was in the region of £100,000. Then he said to me, 'I have heard all these rumours before, nobody has got the bottle to kill me in this city.'

He got heavily tooled up that night before we left his house. I remember his body armour going on him, and he took a shooter and a blade. So he was well kitted out. I had fuck all on me. It did cross my mind that I should also be tooled up, especially being in the company of this fella.

The night was going fairly well, and we visited quite a few of the clubs in the city. It was the usual palaver being greeted by bouncers and club owners, who we both knew.

At about 4.00am when the clubs were starting to close, George Bromley suddenly wanted to go to a casino to have a gamble on the wheel. I wasn't too keen on the idea myself — I hate gambling, especially horses and betting shops. How people can stand in smoke-filled betting shops hoping to win is beyond me. Anyway, we did finally end up in a casino. The place was fairly packed inside. George spotted an empty chair by the gambling table and, just before he sat down, he asked me to mind his knife as it was a bit awkward for him whilst sitting down. I told him discreetly to pass it to me. It was a 12in blade in a sheath. I managed to hide it half-way down my belt and as I had a suit on it was concealed OK.

I was standing next to George's seat when I noticed a few fellas a few yards away looking over and snarling at George and me. They then began to edge towards us. I heard one of them say, 'That is Bromley.' I marked George's card. I also told him not to pull the gun out if there was going to be a kick-off.

Now, in a situation like this, and especially if there is a hit on the fella whose company you are in, a little bit of paranoia sets in. I said to George, 'I'll handle this, but be ready to fuck off out of here fast.' When this gang was just a few feet away, I pulled the blade out in full view of them. They saw the blade and I shouted at them, 'I'll cut you to fucking pieces if you come near us.' After this, they backed off. By now, all eyes were on me and George Bromley. We were surrounded by customers and potential witnesses. I then said to George, 'Come on, let's fuck off out of here.'

Just as we got to the entrance and were about to leave, a crowd of police rushed in, obviously having been alerted. I was nearly out of the door when somebody shouted to the police, 'He's the one with the knife,' and pointed at me. The bizzies all pounced on me. There must have been about eight or ten of them. They got me down on the pavement. By now a crowd had gathered and George Bromley was in the middle of them. I told him to do one. He had no choice but to fuck off, especially as he was carrying a gun as it would have made matters worse. One of the bizzies grabbed my hair. While he held me in this position, another copper squirted CS gas. To have this gas squirted into your eyes is the most excruciating pain imaginable. Not only are your eyes on fire but you are literally choking to death, or so it seems.

I was thrown into a police van and driven to Cheapside Police Station. Once there, that's when the fun really began. First, I was chicken-marched into a cell.

The next morning, a police doctor was called. He asked me how I had received my bruising, and by now there were a few coppers standing around. I then pointed to two of the main ones. One of the coppers said to me, 'Don't be looking at me.' I told him that I never forget a face, especially his. By then, they had found out who I really was. They don't like any come-backs, especially if you find out where they live which wouldn't be very hard.

I told them, 'Aren't you all big, brave young men? I am twice your age but I would still take you all on one at a time.'

They just stayed quiet. I was finally released the next morning. They didn't even take me to court. Ironically, some crowd of bizzies were caught on camera in the city centre in a pub. It was headline news but it was all hushed up as the police had paid a large amount of compensation to the people that they had injured.

Another reason why no charges were brought against the police was that not one of them could be identified because they were wearing helmets, which had visors on them. Then it was suggested later in the Liverpool press that each policeman should have his name printed on his uniform, but the bizzies protested about this and went up in arms. This was mainly because criminals would know who they were and where they lived. They wouldn't like any villains knocking on their doors for a change and sorting them out.

* * *

It was now the beginning of November 1997 and I had turned 57 years of age. When people are getting on a bit, they all say 'time flies' and 'where have all the years gone to?' One thing's for sure — youth is not eternal. So here I am, more or less involved with the modern young villains of the '90s and, believe me, they are a completely different kettle of fish to the way we were. As I've mentioned on numerous occasions, why these young gangsters always want to be in my company, God knows. Maybe it's because of respect for what I once was and what I have done in the past. It's like sort of serving your apprenticeship and achieving good qualifications later on. I've had many young villains saying to me, 'Charlie, I hope I'm like you when I get to your age.' Don't get me wrong, I don't mean to give any of these kids inspiration or encouragement, that is entirely up to them. I am very cautious as to who I want in my company these days. Certainly none of these young flash drug-dealers in their high-powered cars. That sort would bring it on top for you, especially if you were up to something.

There were two people in particular who were socialising with me quite frequently now. One of these was a big young fella called Lee Jones, a powerful keep-fit fanatic, and he could really handle himself, a very staunch loyal kid to me and, above all, he has good principles. At one time, Lee had a good boxing career ahead of him until some dogs shot him while he was sitting in a car. He lost one of his eyes in the shooting and that fucked up his boxing career. Lee got one of these dogs later on and killed him outright. He got charged with murder but at his trial the jury found him guilty of manslaughter, which was a brilliant result. He served a couple of years in jail and had not long been out when he was introduced to me.

The other man was called Joey Owens. Joey had been a suspect over a horrific murder, which had just taken place at the time. A man called Cole was cut to pieces in a local pub and died. He was the head doorman of the Cream nightclub in the city. Cole had shot one of Joey's mates in the mouth. He was lucky that he lived. The bullet went right through his mouth and came out of his cheek. Joey was lucky, too. Witnesses failed to pick him out in an identification parade over the Cole murder. Joey Owens was very different from the rest. Although young and in his thirties, he had that sort of 'old-school' feel about him. First, his manners were impeccable, and the other good asset he possessed was his intelligence. He also showed a lot of respect to his elders.

These two men, Joey and Lee, are well known to all of the Liverpool gangsters and club doormen. And if it came to violence, just don't fuck with them because if they are on your case, especially Joey, you would have to be prepared to face the consequences afterwards. You could even be deceived by Joey's appearance — blue eyes, fair hair, quietly spoken — you just wouldn't be able to dream of what this man was capable of.

* * *

I woke up early. It was Tuesday, 18 November 1997. I had quite a lot of running around to do that day. The weather wasn't too good, a typical November morning, damp and drizzly. George Bromley had said he would call at my home that evening at about teatime. He always seemed to call around teatime, usually around 5.00pm–6.00pm.

After I had taken a shower and had my breakfast, I was all geared up and ready for work, and by that I mean dabbling. The post had just arrived that morning. It was about 9.30am. My phone bill was with some of the mail and on opening it I couldn't believe how high it was. I think it was nearly £300. As I am not one for using the phone in the house a lot, I was furious about it all, not just because of the money but because my daughter Britt, who had just returned to university after spending a week or so at home, had to have been the culprit. I was quite sure about that. I thought to myself I will have to have words with her the next time she's home. My other two daughters are quite different from Britt. Jean is in the medical profession, and Hayley was employed in the jewellery business studying gemmology. They have never lived with me so I never had any problems with them, but Britt, who is the apple of my eye, could be a pain at times. I phoned BT that morning and asked them to send me a breakdown of the bill. After I got through the morning sorting a few things out, my brother James called. We had a little talk and a cup of tea together and off he went about his business. The time must have been about 3.00pm. Not long after my brother had gone, Joey Owens popped round. Joey was another pain like my daughter when it came to using my phone. He was never off it at times. We had a chit-chat and a cup of tea. Joey must have left about 3.30pm. He was only with me for about ten minutes. That was typical of Joey; couldn't stay still for long, always on the go. A lady friend had also called round to see me that day. I won't mention her name in this book. She's a decent sort and, to be honest, she's married, but very unhappily. And her husband is a right dog.

It must have gone past 4.00pm and the winter nights were setting in really fast. I phoned George Bromley to confirm about him calling. He said he would definitely call at teatime. He did arrive on that dark, wet November evening at about ten to six. When I opened my front door to let him in, he had a mountain bike with him and he said to me, 'This is worth a couple of grand, and I don't want to leave it outside in case it goes missing.'

I told him to put it in the recess of my hallway. We then both walked down the hall and passed the big open lounge on the right and into the morning room, which was at the end of the hall, and finally into my kitchen at the back. The route was all in a straight line more or less from the front entrance door. Just as I was about to put the kettle on, George Bromley sat down at the kitchen table. I had purchased two newspapers earlier on that day, the

Morning Post and the early edition of the evening *Liverpool Echo*. They were both lying on my back kitchen table where George sat and the headlines of both papers referred to the Cole murder trial. George said to me, 'This crowd are going to get life for this murder. They've got no chance.' George was engrossed as I started preparing some tea.

I will now tell you my story, the same one I told the police. You, the reader, may believe it and then again you may not. It's entirely up to you to form your own opinion. The Liverpool police murder team didn't believe it and still don't. Here is the way I told it.

Less than three to four minutes after George Bromley had sat down in my back kitchen that night, I heard the doorbell ring. George was still engrossed reading about the Cole murder trial in the newspaper. I made my way through the morning room and then down the hallway to the front entrance door. I opened the door and was confronted by a masked person standing there with a gun. He pointed the gun at my head and told me to get back. I then backed up the hallway a couple of yards and stepped back into the lounge, which was a large, open-plan room to the right of the hallway from the front door. He then took his eyes off me for a brief second. I knew he'd seen George because of his position in the hallway. He could see right through the morning room and into the kitchen from there.

In the next couple of seconds, he ran towards the kitchen where George was sitting. It would have only taken the hit-man three seconds at the most to get to George Bromley.

At that point, I ran through my lounge and out

through my patio doors. As I was going through them, I heard shots being fired. I then ran down my lawned garden and hid in some bushes at the rear end of my garden, which is very secluded and has big conifers and rhododendron bushes and various other plants with evergreen foliage.

After a couple of minutes had gone by, it was all eerie, very quiet. I stood up from where I had been crouching and cautiously made my way back to the house. The lights were all on and, with the curtains not being drawn, I could see right through to the kitchen and the morning room. I could also see my front door still standing open. I finally came back into the house via the patio doors. I walked the length of my lounge and turned back into the hallway and entered the morning room, where I saw George Bromley lying on his back on the tiled kitchen floor. He was in a right mess. Part of his head had been blown away. There was blood all over the floor. It was a miracle he was still alive. He started making gurgling sounds, still breathing heavily.

I picked up my phone and dialled 999. I knew even then there wasn't very much I could do for him. I then went out of my front entrance door and sat down on the steps outside. Within minutes, the paramedics had arrived, together with a gang of armed-response police. Panic and pandemonium had broken out with the police and the paramedics. George Bromley was taken out of the house fairly quickly by stretcher and whisked away at high speed to hospital. He was still alive. I was escorted to the local police station. When I arrived there, I was ushered into an interview room. After about ten minutes or so the murder squad came in to see me. All my clothes were taken away from me immediately. Of course, this was for the forensics. Then they started grilling me about the events leading up to the shooting. Different detectives came in and out asking me all kinds of questions, but none of them seemed to believe me.

At the time I was being interviewed there were no tapes and I had no solicitor present. They then left me alone for a while then, an hour or so later, one of the detectives came into the room and told me George Bromley had just died. He then said, 'It is now murder, Charlie.' He was looking for a reaction in my face. He then leaned over to me and spoke quietly in my ear and said, 'I know you fucking killed him. Don't think you can fool me.'

I was finally cautioned later on and told I was being remanded in police custody on suspicion of murder.

After spending a night in the police cell, the next morning I was taken to another interview room. This time my solicitor was present, along with two detectives and a tape recorder. After answering all their questions and giving them my side of the story again, they told me it didn't add up. Obviously, they didn't believe me. Later on that night, they decided to release me on police bail.

Joey Owens and Lee Jones called on me the next day. I was staying at my brother's, obviously I couldn't go back to my own house, the police had occupied it and were looking for forensic evidence and clues. I asked Joey and Lee to take me to where George Bromley lived. My intention was to give my condolences to his common-law wife Debbie. When we arrived at the house, I noticed the front door was half-open. I gave a knock, pushed the door aside and walked in. This was the usual routine when you called on someone you knew and their door was open.

I could not believe my eyes when I walked into George Bromley's house. His so-called best friend Tommy Wynn was standing there with only his boxer shorts on. Debbie looked dead embarrassed. Now this was a man who had been killed less than 24 hours ago and his fucking best mate was at it with his wife. A bit of an argument developed and I was so disgusted with them, I just left.

That very night, Tommy Wynn started spreading all kinds of rumours in the city, going from club to club telling people it was definitely me who killed George Bromley or had organised for him to be killed. I decided I would have to have a word with this dog Tommy Wynn.

On the Saturday morning, 21 November, I called at his house. Joey Owen and Lee Jones had come with me. Early mornings are always the best time to approach anybody when you want things straightened out; not barging into nightclubs or pubs when the person is full of drink or on the other gear. Cop for them when they're sober. Early in the morning has always been my best method. You always seem to get the same old story from them — I don't remember saying this or I don't remember saying that. Tommy Wynn was fronted up and, of course, he denied it all. I told him to stop spreading rumours about me over the shooting. After I had been arguing with him, he then said to me, 'Look, there's a police document I had hold of last night. It's concerning the murder and it's got all the suspects' names on it who would be capable of shooting George Bromley.'

In other words, it was a hit list. Wynn told me my name wasn't on it. I asked him for this list and he told me a man called Eddie Kelly had it. He also told me that George Bromley and Eddie Kelley had a couple of bizzies on the take, and that's how they got hold of this sensitive document.

After telling Tommy Wynn to behave himself about spreading the rumours, I indicated to Joey and Lee to drive me to Eddie Kelly's house. I wanted that police file badly. It would also take the heat off me once in the hands of my solicitor. Unbeknown to us, Tommy Wynn had phoned the police when we had driven away from his house, and armed police were put on full alert all over the city looking for the three of us. Obviously, Wynn never disclosed to the police we were on the way to pick up a sensitive police file. He pinned his hopes on us being captured before we got to Eddie Kelly's house, and possibly shot, because he told the armed-response team that all three of us had guns and were wearing bullet-proof vests. Luckily for us, I told Lee who was driving to pull over in a side-road while I got a bottle of lemonade from a corner shop. By doing that, it stopped us from getting captured immmediately. After quenching my thirst, we drove on to Eddie Kelly's house. It was only a few minutes away. It must have been about 9.00am by the time we arrived outside the house. It had high electric gates which were locked. I told Joey and Lee to stay put in the car. I would do the fronting up to Eddie, as I wouldn't like him to be scared off or anything. I climbed over his gates, and discovered that he must have been in bed because all the curtains were drawn. So I knocked him up. Eddie came to the front door in his dressing gown. I started explaining to him what had gone on with Tommy Wynn. I then said to him, 'I want to see the police file you have.'

The colour drained from his face; he went white. He said he would go inside and bring it out for me. Just as he was about to do this, the armed police appeared from everywhere. They were screaming at me to put my hands slowly on my head, and Eddie as well. They were everywhere — in neighbours' front gardens, on garage roofs. The armed police then shouted to us to walk slowly towards them. Eddie Kelly's house was situated on a main road. We both walked down his driveway and I saw Joey Owens and Lee Jones in a kneeling position in the middle of the road. Police marksmen were pointing guns at their heads. They made me and Eddie do likewise.

So there we were, all four of us kneeling down in the main road holding up all the traffic. The press were taking photos of us all. How they came to be on the scene I just don't know; what a fucking pantomime they were all having.

And this is the picture the press took of that scene — Joey Owens kneeling down, with the rest of us further down the road, also in kneeling positions.

I just couldn't fathom out what was going on. First, we had no guns on us or any other weapons. Second, we hadn't done a robbery or anything. And with me being out on police bail on suspicion of murder, it wouldn't warrant them to ambush us if they wanted me back in custody.

After the big show was over for all the spectators, especially bus drivers and car owners who were part of the traffic jam, we were hauled off in handcuffs, including Eddie Kelly who still had his dressing gown on.

When we arrived at the police station, I was

interviewed by the Serious Crime Squad. I was later cautioned and charged with threats to kill Tommy Wynn. So, too, were Lee Jones and Joey Owens. Wynn had made a statement against all three of us, saying I was going to shoot him. Here is Tommy Wynn's first statement, which is signed.

NAME: **THOMAS JAMES WYNN**
AGE/DATE OF BIRTH: **31/25-04-1966**
WHO STATES:-

THIS STATEMENT CONSISTING OF 007 PAGES, EACH SIGNED BY ME, IS TRUE TO THE BEST OF MY KNOWLEDGE AND BELIEF AND I MAKE IT KNOWING THAT IF IT IS TENDERED IN EVIDENCE I SHALL BE LIABLE TO PROSECUTION IF I HAVE WILFULLY STATED IN IT ANYTHING WHICH I KNOW TO BE FALSE OR DO NOT BELIEVE IT TO BE TRUE.

DATE: 22-11-97

T WYNN (SIGNED)

I RESIDE AT 22 SQUIRE STREET, LIVERPOOL 8, WITH MY MOTHER, MARGARET WYNN. I HAVE BEEN AT MY MOTHER'S FOR THE PAST 10 MONTHS. I MOVED BACK TO MY DOMESTIC SITUATION. I SPLIT WITH MY COMMON-LAW WIFE WHO IS FROM THE EASTBOURNE AREA.

APPROXIMATELY 7.30AM (0730) ON SATURDAY 22ND NOVEMBER 1997 (22-11-97) I WAS ASLEEP ON THE COUCH IN THE FRONT ROOM OF MY HOME ADDRESS. MY MOTHER AND A RELATIVE WERE ASLEEP UPSTAIRS. I HAD

ARRIVED HOME JUST BEFORE 1AM BUT DIDN'T GO TO BED BECAUSE I HAVEN'T BEEN SLEEPING VERY WELL DUE TO THE MURDER OF MY BEST FRIEND, GEORGE BROMLEY. I WAS THEN AWOKEN BY THE SOUND OF SOMEONE BANGING ON THE LOUNGE WINDOW AND SHOUTING 'TOMMY, TOMMY'. I LOOKED THROUGH THE BLINDS AND SAW JOEY OWENS AND LEE JONES OUTSIDE. JOE OWENS SHOUTED 'WE WANT TO TALK TO YOU'. I OPENED THE FRONT DOOR AND THE TWO OF THEM WALKED TOWARDS ME. LEE JONES SAID TO ME 'COME ON, WE ARE GOING TO SORT ALL THIS OUT'. I ASKED 'SORT WHAT OUT?' AND HE SAID 'THE RUMOURS YOU HAVE BEEN SPREADING ABOUT CHARLIE SEIGA SETTING GEORGE BROMLEY UP'. I SAID 'EVERYONE IN THE CITY THINKS IT'S SUSPICIOUS ABOUT CHARLIE AND IT'S GOT NOTHING TO DO WITH ME'. THERE WAS A GREY TOYOTA CAR PARKED OUTSIDE OUR HOUSE AND I THEN SAW CHARLIE SEIGA GET OUT OF THE BACK OF THE CAR. CHARLIE THEN SAID TO ME 'YOU CARRY ON WITH THESE RUMOURS ABOUT ME AND YOU WILL GET YOURSELF FUCKING KILLED'. JOEY OWENS THEN JUMPED INTO THE CONVERSATION AND SAID 'YOU WILL END UP WITH FUCKING THREE IN YOUR HEAD JUST LIKE GEORGE DID, THE GRASSING BASTARD'. CHARLIE SEIGA THEN WALKED TOWARDS ME AND PRODDED HIS FINGER INTO MY CHEEK. HE WAS WEARING LEATHER GLOVES. HE SAID 'I

AM TELLING YOU NOW, I WILL FUCKING KILL YOU IF YOUR RUMOURS DON'T STOP ABOUT ME KILLING GEORGE BROMLEY'. I WAS VERY SCARED AT THIS TIME. I SAID TO CHARLIE 'I DON'T KNOW ABOUT ANYTHING'. THEN CHARLIE AND JOEY OWENS WERE SHOUTING OBSCENITIES AT ME AND LEE JONES THEN SAID 'IF YOU CLOSE THAT DOOR AND RUN IN WE WILL COME IN RIGHT AFTER YOU'. JOEY OWENS THEN SAID 'IF YOU DON'T STOP THE RUMOURS YOU'LL GET THREE IN THE HEAD LIKE GEORGE GOT'. CHARLIE THEN SAID TO ME 'I DON'T GIVE A FUCK WHETHER YOU LIVE OR DIE, BUT I WILL FUCKING KILL YOU IF THE RUMOURS DON'T STOP'. AT THIS POINT I SAW WHAT I BELIEVED TO BE THE HANDLE OF A GUN IN LEE JONES' RIGHT-HAND POCKET OF HIS JACKET. I ONLY GOT A BRIEF GLIMPSE BECAUSE HE HAD HIS HAND IN HIS POCKET. THE HANDLE OF WHAT I BELIEVED TO BE A GUN WAS BROWN IN COLOUR. LEE JONES THEN SAID TO ME 'WE ARE COMING BACK TO FUCKING DO YOU IF THIS SHIT DOESN'T STOP WHAT YOU'VE BEEN SPREADING'. AT THIS POINT I BECAME VERY FRIGHTENED. I SAID 'PLEASE DON'T INVOLVE ME IN ANY MORE OF THIS. IT'S GOT NOTHING TO DO WITH ME AT ALL'. I ALSO TOLD THEM I HAD NO IDEA WHO KILLED GEORGE. I SAID THIS BECAUSE I WANTED THEM TO GO AWAY. I FEARED FOR THE SAFETY OF MYSELF, MY MOTHER AND MY RELATIVE WHO REMAINED UPSTAIRS

THROUGHOUT THE INCIDENT. THE THREE OF THEM THEN WALKED OFF AND GOT INTO THE TOYOTA CAR. I CLOSED THE FRONT DOOR BEFORE THEY ACTUALLY GOT INTO THE CAR. I IMMEDIATELY TELEPHONED THE POLICE AND REPORTED THE INCIDENT.

IN RESPECT OF WHAT TOOK PLACE IN MY HOUSE THAT THE THREATS MADE TO ME WERE GENUINE AND I FEAR SAFETY OF MYSELF. I HAVE KNOWN JOEY OWENS FOR ABOUT 5 OR 6 MONTHS. I MET HIM THROUGH GEORGE. HE LIVES IN NORRIS GREEN. I HAVE KNOWN LEE JONES ABOUT 6 MONTHS, WHERE HE WORKS AS A DOORMAN IN A CLUB CALLED THE GARAGE NIGHTCLUB. I WOULD DESCRIBE HIM AS WHITE, ABOUT 30 YEARS OLD, SIX FOOT 1 TO 6 FOOT 2 TALL. I HAVE KNOWN CHARLIE SEIGA FOR A NUMBER OF YEARS. I GOT TO KNOW CHARLIE SEIGA THROUGH THE CLUB SCENE IN LIVERPOOL.

I AM PREPARED TO ATTEND COURT AND GIVE EVIDENCE REGARDING THIS INCIDENT IF REQUIRED.

T WYNN (SIGNED)

DATE: **22-11-97**
OFFICER'S SIGNATURE: **DC4284 BOUGHEY**

Eddie Kelly was charged over the stolen document containing sensitive information about the murder suspects. The police had turned his house over and found it inside. It's always a police routine when you have been arrested, your house automatically gets searched. Lee's and Joey's were searched as well. After we had been formally charged, obviously no bail was granted. The police split us all up. Joey was sent to HMP Manchester; I was remanded to Walton Prison, Liverpool, along with Eddie Kelly and Lee Jones.

Well, there I was. After being out of prison all those years, 34 to be precise, back in Walton Jail. It was 1968 the last time I was here and what a difference there is these days. A fucking mad house, that's the only way I can describe it. I must have been one of the oldest villains in there.

The next day, I was allowed out of my cell on to the exercise yard only to be greeted by some of the younger villains. I didn't know most of them but they seemed to know me. Some of them had battle scars on their faces and bodies. One kid's face had a horrific slash across it. He told me that George Bromley had done it to him. Another young fella showed me a bullet hole where he had been shot by Bromley. All these kids were walking around the exercise yard with me saying how glad they were that I had killed George Bromley. I had to put a stop to this immediately. I didn't want any more rumours being spread about me and, besides, I hadn't been charged with the murder yet.

It was 15 December 1997, about 7.00am. The murder squad came for me at Walton Prison. They took me to Wavertree Road Police Station, Liverpool, for more questioning. It was the same as a few weeks before, questions after questions. This grilling went on for nearly two days. Just before the end of the interviews, they hit me with it. They said their forensic scientists had found no traces of soil or grass or any other matter that should have been on my lounge carpet. I couldn't have gone out on to my patio doors and run down my garden and come back the same way. With it being wet that night, the police said I would have certainly left some soil or matter on my shoes and carpet but there was none. Not even a minute bit of grass. They then said the execution of George Bromley had not happened the way I reported it. They went on to say they had also found Joey Owens' fingerprints in my house on the said day of the murder. His fingerprints had been found on a newspaper I had purchased that day, 18 November. They also said I'd phoned BT and asked them if I could block incoming calls. This was a load of rubbish, of course. I phoned BT asking them for a detailed breakdown of my bill. They then said to me, 'Look, Charlie, there's a chance for you here. If somebody else has done it, tell us. Was it Joey Owens?'

I told them definitely not.

They then said, 'Come on, Charlie, think of your family and your daughter.'

Well, I'll give them credit, they tried every trick in the book on me, but I stuck to my guns. I never once changed my story from the beginning. Towards the end of the interview, one of the detectives shouted uncontrollably at me, 'It was an execution, Charlie. BANG ... BANG ... BANG ... Three in the head and for some reason you have carried that out or you have arranged to have it done. It just doesn't add up, Charlie.'

Throughout my life, I have always disciplined and controlled myself. I have never betrayed my feelings when things start getting really hard. But some people lack the ability to work out logical solutions to their problems, to think themselves out of a mess. So they resort to short cuts such as breaking down under pressure, admitting to their guilt, even if they are guilty or not. What they lack, of course, is self-control and common sense.

The next day, 16 December, I was charged with the contract killing of George Bromley. I was also charged with threats to kill Thomas Wynn and a further charge of being in possession of a knife with a 12in blade with intent. Joey Owens was charged with the murder as well, and threats to kill Tommy Wynn. How he was charged with the murder, fuck knows. They only had a fingerprint on a newspaper two hours before the murder had taken place in my house. There were no witnesses or forensic evidence against him. The only thing they had on Joey was Tommy Wynn's statement in which Joey was supposed to have said to Tommy Wynn, 'You will get three in the head like your mate George got.' Don't forget those were the words of a self-confessed criminal, Tommy Wynn, who incidentally had given evidence before over another murder charge a couple of years previously. He also had a record of violence and was on bail himself for violent behaviour and burning down some buildings belonging to his in-laws. Lee Jones was charged with threats to kill only. He was eliminated from the murder charge.

We all made an appearance the next morning in a special magistrates court. The court was packed tight with family and friends and guarded by armed police. I was the first to be indicted. My charges were read out one at a time. First, Charles Anthony Seiga, for being in possession of a 12in knife and making threatening behaviour in a gambling casino how do you plead?

'Not guilty.'

Second, threats to kill Thomas Wynn by shooting him with a gun, how do you plead?

'Not guilty.'

And third, the unlawful murder of George Bromley.

'Not guilty.'

Looking at these charges against me and the reaction on most of the people's faces in court, one would think, What chance have I got? Absolutely none. I know a majority of the spectators in court that day had me down as finished. Never to be set free, will most probably die in prison. All three of us were taken to her HMP Strangeways in Manchester. A special new Cat A block had not long been built there. Lee Jones was allocated to the ordinary prison wing when we arrived, but Joey and I went straight on the Cat A wing.

Chapter Thirteen

Category A prisoners are considered to be the most dangerous criminals in the system. They mostly consist of murderers, armed robbers (not that there are many armed robbers about nowadays), and, last but not least, the drug barons. All of these prisoners are facing long sentences depending on their crimes; for example, life for murder, and 20 years or more for the drug barons. That is, of course, if found guilty of the crime, but, believe me, nearly everybody on the Cat A wing is found guilty. Incidentally, this Cat A wing I am now on is nicknamed the 'Wing of Death' by the prisoners.

It is called that simply because it is rare for a Cat A prisoner to be found not guilty at their trial. The wing itself is like a prison within a prison. I will now describe to you exactly what it is like regarding the rules and regulations.

First, we are all segregated from all of the rest of the prison. There is even a special exercise yard, if you could call it that — try and imagine a massive steel drum cut in half. When you walk around this yard, the curved walls are fenced off with high sheets of galvanised metal, which is to prevent you from seeing or making any contact with any ordinary prisoners. It also has a wire contraption on the top, just in case somebody comes to whisk you away to freedom by helicopter (fat chance of that happening). Escape is virtually impossible from this place.

Back on the wing, the cells are constantly searched, and they are also secretly bugged. They have special search screws, who always carry a bag of tools. When carrying out the search of your cell, it is a regulation for the prisoner to wait outside the cell whilst this search is in progress. But what are the tools for? And why do some searches take up to an hour — furniture maintenance? I don't think so! Obviously, it is to do with the bugging equipment and taping devices. And why do they allow all Cat A prisoners to socialise with each other in each other's cells; is it because they can listen to our conversations? We have often asked the screws if the cells are bugged and they give us the same old answer every time — 'Don't be so paranoid.' Everything a prisoner does is noted and monitored at all times. Every screw carries a little book which looks like a sort of diary and whoever you talk to or whatever you get up to gets written down by that screw in his book. We also have our own separate visiting room. Before you go on a visit, each prisoner is strip-searched and once the visit is over, the prisoner is strip-searched again. Once you are inside the visiting room with your visitors, you are monitored at all times by camera. Every table you sit at has concealed, highly sensitive listening devices. The screw who's monitoring you by camera also has a professional lip-reader sitting next to him! Now whether or not this was true, I certainly wasn't taking any chances. On all my visits, I would discreetly cover my mouth with my hand when I wanted to tell my visitors anything of importance. And I would lean over and whisper in their ears especially if it was something I needed doing outside with regard to my case.

We were also allowed access to phones, but again, whatever your conversation might be on that phone would be recorded on tape at all times. I think deep down this was all to do with the police. They would know by all the information that they had acquired what you might be going to do or say regarding your trial. So, you see, even when trying to put your defence together for court, you still haven't much of a chance.

Having all this knowledge about this regime, I kept my cards close to my chest at all times and the most important thing is to say 'fuck all to anyone in there'. Some prisoners would sell their souls or their mothers to do a deal to get a lighter sentence or to get off their charge altogether. However, I did meet some decent fellas in there but then I also met some dogs, and I mean dogs — in fact the word 'dog' is too good for them.

Well, that's a basic run-down of the negative side of being on a Cat A. Now I'll tell you about the good points it has to offer. First, every prisoner has his own single cell, with a flush toilet and a wash basin with running hot water. We could also take a shower every day, so hygiene was fairly good. Every prisoner was allowed association on the wing, and there are even a couple of pool and table tennis tables. There is also a decent-sized gym with all the latest equipment where you can work out. Or if you preferred to just sit around and have tea or coffee and play cards, this was allowed as well. The cells were unlocked most of the time so we weren't banged up 23 hours a day like the rest of the ordinary prisoners. Another good aspect was that we each had a colour TV in our cells.

Now the way I have described these luxuries in prison, you may think it sounds too good to be true, but it is also quite true. There are all those amenities in there for you when you are on Cat A. But there is one big, big problem that won't go away, no matter how hard you try, and that big problem is your mind. Your head is always completely wrecked! How can anybody concentrate on games, books or TVs when your forthcoming trial is always on your mind, sometimes for hours, days, weeks and months? The only time your mind can rest is when you sleep and that doesn't come very easily because your mind is so active. You are forever thinking what your fate is going to be; will you get life, or will you get 25 years? It is impossible not to worry or think about it.

Some prisoners on Cat A go under with all of this stress. In the first few months on remand, I have witnessed a few who have cracked up. I think another reason which makes it very hard is when you have become friendly with somebody and they have come back from court after being sentenced to life or to 20-odd years or so. Some of them are in deep shock and have to go on strong medication. Yet you get some who've convinced themselves they are innocent and can't be found guilty. The big-time drug-dealers usually have this belief; they just can't control themselves when it comes to boasting about their wealth — even in prison. Some of them have their cell walls covered with photos of all the holiday villas they own in Spain and their Shogun and Mercedes cars. How can they expect to be found not guilty? Normally, the majority of them were living in council houses less than a year before. Even when their trials have started, they go to court wearing different designer clothes and jewellery each day. All of this flashness doesn't go unnoticed by a judge and jury — especially the jury — some of them may work in a 9-to-5 job all year round trying to save for a holiday or a car; I don't think they would be very impressed.

With all this going on around me, I knew that I had to stay strong and think positive, not just for myself but for my family and my daughter. After all, they themselves were under a lot of stress. I had been almost five months on this Cat A remand now. It was coming up to Easter 1998, and my trial wouldn't begin for at least another seven to eight months.

The prison had a small classroom on this Cat A wing, and prisoners were invited to join if they wanted to brush up on their Maths or English, or any other subject they cared to study. I decided to join, solely to keep my mind occupied.

The prison had appointed a couple of outside teachers for this particular class; one was a lady called Val, and the other was a man called Alan. They were both fairly pleasant and I would describe my relationship with them as friendly. Alan said to me one day, 'Charlie, you seem to hold a good conversation and you've been around quite a bit, why don't you write a story or maybe your memoirs? After all, you have the time on your hands and it will help to take your mind off your case or trial.'

I thought it was an excellent idea at first, then paranoia set in. I lost my head a little bit — I thought this could be a trick — anything I write about such as a bit of villainy could be used in court against me later on. Being on a Cat A wing, you cannot afford to trust anybody. Alan then reassured me, and so did Val, that everything would be OK and nobody would know what I'm writing about. They said as far as they were concerned, I would just be brushing up on my English.

Well, that's how it all began; me writing this book in this prison. Val and Alan would give me little exercise books and I would just write and write, even sometimes in my cell late at night. Each time I filled up one of these little exercise books, it would be smuggled out of the prison — don't ask me how. Alan and Val became two very nice, down-to-earth people to me. They gave me a lot of inspiration in writing this book. Here is a note of encouragement from Alan when I first starting writing.

> *Charles, this is an excellent piece of original creative writing. You have a natural story-telling style and the reader's interest is maintained throughout. You have structured your story well, with a detailed introduction, creating plenty of period atmosphere. Continue in this style, it is developing into an exciting narrative. Do not worry unduly about grammar/spelling — this can be modified at a later date. Write as you think and speak — it makes the story more authentic and realistic. Keep it up. I will try and get you an A4 pad.*
>
> *Alan*

Summertime was here now. It was July 1998. I had just

come back from a visit with my solicitor, Kevin Dooley, and my head was totally fucked up. It appeared that Tommy Wynn, the supposed best mate of George Bromley, the man I was charged with killing, had decided to make a further statement against me. What he said in the second statement is a total fabrication, of course, but if it is allowed to be read out at my trial or, even worse, if Tommy Wynn gives evidence and the jury believes him, it could seal my fate. The statement is supposed to be a carbon copy of the murder that took place in my house. Here is Tommy Wynn's second statement:

NAME: **THOMAS JAMES WYNN**
AGE/DATE OF BIRTH: **31/25-04-1966**

WHO STATES:

THIS STATEMENT CONSISTING OF 005 PAGES EACH SIGNED BY ME IS TRUE TO THE BEST OF MY KNOWLEDGE AND BELIEF AND I MAKE IT KNOWING THAT IF IT IS TENDERED IN EVIDENCE I SHALL BE LIABLE TO PROSECUTION IF I HAVE WILFULLY STATED IN IT ANYTHING WHICH I KNOW TO BE FALSE OR DO NOT BELIEVE TO BE TRUE.

DATED: **01-04-98**
SIGNED: **T WYNN**

I AM THE ABOVE NAMED PERSON AND I RESIDE AT 22 SQUIRE STREET, LIVERPOOL 7. I HAVE MADE PREVIOUS STATEMENTS TO THE POLICE DURING THE COURSE OF THEIR INVESTIGATION INTO THE MURDER OF MY BEST FRIEND, GEORGE BROMLEY.

WITHIN THESE STATEMENTS I HAVE BRIEFLY DESCRIBED MY ASSOCIATION AND KNOWLEDGE OF A FELLA, CHARLIE SEIGA, WHICH I KNOW IS NOW ONE OF THE THREE MEN CHARGED WITH GEORGE'S MURDER.

THERE IS SOMETHING I NOW WISH TO SAY ABOUT CHARLIE, WHICH I FEEL IS VERY IMPORTANT INTO THE KILLING OF MY FRIEND.

ABOUT SIX MONTHS BEFORE GEORGE WAS MURDERED, I WAS PRESENT AT CHARLIE SEIGA'S HOUSE WHICH I FREQUENTED AT THAT TIME.

I WAS SAT IN THE KITCHEN HAVING MY TEA WHICH CHARLIE HAD COOKED FOR ME. OBVIOUSLY IT WAS ROUND TEA TIME.

CHARLIE ASKED ME ALL OF A SUDDEN IF I WOULD BE INTERESTED IN TAKING A MILLION QUIDS WORTH OF JEWELS OFF A JEWELLER WHO HE KNEW. I ASKED HIM WHAT HE MEANT AND HE SAID HE KNEW A JEWELLER WHO WAS STUPID AND AN EASY TOUCH.

HE SAID THAT THE FELLA WAS FROM SOUTHPORT AND WOULD COME TO HIS HOUSE WITH THE JEWELS IF HE (CHARLIE) ASKED HIM TO. CHARLIE SAID I WOULD HAVE TO POSE AS A BUYER SO I ASKED WHAT HE MEANT AND HOW HE PROPOSED TO DO IT. HE SAID HE COULD CALL THIS JEWELLER TO THE HOUSE AND ONCE INSIDE I COULD COME TO THE FRONT DOOR, PUT

A GUN TO CHARLIE'S HEAD, MARCH HIM BACK IN AND HANDCUFF HIM AND LIKEWISE TO THE JEWELLER. I THEN COULD TAKE THE JEWELS AND LEAVE THE TWO OF THEM CUFFED. I SAID TO CHARLIE WHAT THE HELL WOULD HE DO WHEN THE POLICE CAME AND HE TOLD ME NOT TO WORRY ABOUT THAT AS IT WAS HIS PROBLEM. I ASKED HIM WHAT HE MEANT AND HE SAID 'WHAT CAN THEY DO TO ME? A FUCKING LIE DOWN. I'LL LIE DOWN FOR A YEAR FOR A MILLION QUID'S WORTH OF STONES MATE.' I TOLD HIM HE WAS MAD TO EVEN SUGGEST THAT SCENARIO. HE SAID IT WAS ALRIGHT AND SAID TO ME AGAIN 'WHO THE FUCK IS GOING TO DO A ROBBERY OF THAT NATURE IN HIS OWN DRUM, THINK ABOUT IT'.

HE OBVIOUSLY THOUGHT THAT THE PLAN WOULD WORK AND I BELIEVED THAT HE REALLY MEANT WHAT HE WAS SAYING. HE FINISHED TELLING ME THAT THE POLICE WOULD NEVER THINK ANYBODY WOULD BE STUPID ENOUGH TO SET UP A JOB LIKE THAT IN THEIR OWN HOUSE AND HE WOULD NEVER BE SUSPECTED OF BEING INVOLVED. I TOLD HIM STRAIGHT THAT I WAS NOT INTERESTED AND TO FORGET IT.

I WOULD ADD THAT CHARLIE HAD ALSO TOLD ME THAT I WOULD HAVE TO WEAR A BALACLAVA IN CASE I WAS SEEN BY ANY OBSERVANT NEIGHBOURS OR PASSERS BY.

LOOKING BACK ON IT NOW AFTER WHAT HAPPENED TO GEORGE, MY BEST MATE, WHO WAS SHOT DEAD IN CHARLIE'S HOUSE, I BELIEVE CHARLIE MIGHT HAVE BEEN TRYING TO SET ME UP TO HAVE DONE TO ME WHAT HE HAD DONE TO GEORGE BECAUSE OF THE THREATS HE MADE TO KILL ME OUTSIDE MY MOTHER'S HOUSE. I FELT IT WAS A CARBON COPY OF THE DEATH OF MY BEST FRIEND, GEORGE BROMLEY. I WANT TO ADD THAT I NOW FULLY BELIEVE CHARLIE SEIGA WANTED TO KILL ME AS WELL AS GEORGE AND THAT IS WHY I AM NOW MAKING THIS STATEMENT. PROVIDING THE APPROPRIATE MEASURES ARE TAKEN FOR MY SAFETY AS HAS BEEN EXPLAINED TO ME BY THE POLICE THEN I WOULD BE WILLING TO GIVE EVIDENCE TO WHAT I HAVE SAID IN THIS STATEMENT.

T WYNN

TIME: **1700**
DATE: **01-04-98**
OFFICER'S SIGNATURE: **DC6802 TOMLINSON**

After reading this vindictive statement against me, I thought, Fuck him. When and if he gets in the witness box, he will be ripped to pieces by my defence lawyer. First, his police record was as bad as they come. Second, it's not the first time this dog Wynn has given evidence in a court of law. He has been a prosecution witness on another murder trial. The evidence he gave in court was so convincing the jury brought in a guilty verdict. The man who stood trial got life. So this was the main problem I had to contend with.

My barrister, Mr Wolfe, said it would be very dangerous if Wynn was to go to court as a prosecution witness against me. At this stage, I needed help badly but being caged up in here my hands were tied. At one point, I began to believe it was the end for me.

A couple more months went by. It was now the beginning of September 1998 and my trial date was drawing near. It was set for the first week in October. A matter of weeks to go, and I've got this cocked-up evidence against me.

I had a visit from my two brothers, Jimmy and Joe. They were so loyal to me, they were always there without fail. I wanted to see them without my daughter being present. When you're on Cat A, your visits are limited to three of your immediate family. You can have no friends, especially if they have criminal records; nobody else is allowed, not even any more family members once that prison document has been signed and you have chosen who will visit.

I put my cards on the table with our Joe and Jimmy on the visit. I told them if I got found guilty and sentenced to life, I would never be set free again. It is one of the highest charges in the land, shooting someone to death. I was 58 years of age and if they did ever consider setting me free, I'd be well into my eighties. I told them both that wasn't for me. My philosophy has always been all or nothing. I have never been a defeatist in my life, but this was something else. There was no way I would rot away in there. So I told them both what I planned to do if the worst happened. I would kill myself. I would choose how I would die. Hanging was out of the question; to hang yourself is like being a cur and to bleed to death by cutting your throat or wrists was also out. I told them I would go out on a hunger strike. It would be a sort of protest at the same time. I would hurry it along, I would make sure I took no water or any other liquids and if I stripped my clothes off each night and lay on the cold floor of the cell at my age, pneumonia would set in fast. I would be gone within ten days or so. I know people might say that's a coward's way out but, believe me, it takes a brave man to kill himself especially if he is still of sound mind.

Then there's also the other side; what about your family, your daughter? That is the reason why I would be doing this — to stop my family suffering over the years. Imagine my family coming to see me year after year and me becoming a senile old man and then after all those years I would most probably die in there anyway. I wouldn't like to end up like the Krays or the Charlie Bronsons. In my eyes, they died long ago.

After I had told my brothers what my plan would be if the worst came to the worst, they fully agreed with me in every respect. After my morbid visit was over, I said to them, 'All's not lost yet; there could still be light at the end of the tunnel.'

One week later, a small miracle happened. Our mate Lee Jones got bail on the threats to kill charge. A few days later, Lee was released. Tommy Wynn had dropped all the charges of the threats to kill in his statement against me. He had also mysteriously disappeared and was never seen again. A special court was convened and myself, Joey Owens, Lee Jones and our lawyers had to appear.

The prosecution offered no evidence against Lee and Joey and so they both walked free from court — Lee from the threats to kill and Joey from the murder through lack of evidence. I had the threats to kill Tommy Wynn dropped, but the murder of George Bromley remained. I was taken back to Strangeways on the Cat A Wing.

That night, back in my cell, I was just about to drop off to sleep after all the events that day — the courts, travelling and so on. I was completely exhausted from it all. Just as I was dozing off, I heard my name being called. The voice was coming from below my cell. Directly below the Cat A cells was where the punishment cells are situated. I got up to my cell window and shouted, 'Who's that calling me?'

I don't make a habit of talking out of the cell window; it is too dangerous, especially discussing your case. You could never tell who might be listening. The person who was shouting to me was a fella called Alan Lea. He was from Liverpool, too. He asked if I could give him some tobacco. I didn't smoke, as I've said, so I told him I would fix him up in the morning with some. I felt a bit sorry for him. He had been down the block quite a bit and once you're down there on your own with fuck all it's quite hard. This is how I met Alan Lea, who was to play a major part in my life later on.

Exactly two days later, early in the morning before any prisoners were unlocked, my cell door was suddenly opened and a gang of screws came in. They told me to get my gear packed. I asked them what was going on but they just ignored me and told me to hurry. I was then ordered to put on a jump suit (like an all-in-one tracksuit). I was then double-handcuffed and taken out of the Cat A and straight into a prison van. In no time at all, I was driven up the motorway with an armed police escort car behind. They wouldn't tell me anything whilst I was on the journey and I did not have a clue what was going on. After what seemed like a couple of hours we finally arrived at Doncaster Prison.

After I was handed over the screws in Doncaster, I was taken on to the prison wing, which was called an 'enhanced' wing. Prisoners have more privileges on these enhanced wings. You can move around more freely and you're treated more humanely by the screws. I still couldn't fathom out what I had done to deserve this. I wasn't even on a Cat A whilst I was in Doncaster. I finally got the answer. They told me it was a Home Office ruling. I asked why. The screw in charge just avoided any more questions from me.

I sort of settled in after a day or so, keeping myself to myself, making sure no dogs or snides got into my company, although I did meet a few cons in there who walked about with me.

One was a lad called Alan Lord. He was one of the so-called ring-leaders of the Manchester riots a few years before. It was hard for Alan. He was in his early thirties but had been inside since he was just 19, a long time, the best years of his life and he still hadn't got a date when he would be released. I still correspond with him. He won't talk to any screws in there and will not entertain any low-life dogs. He just trains and keeps himself to himself. I will say, though, the man has got pride and dignity; it's just a shame he's rotting away in there.

Another fella who socialised with me in there was Steve Gillon from London. He was doing 15 for armed robbery. He was another good lad. He hated any scum dogs around him and he wouldn't entertain any screws. I write to him quite a lot.

Just as I was beginning to settle in this nick, it must have been only a couple of weeks at the most, and I was on the move again. This time I was told where I was getting ghosted to — back to the Cat A wing in Manchester. I just couldn't believe it. What the fuck were they playing at? I was finally put back on to the Cat A in Strangeways and a couple of young mates greeted me as soon as I got on the wing. One was called Paul Massey from Cheetham Hill, Manchester. A fairly handy lad was Paul and he also had good principles. The other young kid was Wayne Hardy. He was a diamond, Wayne. He would do anything for you. They all couldn't understand what it was that caused me to be moved for a couple of weeks to Doncaster.

The truth did emerge when I had a visit the next day from my two brothers. They both looked gutted when they came into the visiting room. My solicitor had been told by the police that I had confessed to the murder of George Bromley.

It appears while I was in Doncaster Prison for that couple of weeks, a prisoner by the name of Blackburn said in a statement that I had shot dead George Bromley and he was willing to testify in court against me. Well, you have got to hand it to them, they don't give up, do they? Every trick in the book has been tried on me. You don't have to be blinded by science to see what's going on here. After I'd been on remand for almost 12 months and very evasive about my case to anybody in there, would I be so silly as to jeopardise everything to a dirty, scum dog prisoner in Doncaster, who I don't even know? My lawyers contacted the Crown Prosecution indicating that there was nothing to substantiate the allegations made by Blackburn. After a lengthy discussion, the prosecution decided not to use it as evidence. Whoever manipulated this plan for that low-life prisoner to fabricate a statement against me backfired on them in a big way.

Chapter Fourteen

Tomorrow, 5 October 1998, my trial begins. In the 12 months I have been caged up in here on remand, I've seen men who have been charged with murder coming back with life sentences. I've also seen robbers and drug dealers coming back with their long stretches, 20 years or more. No wonder the prisoners have christened this place the Wing of Death; everybody seems to come back guilty and now it's my turn to face a judge and jury.

That first day in court I was handcuffed to a screw and taken along with three other screws from the cells below, into a lift and up above to the dock. I was ordered to sit down in the dock and the handcuffs were taken off me. Then the four screws just sort of sat around me. The court was packed tight with family and friends of mine and on the other side of the court sat George Bromley's family, most of them dressed in black mourning clothes. I can't imagine them dressing that way when they go out for a drink in a club or pub in the evening; I wonder who put them up to dress like that in court.

My QC appointed to me was the famous Jonathon Goldberg, a very skilful lawyer. He was supposed to be one of the best in the country. I will say on the first day of the opening he did a brilliant job. He had a lot of important and dangerous points eradicated for me, such as the statements and hearsay evidence that was mentioned about me. Another important point we were successful on was the jury. The police and prosecutor insisted on an outside jury to be brought in (meaning nobody from Liverpool). The Crown Prosecutor said I might know some of them or they might know me. The real reason for them not wanting a Liverpool jury is simply because George Bromley was well known in the city because of the atrocities he had carried out on quite a few ordinary people. I strongly protested; I wanted a Liverpool jury. Most people who live outside of Liverpool are not too keen on Scousers. This is a known fact. What they don't realise is that the majority Liverpool people are good. It's just that the other crowd — the low-life scum — have left a stigma on our city. In the end, the judge allowed a Liverpool jury on one strict condition — that armed police would be present throughout my trial so the jury had police protection. My lawyers didn't want the armed police in court and started to protest, but I insisted on it simply because I knew I could relate to a Liverpool jury and, more to the point, they could relate to me. They swore a jury in which consisted of nine women and three men.

My lawyer turned and said to me we could have done without the women, especially with this violent murder charge. I said I'm quite content with the ladies;

they all looked sensible enough to me, so I asked him to leave things as they were.

Once the trial got off the ground, the police introduced new evidence. According to their forensic scientists, and the police themselves, a new scenario had been formed. Apparently, I am supposed to have left my back kitchen door unlocked and a so-called gunman opened it and shot Bromley from behind as he sat reading the newspaper. They even showed the jury a video with two policemen play-acting the part. This, of course, was completely untrue. That never happened at all. I had already said in my statement from the beginning, my back kitchen door is always, especially at winter times, permanently locked. It is locked due to the fact that it was a temporary, softwood door and when it rained or it was damp the wood would swell and the door was very, very hard to open. One of my neighbours who is of impeccable character and has his own joinery business was called by the prosecutor as a witness on another matter. But when he was cross-examined by my QC, Mr Goldberg, he was asked if Mr Seiga ever called him over to his house at any time to plane his door so it would open and he replied, 'Yes, I did on numerous occasions.' He also added that he'd told Mr Seiga he needed a new hardwood door because the problem would not go away, especially when it rained in winter times, and he did also stress how very hard the door was to open.

When I got into the witness box under cross-examination, the prosecutor would not budge from the scenario about the kitchen door. He kept repeating to me that if I didn't kill him, I had set it up and had a hit-man behind the kitchen door. He kept the pressure up and at one point it did sound feasible.

I then asked, 'Could I say something? After all, I am an English man in an English court.'

He then smirked and said, 'You may if you wish.'

They like you to talk in case you make a slip or tell a lie. Then they can pounce on you and nail you to the ground.

I looked right at the jury, and said, 'Members of the jury, last week you were all invited to go to my house and view the scene of the crime. All the controversy is over my kitchen door, whether it was very hard to push open, or not. You all saw the police acting the part on the video where one policeman is dressed up like the gunman and you see him open that door very quietly to surprise the unsuspecting victim who was sitting reading the paper at the table.

'Well, members of the jury, each and every one of you who went to my house that day, I bet you all wanted to try that kitchen door and to see for yourselves if it would open easily or not because this is the main point in this trial the police and the prosecutor are relying on, that door theory.

'Well, I will tell you, members of the jury, while you all were asked to wait in the jury room, while the debate was going on, arranging to go to my house, my legal team Mr Goldberg asked the prosecutor and the judge could the jury be allowed to try that door and see for themselves, and this judge and Crown Prosecutor said, "Definitely not."'

After I had blurted all this out, the prosecutor got all hot and bothered. He sort of shifted the blame on to the judge and said it was his lordship who'd disallowed it.

The judge then said, 'That's quite true, members of the jury. I simply did not want any play-acting carried out while we were in Mr Seiga's house.'

I then butted in and said to the jury, 'But they have just showed you a video and that was play-acting,' and I added, 'Isn't it funny the way they made that door look easy to open?' Then I said sarcastically, 'But then you can always plane wood off a door, but you can't put it back on.'

I don't think the jury were too pleased with what had gone on regarding them not being allowed to try that kitchen door.

Think about it — if I'm found guilty and that jury found all this out later on, that that door did jam and was very difficult to open, the police theory then would be knocked right on the head. If they then said the gunman took Bromley by surprise by opening the door very quietly, then it would be a miscarriage of justice.

The next important point for the Crown was why there were no traces of soil on my lounge carpet. Again, I had told the police from the beginning that I had run down my garden and hid in some bushes where there was soil and it had also been raining that night. I told them there were armed police in my garden as well that night and several witnesses, including my brother and his wife and neighbours, told the court this, but the police denied they'd been in my garden. Then it was proven in court that they *had* been there, so why weren't their footprints on my carpet as well as mine? Then my QC called a forensic scientist to give evidence on my behalf. He told the court that when he'd examined my boots (the police had had my boots in their possession for nine months) he had found traces of soil and bits of grass on them. So why wasn't any of this soil found on my footwear on the night of the murder? The answer the police gave in court was that they didn't examine my boots for soil and so it seemed as though their evidence was falling apart and becoming very dubious. My brother Jimmy was called as a witness, as well as his wife, Ann, who was very supportive to me throughout the trial. I had a good word with our Jimmy on the phone the night before he was going to give his evidence. I told him it was imperative to tell the court about the policeman who'd been suspended on a corruption charge selling a sensitive document regarding this murder. My brother did tell the court this in his evidence.

Also, Bromley's common-law wife, Debbie Bridson, admitted under oath while giving her evidence to my QC that she had actually handled the police document and passed it to her boyfriend, Tommy Wynn (it's funny that Debbie and Tommy Wynn haven't been charged with handling this document — I wonder why).

Just before the end of the trial, the Crown Prosecutor said to the jury, 'Don't be fooled by this man's cock-and-bull story. He set this murder up; he planned it and it was executed and he is as guilty as the man who pulled the trigger.'

After my QC gave his speech to the jury — it was masterly — the judge, after his summing up, which surprisingly didn't take too long, told the jury to go out and reach a verdict.

The jury filed past me in the dock and when they had gone through the door out of sight, the judge turned on me and said, 'I don't want any more of your outbursts. I want complete silence when that jury returns. Take him down.'

The four screws led me away down to the cells and one of the screws, a big bastard from Yorkshire somewhere, said to me, 'When you get your life sentence after, you're going right down the block.'

I told him to go and fuck himself.

He then just banged me up in one of the cells. About ten minutes later, my cell was unlocked and my lawyers came in to see me. John Browne, my solicitor, who had been a great help and a real good brief, looked a bag of nerves. Mr Wolff, my barrister also looked very gloomy and my QC, Mr Goldberg, wasn't very confident about it at all either. I said, 'What are you all looking so miserable for?'

Then I was told that if I was found guilty, the judge had made a recommendation that I serve 25 years. My QC said to me, 'The judge thinks you're guilty.'

I started pacing up and down the cell. I said to all three of them, 'Well, look, whatever happens I want you all to know I've appreciated everything you have done for me and you've been a brilliant team. I couldn't have asked for any better.'

Then one of them said to me, 'You could get a re-trial or the jury might not consider their verdict today.'

It was a Friday afternoon and I said they would reach a verdict today, I could just feel it.

Just then the cell door was flung open, and the four screws were all telling me to come and hurry, the jury were back with the verdict.

Just before I was led away by the screws, John Browne, my solicitor, put his arms on my shoulders and looked into my eyes and said, 'Charlie, I hope to God you're going to be OK. Good luck.'

My barrister put his arm on mine and shook his head. Walking back through the cellars of the court with those four screws in silence, it was like going to face a firing squad. When I got back into the dock, the court was jam-packed tight. The most weird part of it all was the silence. It was eerie. You could hear a pin drop. The only audible sound was the sobbing of my young daughter. My two brothers were at each side of her, holding her. I looked over and she whispered to me, 'Dad.'

My brother Joe and I made eye contact and he shook his head in disbelief. I then heard a loud knock and the door opened to the left of where I was standing in the dock. The jury filed past me on the left. Not one of them looked up. They all kept their heads down. That's when I thought I was finished. They've found me guilty. I'm a dead man.

Then the jury were asked, 'Have you all agreed on a verdict?'

A young girl stood up holding a piece of paper in her hand; she was trembling. She was asked, 'And what is your verdict?'

Then it all happened. She looked right across at me and said very loudly, 'We find him not guilty.'

For two seconds it was still deathly quiet, and then all pandemonium broke out. All my family and supporters were shouting, 'Yes, yes.' I myself vaulted right out of the dock. I don't know why but I just did. I looked at the judge who was just staring with his mouth open. Then the screw who'd said I would get life grabbed hold of my arm. I told him, 'Get your fucking arm off me. I'm a free man now.'

He let go of me like a hot brick. The court was in uproar. I looked across at my daughter. She was smiling with the tears still running down her face. I shouted to her, 'I will be with you in five minutes.' The Bromley family started shouting, 'Murderer, gangster,' and all other kinds of names under the sun. After ten minutes I walked out of there a free man, found not guilty by a unanimous verdict.

Here's the summary my QC, Mr Jonathan Goldberg, wrote after my trial.

IN THE LIVERPOOL CROWN COURT
Regina V Charles Seiga
Particulars in support of Reg.9(5) (B)

I gratefully adopt the case summary prepared by my junior Michael Wolff Esq.

I would add this. This was all in all as gruelling and hard-fought a murder trial as any I can remember in my 27 years at the criminal bar, in which time I have defended in literally dozens of important murder trials.

It was a real 'whodunnit'. Every detail of the intricate circumstantial evidence was battled over inch by inch. The Crown gave no quarter. Mr Richard Henriques QC is no mean opponent. He took every point. We had to counter every point — and we did.

My final speech lasted over a full day, and I believe not a word was wasted, detailing the evidence bit by bit and criticising it. In his summing-up, the learned judge termed my final speech 'masterly'.

The Crown called no less than 6 experts and scene of crime officers. We Called 3. Their evidence was vital, contentious, and bitterly fought over.

Our client himself was difficult and demanding. I think he was that rare breed, but he behaved like a cat on a hot tin roof!

He was well-nigh uncontrollable in chief — I understand the court officer made sympathetic entries on the court log regarding my efforts to control him and present his evidence in some kind of comprehensible order, which was not easy.

Other unpleasant suggestions were floated by the Crown that they had represented several accused originally despite a conflict of interests, and had tipped off Seiga about what another defendant was saying in a separate police interview. I raise this because it exemplifies the hostile atmosphere in which this trial was conducted, and which I would not care to relive. Whilst I was happy to do so because I think they were treated with great unfairness and unjustified hostility, the fact is I had to defend my lay client on the one hand and my professional clients on the other from unwarranted attacks. This was hard work.

This was a trial which demanded long hours of preparation at nights, weekends and in the early mornings in my hotel room to prepare for the cross-examination, legal arguments and speeches of the day ahead. It was won against high odds by excellent cross-examination above all else, if I say so myself!

It was a dramatic and even a thrilling case. Nobody present will ever forget its atmosphere or the scenes of pandemonium in the public gallery which accompanied the final not guilty verdict.

I had dedicated and willing assistance from my junior, Mr Wolff, and my solicitor, Mr John Brown. We all had to work very hard. We did so gladly because we all realised this to be a rare case indeed.

This trial lasted 19 working days in all and I have to say I underestimated both its length and factual difficulties at the outset.

This was, in summary, in the very top league of contested murder trials in this country.

Jonathan Goldberg
3/11/98

I can now give you an insight into what George Bromley and his cronies did to certain people. And what I state are true facts, known by many other villains in Liverpool. I cannot mention the true identities of most of these people because of any reprisals.

There's a man called Jimmy O'Callaghan. He was severely disembowelled; the mutilation was so bad that all his organs inside him were cut away. He is now permanently in a wheelchair with a colostomy bag attached to him.

Another person, Tony M, just an ordinary working man, was severely beaten up, but worse was his pregnant wife who was almost kicked to death in her stomach. When he heard of the death of George Bromley, Tony M went out and celebrated in style.

Another man, young John White whose father was a good mate of mine, can hardly walk. He had to have two ribs taken out to try and repair the mutilation that George Bromley inflicted on him.

Then there is a man called Steven. I know Stevie, he is a fairly decent fella and he can also handle himself. But George Bromley, together with Kevin Maguire (who was shot dead a few months after George), went round to Stevie's house and fired over 100 rounds of ammo into his lounge. Stevie's pregnant wife was lucky not to have been killed, but the shock of it all was believed to have led her to miscarry.

Another young couple were at the mercy of George Bromley, who had actually brought a body bag round to the couple and forced the woman inside it. This couple do not want to be named. The woman is still severely traumatised.

A young teenager was also kidnapped by George Bromley and company. He was kept in a cellar for two days while the kid's dad tried to get money for them. What the young lad went through I can't repeat, and I promised not to mention their names.

I know you, the reader, might think, Well, you are just as bad, after all, you yourself have damaged people. What I say to that is, 'Yes, I have and I don't regret it one bit, but I didn't hurt the ordinary man, woman or child in the street.' The people I damaged were scum and bullies.

I can now state that I never killed George Bromley or had anything to do with his murder. His family think differently. They still think I killed him. So do the police. They're looking for no one else, so that's leaving me with the stigma.

Let's look at it all logically. First, I had no motive for the murder of George Bromley. Second, nobody saw me do it or that I had anything to do with it because there were no witnesses. Third, there were no forensics on any of my clothes, which were taken off me within minutes after the shooting. And last but not least, the most important point is that a jury unanimously found me not guilty.

Only two people know what really went on in my house that night. One is dead (obviously) and the other is the hit-man, whoever he may be.

Epilogue

Throughout my life as a criminal, my first priority was to have money, and when I say money, I mean plenty of it. In my opinion, money is a very powerful thing. It can enable you to have practically anything you desire. Some people say that money cannot buy love or bring happiness, but my answer to that is — give me a couple of million and I will show you just how happy it can make you.

Ever since my youth, I craved for the good things that life could offer — beautiful women, nice cars, good clothing, expensive jewellery, lavish holidays and, most importantly, a nice house, home and family. I would never have been able to have achieved or sampled these lovely things without money.

However, money does not come easily, and it never was just handed to me on a plate. I went out and committed some of the most serious offences and crimes in the country in order to have money; armed robberies on banks, security vans, hijacking lorries, safe-breaking and many other serious crimes. I did it all, but at times it was a terrifying business. It certainly was not glamorous and I never got a kick out of it or excitement from it all. In fact, for me, it was the reverse. In a way, it was a means of support as well as a gamble. Every time I did one of those armed blags I was taking a risk and gambling. In fact, I was gambling with my life — my young life at that.

I was always fully aware that, if I was captured, then I would be facing a long time in prison — 20 years at least — or, worse still, I could have been ambushed by the armed-response police and been shot dead.

As I have previously stated, nowadays, if I were still at it, I think I would find it difficult in comparison to how it used to be. I would just like to say to these young villains — and by that, I am not referring to or talking about the low-life, degenerate scum and perverts who abuse women and children and hurt the innocent. Those types of pricks can go and fuck themselves. I am talking about the young villains of today who do still have decent qualities and principles of respect, which they have adopted from the old-school villain. Yes, these types of villains still do exist, although there are not as many of them now, and it is to those kids that I would say, before you go down that road, have a good think about it, because personally I think that these days the bizzies seem to have boxed it off.

Just look at the sophisticated computer systems and equipment that they have today — helicopters, high-tech cameras, armed-response teams and advance forensics, such as DNA testing. They even have sensitive listening devices and bugging systems, as well as tracking devices; and these are only some of the things you are aware of. Police technology is far more advanced today. To sum it all up, in my opinion it is the end of an era.

The other side of my criminal life involved violence. I had to deal with violence along the way. I have never wanted it but, when it came, I had no choice but to use it and to use it in the best way I knew how. I have had many street fights throughout my life, and in some of those I have come off best and then there have been others where I have come badly unstuck. But, then again, I have never professed or claimed to be a hard-case. There is no shame or embarrassment if a man loses a fight. At least he can hold his head up high and say that he has had a go. You can always go back and have a straightener, but these days that is a very rare occurrence and, in my opinion, straighteners do not exist any more.

Everybody in and around the city of Liverpool who knows me will back me up when I say that I have never deliberately or intentionally gone out of my way and picked a fight with anybody. There have been many occasions when I have walked away from somebody with whom I have been arguing over something trivial, such as getting pushed in a queue or a disagreement with another driver. In these circumstances or situations, I have always been the one to apologise first; but do not misunderstand me — if a person went too far and took my apology as a sign of weakness instead of manners, or even if they overstepped the mark by laying their hands on me, then in my younger days I would have fucking killed them (not literally, obviously).

One thing I have always believed is that nobody, no matter who they are, should never underestimate another person's capabilities. Appearances, as they say, can be deceptive. And once you have reputation, no matter what it is for, it is very hard to shake off.

I am fully aware that certain people and authorities have used this fact in order to associate me with a whole range of crimes. If I were to list everything I have ever done or been involved in or charged with, believe me, the list would be endless.

Again, do not misunderstand me — I am no angel and I was obviously involved in a wide range of criminal activities for a long time. During my life, I have been charged with using and being in possession of firearms, as well as many other offensive and dangerous weapons such as hatchets, machetes, hammers and knives to name just a few. You name them and I have used them. I have also been charged for GBH several times, as well as threats to kill, attempted murders and murder. There have been numerous occasions when I have been questioned in relation to murders which have been committed in and around the Liverpool and north-west area.

I can even go far back to the early Seventies when the murder squad came to see me over a killing which had taken place in Cumbria — a man was found dead in one of the lakes up there with both of his hands severed from his body. I can come right up to the 1990s, when shootings have occurred in my area and the police have had the audacity to warn me and my so-called associates that they believe us to have been involved. I have been ambushed by the armed-response unit in my own neighbourhood in broad daylight, in front of women and kids. Obviously, they had been incorrectly informed that I was armed, and so they forced me to kneel in the middle of the road with guns pointing at my head, whilst the public looked on and the press took photographs. Who the fuck do the police think I am?

I have been taken to court and charged with the aforementioned offences. The only convictions I have are three GBHs, the last of them being in 1966, some 35 years ago.

And why have I never been convicted of these offences? Because a Liverpool jury has always believed in my innocence. But the police, on the other hand, have not and never will.

I am also aware that various people have branded me a killer. I would like to state that I am not a psychopath and would not get a thrill out of killing somebody just for the sake of it. I am not a callous or cold-blooded person. I, too, have feelings. I love my children and family and my true friends. But I do believe that nearly every one of us — especially men — have the killer instinct inside us.

Just recently I heard that the Home Secretary Jack Straw is now urging the public not to turn a blind eye to crimes which are being committed and to 'have a go', meaning that you should go to the aid of somebody who is being attacked or who is a victim of the crime itself.

I have been having a go for years, going to the aid of the defenceless old people and women who have been the victims of violence and beatings by low-life scum. It is all very well for Jack Straw urging people to have a go, but what guarantees does he give for protection? Just supposing a person goes to help someone who is being viciously attacked, mugged or raped, and accidentally killed the low-life scumbag who is committing the offence? The police would have no hesitation in charging him with manslaughter, if not murder, even if he was protecting his own family.

Finally, I am always being asked if crime pays. Well, that is easy to sum up, isn't it? Look at all of the old gangsters. For instance, the Great Train Robbers, poor bastards! Most of them ended up serving 30 years in prison and came to fuck all.

Next, take, say, Frankie Fraser — he has wasted almost 40 years of his life behind bars, as have a fair number of his mates.

And, finally, there are the Krays — they got sent down when they were young men in their prime. They were caged up for over 30 years only to come out in boxes — dead.

Obviously, crime did not pay for all of these guys. Time and again, you will hear the same old reasons or excuses, the 'what ifs ...' and 'but if only ...'. Maybe it could have paid for all of these old villains, but they were all careless or made major mistakes somewhere along the line, like we all do sometimes.

To put your trust in somebody is a very big risk to take. It was true in those days and is even more so nowadays. I did, and came very badly unstuck. I was enticed, or tricked, from my home in broad daylight and then ambushed in a house by a gang of young, drug-crazed scum. I was held for two days and tortured.

But my ordeal was fuck-all compared to what these perverted sick bastards did to the ordinary, inoffensive families around the city — but that is another story!

Charlie Seiga
Huyton, 2002

Confidential police memo

Liverpool Police Force, 1998

Charles Anthony Seiga

D.O.B 7/4/1940

I retired from the Merseyside Police in February 1997 having served for 27 years. The majority of the time, some 23 years were spent as a detective and 15 of those years as a Detective Sergeant.

I spent two long periods on the Serious Crime Squad and have dealt with every type of crime from armed robberies through to murder.

I spent all of my working life as a police officer in the Merseyside area and during that time came across numerous characters that I dealt with. In fact, Merseyside over the years has produced a magnitude of violent and career criminals who were into heavy crime.

By that I mean armed robberies, kidnappings, serious woundings, lorry heists and contract killings to name just some.

When I first joined the police in 1971, I was stationed at Kirkby on the outskirts of Liverpool and was part of that division that covered the Huyton area, another part of Liverpool.

When I first joined the police it was my ambition to become a Detective. I was in awe of the C.I.D. and the Regional Crime Squad Detectives who frequented my Police Station.

They were dealing with what were then known as 'Target Criminals'. That is, the criminals who fell into the above categories.

Names of these villains were bandied about and one day, I thought, I would be looking into those sorts of people.

One of the names mentioned was that of Charles Anthony Seiga. He was a Huyton villain, whose name was constantly coming up every than an armed robbery or violent crime was committed. However, he had used his brains and moved out of the area and gone to live in Wales, as he was too well known in his home town.

It didn't take the North Wales Police long to realise that he was in their area as the crime rate suddenly started to go up for high class burglaries and antiques robberies.

The amount of antiques that were stolen by Liverpool villains in the early '70s was so great that the Regional Crime Squad set up a separate Antiques Squad looking into these thefts that were allegedly controlled by Charlie Seiga.

On his return to Liverpool from North Wales, Seiga then had a reputation for being a violent character. Intelligence was constantly being received of stabbings and shootings being perpetrated by this man, but very rarely would anyone come forward to complain about him.

He was known to be a careful planner and always seemed to provide a back door for himself when he knew he was to be arrested. He would often disappear after such events, and when the heat had died down, would calmly walk into a police station and give himself up, knowing full well that the complaint had either been withdrawn or that the complainant, through fear, had been bought off.

He would vent his violence on other criminals who harmed or tried to bully any of his friends or family, and he did come from a very large family. The police were always warned to be careful when approaching him as he was known to constantly carry knives and other weapons about him.

Having left the police force and now retired, it came as no surprise to me when I read about Seiga being arrested for a contract killing. How he got out of that one I do not know, and the secret of that job, along with many others, will no doubt be carried with him to his grave. The police are not looking for anyone else in relation to this matter and, in my experience, they must be more than satisfied that they had the correct man in the dock.

He was commonly known as Charlie Seiga, but we had another name for him – Killer.